Fundamentals of Engineering Mechanics

Basic Concepts in:
Statics
Mechanics of Materials
Dynamics

David A. Cicci
Darby A. Cicci

Copyright © 2019, by David A. Cicci and Darby A. Cicci

Copyright Registration Number: TXu 2-134-792

All rights reserved. No part of this publication may be copied, reproduced, stored in a retrieval system, or transmitted, in any form or by any means, electronic, mechanical, photocopying, scanning, recording, or otherwise, without the prior written permission of Dynamic Solutions Publishing. Violations of the copyright laws of the United States by any of the actions stated above will be prosecuted to the fullest extent of the law.

Dynamic Solutions Publishing
Auburn, AL

Printed in the United States of America

PREFACE

Fundamentals of Engineering Mechanics was developed to present three topics in engineering mechanics: statics, mechanics of materials, and dynamics, to undergraduate students in non-mechanics oriented engineering disciplines. It was not originally designed for students in the more mechanics-based engineering disciplines such as aerospace, mechanical, or civil engineering.

The three subjects presented are traditionally taught in a three-course sequence of undergraduate courses which allows for in-depth study and a more comprehensive learning experience. The result of combining three subjects into a one semester-long course is that a very limited amount of time is available for each particular subject. Therefore, a less in-depth approach to the subject matter is presented in this textbook. It's primarily intended as an introduction for individuals with little or no background in these topics, although it is assumed that students have a strong background in mathematics, through differential and integral calculus and differential equations. In addition, this textbook can also be used as a review for students or professionals who've previously been exposed to these subjects. That being the case, it can also be used as a preparation for the Fundamentals of Engineering (FE) Examination or the Principles and Practice of Engineering (PE) Examination, both of which are required for board certification of practicing engineers.

This publication presents the subject matter in a module-based learning approach. Each module presents a few concepts in the manner that an instructor might present the material during in-class lectures. The basic concepts are explained using simple illustrations to help facilitate understanding of the subjects. Example problems are included within the module to demonstrate the concepts and enhance the learning experience. A problem set, with answers provided, is also included at the end of each module. The material is presented from an applications-oriented viewpoint with a minimal amount of accompanying theory and mathematical derivations of the formulas. This type of presentation is more suitable for the students to develop the understanding of the applications encountered on the FE and PE examinations.

If this textbook is used for an academic course, the material can be covered in a full semester consisting of approximately 15 weeks, or 45 class-hours, and each module can generally be covered in a one-hour period. The three subjects presented are broken down as follows: 13 modules in statics, 13 modules in mechanics of materials, and 14 modules in dynamics. The additional five class-hours could be used for examinations/quizzes, reviews, more in-depth discussions of certain material, or the presentation of additional material of interest to the students. The instructor may also choose to provide additional lecture material to cover certain modules in more detail or skip some modules to modify the course content as desired. Flexibility is built into the module-based structure to allow the instructor freedom to adjust the syllabus, the number of examinations/quizzes, review sessions, and whether or not to include in-class exercises as part of the learning experience.

The material is presented in a way that students should be able to read and understand the material on their own outside of class and only meet with the class on a limited basis for questions, discussions, reviews, quizzes, or examinations, if desired by the instructor. Again, the manner in which the course is conducted is at the discretion of the instructor since the module-based approach offers flexibility in possible methods employed to adequately cover the material.

TABLE OF CONTENTS

Module   Page

PART I - STATICS

1. Introduction to Vectors..3
2. Vector Operations..9
3. Moment of a Force...15
4. Force-Couple Systems..21
5. Coplanar Force Systems...27
6. Equilibrium of Coplanar Force Systems..33
7. Equilibrium of Coplanar Force Systems (cont.)..41
8. Trusses..47
9. Friction...53
10. Friction (cont.)..59
11. Centroids of Areas..65
12. Distributed Loads on Beams..71
13. Distributed Loads on Beams (cont.)...77

PART II - MECHANICS OF MATERIALS

14. Stress and Strain...85
15. Stress and Strain (cont.)...95
16. Direct Shear Stress...101
17. Area Moments of Inertia..107
18. Torsion..115
19. Shear Forces and Bending Moments in Beams...119
20. Shear Forces and Bending Moments in Beams (cont.)..127
21. Bending Stresses in Beams..131
22. Beam Deflections in Bending..135
23. Stresses Under Combined Loading Conditions...141
24. Principal Stresses...147
25. Mohr's Circle for Plane Stress...151
26. Buckling...157

TABLE OF CONTENTS (CONT.)

<u>Module</u> <u>Page</u>

PART III - DYNAMICS

27.	Kinematics of Particles...	163
28.	Kinematics of Particles (cont.)...	169
29.	Constrained Motion of Connected Particles..	175
30.	Kinetics of Particles..	181
31.	Kinetics of Particles (cont.)..	187
32.	Kinetics of Particles (cont.)..	191
33.	Work and Energy Methods...	195
34.	Impulse and Momentum Methods..	201
35.	Kinematics of Rigid Body Plane Motion...	205
36.	Kinematics of Rigid Body Plane Motion (cont.)...	211
37.	Mass Moments of Inertia..	217
38.	Kinetics of Rigid Body Plane Motion..	225
39.	Kinetics of Rigid Body Plane Motion (cont.)..	231
40.	Kinetics of Rigid Body Plane Motion (cont.)..	239
	INDEX..	243

PART I - STATICS

MODULE 1: Introduction to Vectors

The study of engineering mechanics deals primarily with two types of quantities, scalars and vectors. Scalar quantities are ones that only have a magnitude, while vector quantities are those that have both a magnitude and a direction. Examples of scalar quantities are time, distance, area, volume, density, speed, mass, and energy. Examples of vector quantities are displacement, velocity, acceleration, force, moment, and momentum.

A vector quantity is generally indicated by a boldface character or by a lightface character having an arrow or line drawn above it, while a scalar quantity is simply indicated by a lightface character. Graphically, a vector quantity **P** is represented by a line segment in a specific direction, with an arrowhead on one end to indicate the sense of the vector, as shown in Figure 1.1. The magnitude of **P**, indicated by $|\mathbf{P}|$ or P, is a scalar quantity.

Figure 1.1

Vectors are combined using the parallelogram law. For example, the sum or resultant, **R**, of two vectors, $\mathbf{P}_1$ and $\mathbf{P}_2$, can be expressed analytically by the vector equation

$$\mathbf{R} = \mathbf{P}_1 + \mathbf{P}_2 = \mathbf{P}_2 + \mathbf{P}_1$$

Figure 1.2 shows this vector addition using the parallelogram law, which is obtained by placing the tail of one vector at the head of the second vector. The sum of more than two vectors will follow the same procedure and the resultant will form a closed polygon having the number of sides equal to the number of forces plus one for the resultant.

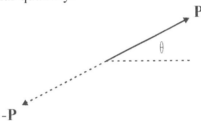

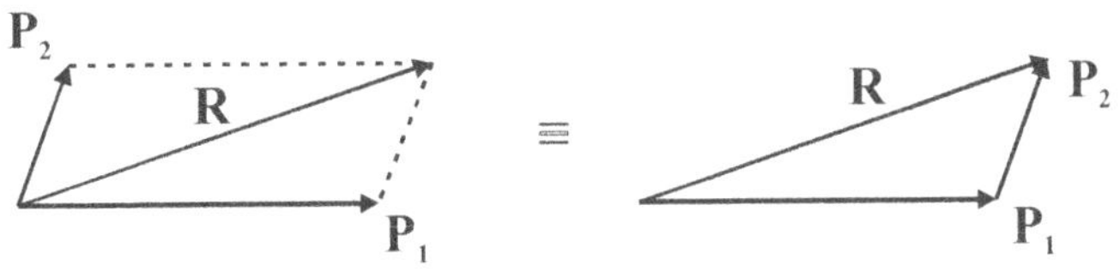

Figure 1.2

The difference between two vectors can be expressed as the sum of one positive vector and one negative vector, as shown by

$$\mathbf{R} = \mathbf{P}_1 - \mathbf{P}_2 = \mathbf{P}_1 + (-\mathbf{P}_2)$$

Graphically, the difference between vectors $\mathbf{P}_1$ and $\mathbf{P}_2$ is shown in Figure 1.3.

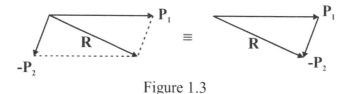

Figure 1.3

Vector quantities must be defined in a particular coordinate system. The most common is the Cartesian coordinate system, consisting of an xyz axes system having unit vectors $\mathbf{i}$, $\mathbf{j}$, and $\mathbf{k}$ in the x, y, and z directions, respectively. The magnitude of each of these unit vectors is 1. This coordinate system is shown in Figure 1.4 below.

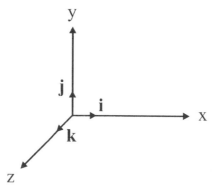

Figure 1.4

The three-dimensional vector $\mathbf{P}$ described in Cartesian coordinates using these unit vectors is shown in Figure 1.5.

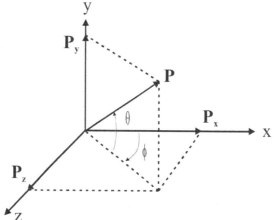

Figure 1.5

This vector can be expressed as

$$\mathbf{P} = P_x\,\mathbf{i} + P_y\,\mathbf{j} + P_z\,\mathbf{k}$$

where the components of $\mathbf{P}$, i.e., P_x, P_y, and P_z, are each expressed as a scalar quantity times a unit vector. The magnitudes of the vector components are given by

$$P_x = P \cos \theta \cos \phi$$
$$P_y = P \sin \theta$$
$$P_z = P \cos \theta \sin \phi$$

and

$$P = |\mathbf{P}| = [P_x^2 + P_y^2 + P_z^2]^{1/2}$$

Consider the coplanar case, i.e., all forces lie in the same plane, as shown in Figure 1.6.

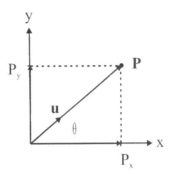

Figure 1.6

As in the three-dimensional case, the vector **P** can be written in terms of unit vectors **i** and **j** as

$$\mathbf{P} = P_x \mathbf{i} + P_y \mathbf{j} = P \cos \theta \, \mathbf{i} + P \sin \theta \, \mathbf{j}$$

The relationship between the vector components and the orientation angle θ is

$$\tan \theta = P_y / P_x$$

Vector **P** can also be written in terms of a unit vector in the **P** direction, **u**, as $\mathbf{P} = P \mathbf{u}$. This unit vector can be determined from the coordinates of any two points, A and B, which lie on the line-of-action of **P** as shown in Figure 1.7.

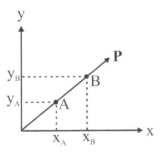

Figure 1.7

The unit vector **u** can then be calculated using the formula

$$\mathbf{u} = [(x_B - x_A) \mathbf{i} + (y_B - y_A) \mathbf{j}] / [(x_B - x_A)^2 + (y_B - y_A)^2]^{1/2}$$

where (x_A, y_A) and (x_B, y_B) are the coordinates of points A and B, respectively. This unit vector is equivalent to the vector from A to B divided by distance between points A and B. To determine a unit vector in three-dimensional space, the formula above will be modified as

$$\mathbf{u} = [(x_B - x_A)\mathbf{i} + (y_B - y_A)\mathbf{j} + (z_B - z_A)\mathbf{k}] / [(x_B - x_A)^2 + (y_B - y_A)^2 + (z_B - z_A)^2]^{1/2}$$

Example 1.1

In the figure below, the resultant of the three forces shown is 25 **j** lb. Determine the magnitudes of both **P** and **F**.

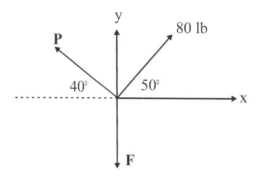

Solution: $\mathbf{R} = \mathbf{F} + \mathbf{P} + 80\cos 50°\,\mathbf{i} + 80\sin 50°\,\mathbf{j}$ lb
   $25\,\mathbf{j} = -F\,\mathbf{j} - P\cos 40°\,\mathbf{i} + P\sin 40°\,\mathbf{j} + 80\cos 50°\,\mathbf{i} + 80\sin 50°\,\mathbf{j}$
   $= -F\,\mathbf{j} - 0.766P\,\mathbf{i} + 0.643P\,\mathbf{j} + 51.42\,\mathbf{i} + 61.28\,\mathbf{j}$
   $\Rightarrow 25\,\mathbf{j} = (51.42 - 0.766P)\,\mathbf{i} + (61.28 + 0.643P - F)\,\mathbf{j}$

Setting the **i** and **j** components on each side of this equation equal gives the two component equations as

i dir: $0 = 51.42 - 0.766P$, **j** dir: $25 = 61.28 + 0.643P - F$

Solving these equations simultaneously for P and F, gives $P = 67.13$ lb and $F = 79.44$ lb.

Example 1.2

Calculate the magnitude of **P** and the angles θ and ϕ (as defined in Figure 1.5) for the force $\mathbf{P} = 200\,\mathbf{i} - 500\,\mathbf{j} + 700\,\mathbf{k}$ N.

Solution: The magnitude of the force is found by

$$P = |\mathbf{P}| = [P_x^2 + P_y^2 + P_z^2]^{1/2} = [(200)^2 + (-500)^2 + (700)^2]^{1/2}$$
$\Rightarrow P = 883.18$ N

Knowing the magnitude of **P**, the angle θ can be calculated from the expression

$P_y = P \sin \theta$
$-500 = 883.18 \sin \theta$
$\Rightarrow \theta = -34.48°$

Similarly, the angle ϕ can be found from the expression

$P_x = P \cos \theta \cos \phi$
$200 = 883.18 \cos(-34.48°) \cos \phi$
$\Rightarrow \phi = 74.05°$

Example 1.3

Determine the unit vector in the direction of a line that passes through two points whose coordinates are (-5,3) and (5,2).

Solution: $\mathbf{u} = [(x_B - x_A)\mathbf{i} + (y_B - y_A)\mathbf{j}] / [(x_B - x_A)^2 + (y_B - y_A)^2]^{1/2}$
$= [(5 - (-5))\mathbf{i} + (2 - 3)\mathbf{j}] / [(5 - (-5))^2 + (2 - 3)^2]^{1/2}$
$\Rightarrow \mathbf{u} = 0.995\,\mathbf{i} - 0.100\,\mathbf{j}$

As a check, the magnitude of $\mathbf{u}$ is

$u = [(0.995)^2 + (-0.001)^2]^{1/2} = 1.00$

Problems

1.1 The resultant of two forces, one in the positive x direction and the other in the positive y direction, is 120 lb at an angle of 55° measured counterclockwise from the positive x axis. Determine the two forces.
(Ans. $\mathbf{F}_1 = 68.83\,\mathbf{i}$ lb, $\mathbf{F}_2 = 98.30\,\mathbf{j}$ lb)

1.2 Determine the resultant force on the eyebolt below.
(Ans. $\mathbf{R} = 266.55\,\mathbf{i} + 33.22\,\mathbf{j}$ N)

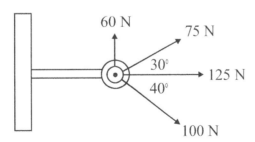

1.3 For a force given as $\mathbf{P} = 400\,\mathbf{i} + 600\,\mathbf{j} + 800\,\mathbf{k}$ N, calculate the magnitude of $\mathbf{P}$ and determine the angles θ and ϕ as defined in Figure 1.5.
(Ans. P = 1,077.03 N, θ = 33.85°, ϕ = 63.43°)

7

1.4 A force is given as **P** = 200 **i** - 175 **j** + 380 **k** N. Determine the magnitude of **P** and the unit vector **u** in the direction of **P**.
(Ans. P = 463.71 N, **u** = 0.431 **i** - 0.377 **j** + 0.819 **k**)

1.5 The magnitude of the force shown is 200 N. Determine the unit vector **u** in the direction of the force and write **F** as a vector.
(Ans. **u** = 0.707 **i** + 0.707 **j**, **F** = 141.42 **i** + 141.42 **j** N)

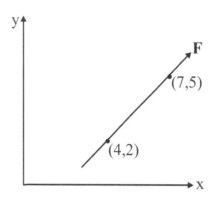

1.6 The resultant of the system of forces shown below is **R** = 387 **j** lb. Determine the possible values of P and θ.
(Ans. P = 522.28 and 164.42 lb, θ = 43.39° and -84.27°)

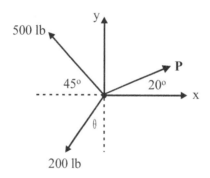

1.7 Three forces applied to an eyebolt are F_1 = 100 **i** + 200 **j** N, F_2 = -500 **i** + 300 **j** N, and F_3 = 600 **i** + 100 **j** N. Determine the resultant force and the angle θ it makes with the horizontal. Write the resultant as the product of a magnitude and a unit vector.
(Ans. **R** = 200 **i** + 600 **j** N, θ = 71.57°, **R** = 632.46(0.316 **i** + 0.949 **j**) N)

1.8 In Problem 1.6, if the 500 lb force shown has an unknown magnitude F, and θ has a value of 14°, find the magnitudes of forces F and P.
(Ans. F = 584.50 lb, P = 491.01 lb)

MODULE 2: Vector Operations

Consider two three-dimensional vectors **P** and **Q**, where θ is the angle between them. The scalar (or dot) product of **P** and **Q** is defined as

$$\begin{aligned}\mathbf{P} \cdot \mathbf{Q} = \mathbf{Q} \cdot \mathbf{P} &= PQ \cos \theta \\ &= (P_x \mathbf{i} + P_y \mathbf{j} + P_z \mathbf{k}) \cdot (Q_x \mathbf{i} + Q_y \mathbf{j} + Q_z \mathbf{k}) \\ &= P_x Q_x + P_y Q_y + P_z Q_z \\ \Rightarrow \mathbf{P} \cdot \mathbf{Q} &= PQ \cos \theta \end{aligned}$$

since $\mathbf{i} \cdot \mathbf{i} = \mathbf{j} \cdot \mathbf{j} = \mathbf{k} \cdot \mathbf{k} = 1$, and $\mathbf{i} \cdot \mathbf{j} = \mathbf{j} \cdot \mathbf{i} = \mathbf{i} \cdot \mathbf{k} = \mathbf{k} \cdot \mathbf{i} = \mathbf{j} \cdot \mathbf{k} = \mathbf{k} \cdot \mathbf{j} = 0$.

The scalar product can also be used to find the 'projection' of a vector in a certain direction. For example, the vector components of **P** can be determined by finding the projections of **P** in the **i**, **j**, and **k** direction using the relationships

$$P_x = \mathbf{P} \cdot \mathbf{i} \quad , \quad P_y = \mathbf{P} \cdot \mathbf{j} \quad , \quad P_z = \mathbf{P} \cdot \mathbf{k}$$

The vector (or cross) product of **P** and **Q** is defined as

$$\begin{aligned}\mathbf{P} \times \mathbf{Q} = -\mathbf{Q} \times \mathbf{P} &= (PQ \sin \theta) \mathbf{u} \\ &= (P_x \mathbf{i} + P_y \mathbf{j} + P_z \mathbf{k}) \times (Q_x \mathbf{i} + Q_y \mathbf{j} + Q_z \mathbf{k}) \\ &= (P_y Q_z - P_z Q_y) \mathbf{i} + (P_z Q_x - P_x Q_z) \mathbf{j} + (P_x Q_y - P_y Q_x) \mathbf{k} \\ \Rightarrow \mathbf{P} \times \mathbf{Q} &= (PQ \sin \theta) \mathbf{u} \end{aligned}$$

which is determined using the relationships

$$\begin{aligned} \mathbf{i} \times \mathbf{i} &= \mathbf{j} \times \mathbf{j} = \mathbf{k} \times \mathbf{k} = 0 \\ \mathbf{i} \times \mathbf{j} &= \mathbf{k} \; , \; \mathbf{j} \times \mathbf{i} = -\mathbf{k} \\ \mathbf{j} \times \mathbf{k} &= \mathbf{i} \; , \; \mathbf{k} \times \mathbf{j} = -\mathbf{i} \\ \mathbf{k} \times \mathbf{i} &= \mathbf{j} \; , \; \mathbf{i} \times \mathbf{k} = -\mathbf{j} \end{aligned}$$

The vector product of any two vectors yields a vector that is perpendicular (or normal) to both vectors. For a vector product of two-dimensional or coplanar vectors, the result will simply be a vector in the **k** direction.

Units

Engineering mechanics deals primarily with four fundamental quantities; length, mass, force, and time. The measurement of these quantities can be described in several different systems of units. The two systems most commonly used in science and engineering will be used in this text. These systems are the International System of Units (SI), or metric system, and the U.S. Customary system, or English (or British) system. Table 1.1 provides the units that will be used for each of the four quantities in both the SI and U.S. Customary systems.

Table 2.1 Systems of Units

Quantity	SI	U.S. Customary
Mass	kilograms, kg	slugs
Length	meters, m	feet, ft
Force	newtons, N	pounds, lb
Time	seconds, s	seconds, sec

Units in any system must satisfy the requirements of Newton's Second Law, that states that force is equal to the mass times the acceleration, given by

$$\mathbf{F} = m\mathbf{a}$$

Therefore, in SI units, this equivalence shows

$$N = kg\ m/s^2$$

and in U.S. Customary units, this equivalence shows

$$lb = slugs\ ft/sec^2$$

In U.S. units, values of mass will occasionally be provided in units of pounds mass, lb_m, rather than slugs. To avoid conversion difficulties in this case, the best practice is to convert pounds mass to slugs prior to making any calculations, using the conversion

$$1\ slug = 32.174\ lb_m$$
$$1\ lb_m = 0.031\ slug$$

All subsequent calculations should then be performed using units of slugs for mass rather than pounds mass. Other useful conversions are

$$1\ ft = 0.3028\ m\quad,\quad 1\ slug = 14.594\ kg\quad,\quad 1\ lb = 4.4482\ N$$

Weight

Since weight is a force, the weight vector can be represented by a mass times the gravitational acceleration, **g**, in the downward direction. In Cartesian coordinates, where the positive y axis is defined upwards, the proper representation of the weight vector would be

$$\mathbf{W} = -mg\,\mathbf{j}$$

Standard values for the acceleration of gravity, g, which are set at sea level and at a latitude of 45°, are given as

$$\text{SI units: } g = 9.807\ m/s^2\quad,\quad \text{U.S. units: } g = 32.174\ ft/sec^2$$

Approximate values of 9.81 m/s² and 32.2 ft/sec² are generally adequate for most engineering calculations. When weight is discussed, only the magnitude of the weight is usually mentioned since the downward direction is assumed to be known.

Example 2.1

Find the projection of the force **P** = 12 **i** - 7 **j** N, in the direction of the unit vector
u = 0.995 **i** - 0.100 **j**.

Solution: The projection of **P** in the **u** direction is defined as

$$\mathbf{P} \cdot \mathbf{u} = (12\,\mathbf{i} - 7\,\mathbf{j}) \cdot (0.995\,\mathbf{i} - 0.100\,\mathbf{j})$$
$$= (12)(0.995) + (-7)(-0.100)$$
$$\Rightarrow \mathbf{P} \cdot \mathbf{u} = 12.64 \text{ N}$$

Example 2.2

Given the vectors **P** = 10 **i** - 20 **j** + 30 **k** ft, and **Q** = -7 **i** + 3 **j** - 15 **k** ft, calculate **P** · **Q**, **P** x **Q**, and the angle between **P** and **Q**.

Solution:
$$\mathbf{P} \cdot \mathbf{Q} = (10\,\mathbf{i} - 20\,\mathbf{j} + 30\,\mathbf{k}) \cdot (-7\,\mathbf{i} + 3\,\mathbf{j} - 15\,\mathbf{k})$$
$$= (10)(-7) + (-20)(3) + (30)(-15) = -70 - 60 - 450$$
$$\Rightarrow \mathbf{P} \cdot \mathbf{Q} = -580 \text{ ft}^2$$

$$\mathbf{P} \times \mathbf{Q} = (10\,\mathbf{i} - 20\,\mathbf{j} + 30\,\mathbf{k}) \times (-7\,\mathbf{i} + 3\,\mathbf{j} - 15\,\mathbf{k})$$
$$= (10)(3)(\mathbf{i} \times \mathbf{j}) + (10)(-15)(\mathbf{i} \times \mathbf{k}) + (-20)(-7)(\mathbf{j} \times \mathbf{i}) + (-20)(-15)(\mathbf{j} \times \mathbf{k})$$
$$+ (30)(-7)(\mathbf{k} \times \mathbf{i}) + (30)(3)(\mathbf{k} \times \mathbf{j})$$
$$= 30\,\mathbf{k} - 150\,(-\mathbf{j}) + 140\,(-\mathbf{k}) + 300\,\mathbf{i} - 210\,\mathbf{j} + 90\,(-\mathbf{i})$$
$$\Rightarrow \mathbf{P} \times \mathbf{Q} = 210\,\mathbf{i} - 60\,\mathbf{j} - 110\,\mathbf{k} \text{ ft}^2$$

Since **P** · **Q** = PQ cos θ, then

$$P = |\mathbf{P}| = [P_x^2 + P_y^2 + P_z^2]^{1/2} = [(10)^2 + (-20)^2 + (30)^2]^{1/2}$$
$$\Rightarrow P = 37.42 \text{ ft}$$
$$Q = |\mathbf{Q}| = [Q_x^2 + Q_y^2 + Q_z^2]^{1/2} = [(-7)^2 + (3)^2 + (-15)^2]^{1/2}$$
$$\Rightarrow Q = 16.82 \text{ ft}$$

$$\theta = \cos^{-1}[\mathbf{P} \cdot \mathbf{Q} / PQ] = \cos^{-1}[-580 / (37.42)(16.82)]$$
$$\Rightarrow \theta = 157.15°$$

Example 2.3

Find the projection of $\mathbf{P} = 10\,\mathbf{i} - 8\,\mathbf{j} + 14\,\mathbf{k}$ lb in the direction of a line that passes through the points (2,-5,3) and (5,2,-4).

Solution: The unit vector passing through the designated points is found by

$$\mathbf{u} = [(x_B - x_A)\,\mathbf{i} + (y_B - y_A)\,\mathbf{j} + (z_B - z_A)\,\mathbf{k}] / [(x_B - x_A)^2 + (y_B - y_A)^2 + (z_B - z_A)^2]^{1/2}$$
$$= [(5 - 2)\,\mathbf{i} + (2 - (-5))\,\mathbf{j} + (-4 - 3)\,\mathbf{k}] / [(5 - 2)^2 + (2 - (-5))^2 + (-4 - 3)^2]^{1/2}$$
$$= [3\,\mathbf{i} + 7\,\mathbf{j} - 7\,\mathbf{k}] / [107]^{1/2}$$
$$\Rightarrow \mathbf{u} = 0.29\,\mathbf{i} + 0.68\,\mathbf{j} - 0.68\,\mathbf{k}$$

The projection of $\mathbf{P}$ in the $\mathbf{u}$ direction is then

$$\mathbf{P} \cdot \mathbf{u} = (10\,\mathbf{i} - 8\,\mathbf{j} + 14\,\mathbf{k}) \cdot (0.29\,\mathbf{i} + 0.68\,\mathbf{j} - 0.68\,\mathbf{k})$$
$$= 10(0.29) + (-8)(0.68) + 14(-0.68)$$
$$\Rightarrow \mathbf{P} \cdot \mathbf{u} = -12.06 \text{ lb}$$

Problems

2.1 Given the vectors $\mathbf{P} = 7\,\mathbf{i} - 4\,\mathbf{j} + P_z\,\mathbf{k}$ m, and $\mathbf{Q} = 4\,\mathbf{i} + 2\,\mathbf{j} - 1\,\mathbf{k}$ m, determine the value of P_z so that the scalar product of the two vectors will be 50 m².
(Ans. $P_z = -30$ m)

2.2 Determine the projection of the force $\mathbf{P} = 10\,\mathbf{i} - 20\,\mathbf{j} - 30\,\mathbf{k}$ N, in the direction of a line drawn from point (2,1,-1) through point (0,1,6).
(Ans. $P_u = -31.61$ N)

2.3 Given two vectors $\mathbf{P} = 10\,\mathbf{i} + 20\,\mathbf{j} + 30\,\mathbf{k}$ lb, and $\mathbf{Q} = 50\,\mathbf{i} - 40\,\mathbf{j} - 25\,\mathbf{k}$ lb, determine the quantities $\mathbf{P} \cdot \mathbf{Q}$, $\mathbf{P} \times \mathbf{Q}$, and the angle between $\mathbf{P}$ and $\mathbf{Q}$.
(Ans. $\mathbf{P} \cdot \mathbf{Q} = -1{,}050$ lb², $\mathbf{P} \times \mathbf{Q} = 700\,\mathbf{i} + 1{,}750\,\mathbf{j} - 1{,}400\,\mathbf{k}$ lb², $\theta = 114.12°$)

2.4 Given the vectors $\mathbf{P} = 8\,\mathbf{i} + P_y\,\mathbf{j}$ m and $\mathbf{Q} = 15\,\mathbf{i} - Q_y\,\mathbf{j}$ m. Determine the possible values of P_y and Q_y if the vector product of $\mathbf{P}$ and $\mathbf{Q}$ is $-10\,\mathbf{k}$ m² and the scalar product of $\mathbf{P}$ and $\mathbf{Q}$ is 135 m².
(Ans. $P_y = -2.52$ and 3.18 m, $Q_y = 5.97$ and -4.72 m)

2.5 Two vectors are given as $\mathbf{P} = 30\,\mathbf{i} + P_y\,\mathbf{j} + 20\,\mathbf{k}$ ft and $\mathbf{Q} = Q_x\,\mathbf{i} + 50\,\mathbf{j} + Q_z\,\mathbf{k}$ ft. If $\mathbf{P} \times \mathbf{Q} = -1{,}125\,\mathbf{i} + 1{,}050\,\mathbf{j} - 500\,\mathbf{k}$ ft², determine the values of P_y, Q_x, and Q_z.
(Ans. $P_y = 41.67$ ft, $Q_x = 48.00$ ft, $Q_z = -3.00$ ft)

2.6 Three vectors are given as **P** = 5 **i** - 7 **j** - 9 **k** N, **Q** = 7 **i** + 2 **j** + 6 **k** N, and
R = -3 **i** + 4 **j** + 3 **k** N. Calculate the quantities (**P** x **Q**) x **R**, **P** x (**Q** x **R**), (**P** x **Q**) · **R**, and (**Q** x **R**) · **P**.
(Ans. (**P** x **Q**) x **R** = -515 **i** - 105 **j** - 375 **k** N^3, **P** x (**Q** x **R**) = -589 **i** - 8 **j** - 321 **k** N^3,
(**P** x **Q**) · **R** = -123 N^3, (**Q** x **R**) · **P** = -123 N^3)

2.7 Three vectors are given as **P** = 4 **i** + 8 **j** - **k** N, **Q** = -6 **i** - 7 **j** + 2 **k** N, and
R = 10 **i** + 5 **j** + 9 **k** N. Calculate the vector triple products **Q** · (**P** x **R**), **P** · (**R** x **Q**), and
R · (**Q** x **P**).
(Ans. **Q** · (**P** x **R**) = -260.0 N^3, **P** · (**R** x **Q**) = -260.0 N^3, **R** · (**Q** x **P**) = 260.0 N^3)

2.8 Two vectors are given as **P** = P_x **i** + 45 **j** + P_z **k** m and **Q** = 40 **i** + Q_y **j** + 15 **k** m. If
P x **Q** = 700 **i** - 75 **j** - 1,200 **k** m^2, determine the values of P_x, P_z, and Q_y.
(Ans. P_x = 4.5 m, P_z = -0.19 m, Q_y = 133.33 m)

MODULE 3: Moment of a Force

While a force has the tendency to move a body in the direction in which the force is applied, it may also tend to rotate the body about an axis that does not intersect the line-of-action of the force. This tendency to rotate the body about an axis is known as the moment **M** of the force. In Figure 3.1, the two-dimensional force **F** is applied such that its line-of-action passes through point A. Since the line-of-action of **F** does not pass through the origin O of the coordinate system, **F** will tend to create a rotation about an axis that passes through point O and is perpendicular to both the x and y axes.

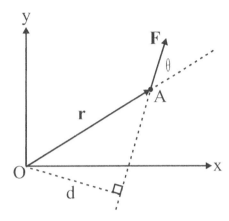

Figure 3.1

The moment **M** created about the rotational axis is determined by the vector product

$$\mathbf{M} = \mathbf{r} \times \mathbf{F}$$

where **r** is the position vector from O to <u>any</u> point on the line-of-action of **F**. It is important to note that the order of **r** x **F** must be maintained because **F** x **r** would produce a moment having the opposite sense, resulting in **F** x **r** = - **M** instead. Since the moment is equal to the vector product of **r** and **F**, the magnitude of the moment M can be expressed as the scalar quantity

$$M = |\mathbf{M}| = Fr \sin \theta$$

Often the perpendicular distance d between O and the line-of-action of **F** is used in this formula. That corresponds to the case where $\theta = 90°$, therefore $\sin \theta = 1.0$ and

$$M = Fd$$

In the general three-dimensional case, the moment of **F** about an axis through point O as

$$\begin{aligned}\mathbf{M} &= \mathbf{r} \times \mathbf{F} \\ &= (x\,\mathbf{i} + y\,\mathbf{j} + z\,\mathbf{k}) \times (F_x\,\mathbf{i} + F_y\,\mathbf{j} + F_z\,\mathbf{k}) \\ &= (yF_z - zF_y)\,\mathbf{i} + (zF_x - xF_z)\,\mathbf{j} + (xF_y - yF_x)\,\mathbf{k} \\ \Rightarrow \mathbf{M} &= M_x\,\mathbf{i} + M_y\,\mathbf{j} + M_z\,\mathbf{k}\end{aligned}$$

Here, M_x, M_y, and M_z are called the components of the moment **M**. The units of a moment are force times distance, so in the SI system a moment will have units of N-m and in the U.S. Customary system a moment will have units of lb-ft. The sense or direction of a moment can be determined by the 'right-hand' rule. This rule states that when the fingers of the right hand are curled in the direction of the tendency to rotate, the thumb will point in the direction of the moment. For example, in a coplanar case when the rotation tends to be counterclockwise, the direction of the moment will be perpendicular to the xy plane and pointing in the positive z direction. This sense is generally used to designate a positive moment. If the tendency to rotate is clockwise, the direction of the moment will be in the negative z direction. Consequently, this is generally used to designate a negative moment. If a single force acts at a location on a body that creates a tendency to rotate the body about a particular axis, an equivalent system of loads consisting of a force applied at the rotation axis and a moment applied about the rotation axis can be determined. In this case, the applied moment is calculated by **M** = **r** x **F**. These equivalent systems are shown in Figure 3.2.

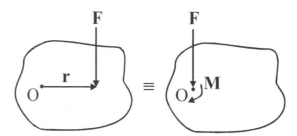

Figure 3.2

The projection of a moment in particular directions, i.e., about specified axes, can also be determined using a scalar product in the same manner as was done for forces. For example, the projection of moment **M** in the direction of unit vector **u**, can be determined by

$$M_u = \mathbf{M} \cdot \mathbf{u}$$

For a three-dimensional moment, the vector components of this moment in the x, y, and z directions can be found using the relationships

$$M_x = \mathbf{M} \cdot \mathbf{i} \quad , \quad M_y = \mathbf{M} \cdot \mathbf{j} \quad , \quad M_z = \mathbf{M} \cdot \mathbf{k}$$

Example 3.1

For **r** = 5 **i** + 3 **j** m, and **F** = 100 **i** + 150 **j** N, compute the moment about O created by **F**.

Solution: **M** = **r** x **F** = (5 **i** + 3 **j**) x (100 **i** + 150 **j**) = (5)(150) **k** + (3)(100) (-**k**)
⇒ **M** = 450 **k** N-m

Example 3.2

A force is given as $\mathbf{F} = 68.7\,\mathbf{i} + 22.9\,\mathbf{j} - 68.7\,\mathbf{k}$ N and is acting through point B (5,1,1) m. Determine the moment of this force about point C (3,4,-1) m.

Solution: The moment about C can be calculated using a position vector from C to any point on the line-of-action of **F**. The position vector from C to B can therefore be written as

$$\mathbf{r} = (x_B - x_C)\,\mathbf{i} + (y_B - y_C)\,\mathbf{j} + (z_B - z_C)\,\mathbf{k}$$
$$= (5 - 3)\,\mathbf{i} + (1 - 4)\,\mathbf{j} + (1 - (-1))\,\mathbf{k}$$
$\Rightarrow \quad \mathbf{r} = 2\,\mathbf{i} - 3\,\mathbf{j} + 2\,\mathbf{k}$ m

The moment of **F** about point C is then

$$\mathbf{M}_C = \mathbf{r} \times \mathbf{F} = (2\,\mathbf{i} - 3\,\mathbf{j} + 2\,\mathbf{k}) \times (68.7\,\mathbf{i} + 22.9\,\mathbf{j} - 68.7\,\mathbf{k})$$
$$= [(-3)(-68.7) - (2)(22.9)]\,\mathbf{i} + [-(2)(-68.7) + (2)(68.7)]\,\mathbf{j}$$
$$+ [(2)(22.9) - (-3)(68.7)]\,\mathbf{k}$$
$\Rightarrow \quad \mathbf{M}_C = 160.30\,\mathbf{i} + 274.80\,\mathbf{j} + 251.90\,\mathbf{k}$ N-m

Example 3.3

Determine the projection of the moment of the force $\mathbf{F} = 3\,\mathbf{i} + 4\,\mathbf{j} - 5\,\mathbf{k}$ N, acting through point A, having coordinates (4,1,1), in the direction of a line passing from point B (2,5,-2) to point C (4,-1,1).

Solution: First, the moment about a point on line BC must be determined. This can be done with respect to either point B or point C. Using point B, the position vector from B to A is

$$\mathbf{r} = (x_A - x_B)\,\mathbf{i} + (y_A - y_B)\,\mathbf{j} + (z_A - z_B)\,\mathbf{k} = (4 - 2)\,\mathbf{i} + (1 - 5)\,\mathbf{j} + (1 - (-2))\,\mathbf{k}$$
$\Rightarrow \quad \mathbf{r} = 2\,\mathbf{i} - 4\,\mathbf{j} + 3\,\mathbf{k}$ m

The moment of **F** about point B is then

$$\mathbf{M} = \mathbf{r} \times \mathbf{F} = (2\,\mathbf{i} - 4\,\mathbf{j} + 3\,\mathbf{k}) \times (3\,\mathbf{i} + 4\,\mathbf{j} - 5\,\mathbf{k})$$
$\Rightarrow \quad \mathbf{M} = 8\,\mathbf{i} + 19\,\mathbf{j} + 20\,\mathbf{k}$

Next, the unit vector in the direction from point B to point C must be determined from

$$\mathbf{u} = [(x_C - x_B)\,\mathbf{i} + (y_C - y_B)\,\mathbf{j} + (z_C - z_B)\,\mathbf{k}]/[(x_C - x_B)^2 + (y_C - y_B)^2 + (z_C - z_B)^2]^{1/2}$$
$$= [(4 - 2)\,\mathbf{i} + (-1 - 5)\,\mathbf{j} + (1 - (-2))\,\mathbf{k}]/[(4 - 2)^2 + (-1 - 5)^2 + (1 - (-2))^2]^{1/2}$$
$\Rightarrow \quad \mathbf{u} = 0.29\,\mathbf{i} - 0.86\,\mathbf{j} + 0.43\,\mathbf{k}$

Taking the projection of the moment in the direction of **u** gives

$$M_u = \mathbf{M} \cdot \mathbf{u} = (8\,\mathbf{i} + 19\,\mathbf{j} + 20\,\mathbf{k}) \cdot (0.286\,\mathbf{i} - 0.857\,\mathbf{j} + 0.429\,\mathbf{k})$$
$$= (8)(0.29) + (19)(-0.86) + (20)(0.43)$$
$$\Rightarrow M_u = -5.42 \text{ N-m}$$

Problems

3.1 Determine the moment of the force $\mathbf{F} = 2\,\mathbf{i} + 3\,\mathbf{j} + 4\,\mathbf{k}$ lb, acting through point A (3,0,1) ft in the direction of a line passing from point B (-2,5,5) ft to point C (-3,0,1) ft.
(Ans. $M_u = 7.42$ lb-ft)

3.2 A force $\mathbf{F} = F_x\,\mathbf{i} + 500\,\mathbf{j} + 700\,\mathbf{k}$ N, is acting through point A (0,0,0) m. If **F** creates a moment component of -2,000 N-m in the direction of a line passing from point B (2,4,5) m to point C (-3,6,8) m, determine the value of F_x.
(Ans. $F_x = -6,696.67$ N)

3.3 In the figure below, if M = 250 kg, determine the magnitude of **P** if the sum of the moments about O is zero.
(Ans. P = 766.38 N)

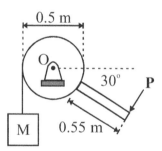

3.4 The plate below consists of 1-ft squares and the forces are applied shown. Calculate the moment about point B due to these forces.
(Ans. $\mathbf{M_B} = -195.22\,\mathbf{k}$ lb-ft.)

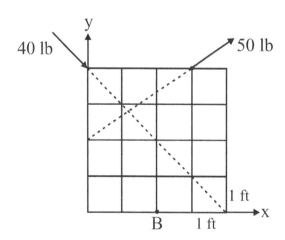

3.5 For the boom shown below, determine the tension in cable AB if the sum of the moments about point O of the boom is zero and $\theta = 38°$.
(Ans. T = 5,083.87 lb)

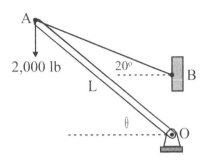

3.6 Determine the moments about both points O and A due to the applied force.
(Ans. $\mathbf{M}_A$ = -14,977.55 **k** lb-in, $\mathbf{M}_O$ = 449.17 **k** lb-in)

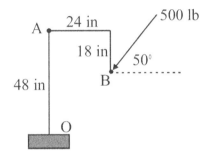

3.7 The force **F** = 5 **i** - 6 **j** - 2 **k** N is acting through point A (-2, 5, -3) m. Determine the component of the moment created by this force along a line from point B (1, 3, 5) m to point C (2, 6, 10) m.
(Ans. M_{BC} = -25.35 N-m)

3.8 If **F** = -300 **i** + 500 **j** + F_z **k** N in Problem 3.2, determine the value of F_z.
(Ans. F_z = -80.39 N)

MODULE 4: Force-Couple Systems

A force acting on a body tends to move the body in the direction the force is applied, and to rotate the body about an axis within the body. These effects can better be visualized through the use of couples. A couple is created when two equal forces act in the opposite direction a distance d apart. This situation is shown in Figure 4.1.

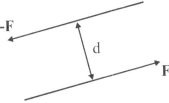

Figure 4.1

Since d is perpendicular to both forces, the magnitude of the couple M is found by

$$M = Fd$$

The direction of the couple is again determined by the right-hand rule. A couple applied at one point on a body exerts the same resultant at every point on the body.

Figure 4.2 shows a force **F** acting at point A on the body, which will create a rotation about point B on the body. Forces equal and opposite to **F** can then be applied at point B to form an equivalent system of forces acting on the body. Then, the original force **F** applied at A and **-F** applied at B can be replaced by a counterclockwise couple **M** as shown.

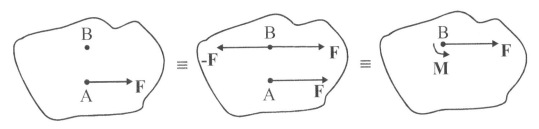

Figure 4.2

Therefore, the original applied force at A has been replaced by an equivalent system consisting of a force and a couple at B, without altering the effects of the original force on the body. This is known as a force-couple system. The process of forming equivalent systems is one that is widely used in the study of engineering mechanics and will be very important in the modules that follow.

Example 4.1

Replace the 15 N force at point A with a force-couple system (a) at point O, and (b) at point B.

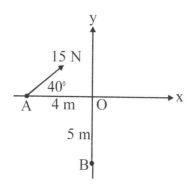

Solution: (a) The 15 N force applied at A can be replaced with a force and couple applied at point O equal to

$\mathbf{F} = F \cos\theta\, \mathbf{i} + F \sin\theta\, \mathbf{j} = 15 \cos 40° \, \mathbf{i} + 15 \sin 40° \, \mathbf{j}$
$\Rightarrow \mathbf{F} = 11.49\, \mathbf{i} + 9.64\, \mathbf{j}$ N

$\mathbf{M_O} = \mathbf{r_{OA}} \times \mathbf{F} = -4\, \mathbf{i} \times (11.49\, \mathbf{i} + 9.64\, \mathbf{j})$ N-m
$\Rightarrow \mathbf{M_O} = -38.57\, \mathbf{k}$ N-m

(b) The 15 N force applied at A can also be replaced with a force applied at point B equal to

$\mathbf{F} = 11.49\, \mathbf{i} + 9.64\, \mathbf{j}$ N

plus a couple at B equal to

$\mathbf{M_B} = \mathbf{r_{BA}} \times \mathbf{F} = (-4\, \mathbf{i} + 5\, \mathbf{j}) \times (11.49\, \mathbf{i} + 9.64\, \mathbf{j}) = (-4)(9.64)\, \mathbf{k} + (5)(11.49)(-\mathbf{k})$
$\Rightarrow \mathbf{M_B} = -96.01\, \mathbf{k}$ N-m

Example 4.2

For the block loaded as shown, replace the applied force and couple with an equivalent force and a couple at point O.

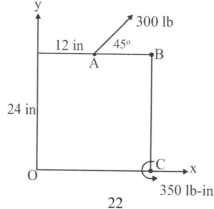

Solution: The single force placed at O will be the resultant of the applied forces calculated by

$$\mathbf{R} = 300 \cos 45° \mathbf{i} + 300 \sin 45° \mathbf{j} \text{ lb}$$
$$\Rightarrow \mathbf{R} = 212.13 \mathbf{i} + 212.13 \mathbf{j} \text{ lb}$$

The couple to be placed at point O will be equal to the sum of the moments of the applied force and the applied moment calculated by

$$\mathbf{M}_O = \mathbf{r}_{OA} \times (300 \cos 45° \mathbf{i} + 300 \sin 45° \mathbf{j}) + 350 \mathbf{k}$$
$$= (12 \mathbf{i} + 24 \mathbf{j}) \times (212.13 \mathbf{i} + 212.13 \mathbf{j}) + 350 \mathbf{k}$$
$$= (12)(212.13) \mathbf{k} + (24)(212.13)(-\mathbf{k}) + 350 \mathbf{k}$$
$$\Rightarrow \mathbf{M}_O = -2{,}195.58 \mathbf{k} \text{ lb-in}$$

Example 4.3

Determine the magnitude of the force **F** so that the moment at point A is zero.

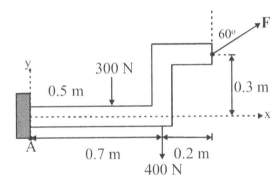

Solution:
$$\mathbf{M}_A = \mathbf{r}_1 \times \mathbf{F}_1 + \mathbf{r}_2 \times \mathbf{F}_2 + \mathbf{r}_3 \times \mathbf{F}$$
$$= 0.5 \mathbf{i} \times (-300 \mathbf{j}) + 0.7 \mathbf{i} \times (-400 \mathbf{j})$$
$$+ (0.9 \mathbf{i} + 0.3 \mathbf{j}) \times (F \sin 60° \mathbf{i} + F \cos 60° \mathbf{j})$$
$$= -150 \mathbf{k} - 280 \mathbf{k} + [(0.9)(0.5) - (0.3)(0.866)]F \mathbf{k}$$
$$= -430 + 0.19F \mathbf{k}$$
$$0 = -430 + 0.19F$$
$$\Rightarrow F = 2{,}260.78 \text{ N}$$

Problems

4.1 For the case of F = 100 N, compute the combined moment of these forces about point O and point B.
(Ans. $\mathbf{M_O} = \mathbf{M_B} = 1{,}300 \, \mathbf{k}$ N-m)

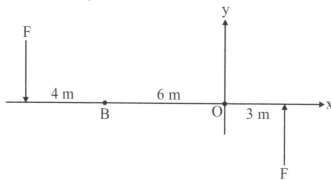

4.2 For Example 4.2 above, replace the given system of a force and a moment with a single force and a couple at point B.
(Ans. $\mathbf{R} = 212.13 \, \mathbf{i} + 212.13 \, \mathbf{j}$ lb, $\mathbf{M_B} = -2{,}195.58 \, \mathbf{k}$ lb-in)

4.3 Replace the applied forces and moment with an equivalent system of a single force, **R**, and couple $\mathbf{M_O}$ at the center of the wheel. The applied moment M has a value of 2,000 lb-in. and the outside diameter of the wheel is 7.0 ft.
(Ans. $\mathbf{R} = 100 \, \mathbf{i} + 692.82 \, \mathbf{j}$ lb, $\mathbf{M_O} = 27{,}098.44 \, \mathbf{k}$ lb-in)

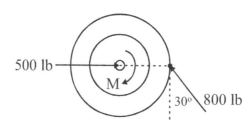

4.4 In Example 4.3, determine the moment about point A if $\mathbf{F} = 866.0 \, \mathbf{i} + 500 \, \mathbf{j} - 600 \, \mathbf{k}$ N.
(Ans. $\mathbf{M_A} = -180 \, \mathbf{i} + 540 \, \mathbf{j} - 239.80 \, \mathbf{k}$ N-m)

4.5 For the structure shown below, replace the applied forces with a single force and couple applied at point O to form an equivalent system.
(Ans. $\mathbf{R} = 3{,}000 \, \mathbf{i} - 5{,}000 \, \mathbf{j}$ N, $\mathbf{M_O} = -515 \, \mathbf{k}$ N-m)

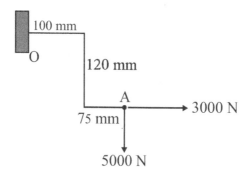

4.6 Determine the value of d in the figure below so that the force and couple shown can be replaced by a single force applied at point A to form an equivalent system. Let F = 400 N. (Ans. d = 0.399 m)

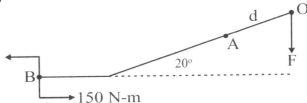

4.7 In Problem 4.6, determine the magnitude of the force **F** for the case of d = 0.55 m. (Ans. F = 290.14 N)

4.8 Solve Example 4.3 for the case where **F** makes an angle of 20° with the horizontal. (Ans. F = 16,666,67 N)

MODULE 5: Coplanar Force Systems

A coplanar system of forces is one in which all forces lie in the same plane. These forces can be concurrent or parallel. A concurrent system of forces is one where the lines-of-action of all the forces intersect at a point as shown in Figure 5.1.

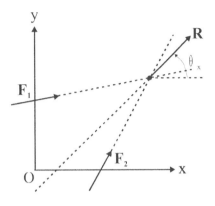

Figure 5.1

A parallel system of forces is one where the lines-of-action of the forces do not intersect, as shown in Figure 5.2.

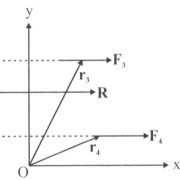

Figure 5.2

The resultant of a combined concurrent and parallel force system is both a resultant force and moment applied at point O. The resultant force is determined by

$$\mathbf{R} = \Sigma \mathbf{F}$$

whose magnitude and angle of orientation are given by

$$R = |\mathbf{R}| = [\Sigma(F_x)^2 + \Sigma(F_y)^2]^{1/2} \quad , \quad \theta_x = \tan^{-1}[\Sigma F_y / \Sigma F_x]$$

and the resultant moment is determined by

$$\Sigma \mathbf{M}_O = \Sigma(\mathbf{r} \times \mathbf{F})$$

A system of forces that includes both concurrent and parallel forces is shown in Figure 5.3.

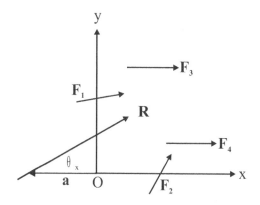

Figure 5.3

This system can be replaced by an equivalent system consisting of a single resultant force, located by position vector **a**, so that the resultant force creates a moment about point O equal to the resultant moment. Vector **a**, locating the line-of-action of the resultant force, can be obtained by satisfying the relationship

$$\mathbf{a} \times \mathbf{R} = \Sigma \mathbf{M}_O = \Sigma(\mathbf{r} \times \mathbf{F})$$

Therefore, for the system of forces shown in Figure 5.3

$$\mathbf{R} = \mathbf{F}_1 + \mathbf{F}_2 + \mathbf{F}_3 + \mathbf{F}_4 = \Sigma \mathbf{F} \quad , \quad R = |\mathbf{R}| = [\Sigma(F_x)^2 + \Sigma(F_y)^2]^{1/2}$$

$$\mathbf{M}_O = \mathbf{r}_1 \times \mathbf{F}_1 + \mathbf{r}_2 \times \mathbf{F}_2 + \mathbf{r}_3 \times \mathbf{F}_3 + \mathbf{r}_4 \times \mathbf{F}_4 = \Sigma(\mathbf{r} \times \mathbf{F})$$

$$\theta_x = \tan^{-1}[\Sigma F_y / \Sigma F_x]$$

$$\mathbf{a} \times \mathbf{R} = \Sigma \mathbf{M}_O = \Sigma(\mathbf{r} \times \mathbf{F})$$

Any moments that are applied directly to the body, indicated by $\Sigma \mathbf{M}$, must be added to the moment calculation as

$$\Sigma \mathbf{M}_O = \Sigma(\mathbf{r} \times \mathbf{F}) + \Sigma \mathbf{M}$$

Example 5.1

For the block loaded as shown below, replace the applied forces and moments with a single force and a couple at point O.

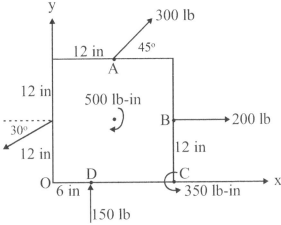

Solution: The single force to be placed at O will be the resultant of the applied forces calculated by

$\mathbf{R} = 300 \cos 45° \, \mathbf{i} + 300 \sin 45° \, \mathbf{j} + 200 \, \mathbf{i} + 150 \, \mathbf{j} - 250 \cos 30° \, \mathbf{i} - 250 \sin 30° \, \mathbf{j}$
$= 212.13 \, \mathbf{i} + 212.13 \, \mathbf{j} + 200 \, \mathbf{i} + 150 \, \mathbf{j} - 216.51 \, \mathbf{i} - 125 \, \mathbf{j}$
$\Rightarrow \mathbf{R} = 195.62 \, \mathbf{i} + 237.13 \, \mathbf{j}$ lb

The couple to be placed at point O will be equal to the sum of the moments of each of the applied forces and the applied moments calculated by

$\mathbf{M}_O = \mathbf{r}_{OA} \times (300 \cos 45° \, \mathbf{i} + 300 \sin 45° \, \mathbf{j}) + \mathbf{r}_{OB} \times 200 \, \mathbf{i} + \mathbf{r}_{OD} \times 150 \, \mathbf{j}$
$\quad + \mathbf{r}_{OE} \times (-250 \cos 30° \, \mathbf{i} - 250 \sin 30° \, \mathbf{j}) - 500 \, \mathbf{k} + 350 \, \mathbf{k}$
$= (12 \, \mathbf{i} + 24 \, \mathbf{j}) \times (212.13 \, \mathbf{i} + 212.13 \, \mathbf{j}) + (24 \, \mathbf{i} + 12 \, \mathbf{j}) \times 200 \, \mathbf{i} + 6 \, \mathbf{i} \times 150 \, \mathbf{j}$
$\quad + 12 \, \mathbf{j} \times (-216.51 \, \mathbf{i} - 125 \, \mathbf{j}) - 500 \, \mathbf{k} + 350 \, \mathbf{k}$
$= (12)(212.13) \, \mathbf{k} + (24)(212.13)(-\mathbf{k}) + (12)(200)(-\mathbf{k}) + (6)(150) \, \mathbf{k}$
$\quad + (12)(-216.51)(-\mathbf{k}) - 500 \, \mathbf{k} + 350 \, \mathbf{k}$
$\Rightarrow \mathbf{M}_O = -1{,}597.44 \, \mathbf{k}$ lb-in

where the negative sign indicates a clockwise moment about point O.

Example 5.2

For the parallel system of forces shown below, find the resultant force **R** and determine its location by finding the vector **a** (measured as shown) relative to point O as shown.

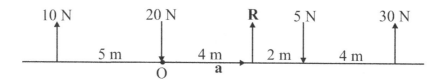

Solution: $\mathbf{R} = \Sigma\mathbf{F} = 10\,\mathbf{j} - 20\,\mathbf{j} - 5\,\mathbf{j} + 30\,\mathbf{j}$ N
⇒ $\mathbf{R} = 15\,\mathbf{j}$ N

$\mathbf{a} \times \mathbf{R} = \mathbf{M}_O = \Sigma(\mathbf{r} \times \mathbf{F})$
$a\,\mathbf{i} \times 15\,\mathbf{j}$ N-m $= -5\,\mathbf{i} \times 10\,\mathbf{j} + 6\,\mathbf{i} \times (-5\,\mathbf{j}) + 10\,\mathbf{i} \times 30\,\mathbf{j}$
$15\,a\,\mathbf{k} = -50\,\mathbf{k} - 30\,\mathbf{k} + 300\,\mathbf{k}$
$a = 14.67$ m
⇒ $\mathbf{a} = 14.67\,\mathbf{i}$ m

Example 5.3

For the force-couple system applied to the structural beam below, calculate a single resultant force and locate this force relative to point A.

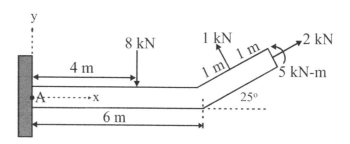

Solution: The resultant force is found by summing the applied forces as

$\mathbf{R} = -8{,}000\,\mathbf{j} + 1{,}000\,(-\cos 65° \,\mathbf{i} + \sin 65° \,\mathbf{j}) + 2{,}000(\cos 25° \,\mathbf{i} + \sin 25° \,\mathbf{j})$
$= -8{,}000\,\mathbf{j} - 422.62\,\mathbf{i} + 906.31\,\mathbf{j} + 1{,}812.62\,\mathbf{i} + 845.24\,\mathbf{j}$
⇒ $\mathbf{R} = 1{,}390.00\,\mathbf{i} - 6{,}248.46\,\mathbf{j}$ N

The corresponding moment at A created by the applied forces is found by

$\mathbf{M}_A = 4\,\mathbf{i} \times (-8{,}000\,\mathbf{j}) + [(6 + \cos 25°)\,\mathbf{i} + \sin 25°\,\mathbf{j}] \times (-422.62\,\mathbf{i}$
$+ 906.31\,\mathbf{j}) + 6\,\mathbf{i} \times (1{,}812.62\,\mathbf{i} + 845.24\,\mathbf{j}) + 5{,}000\,\mathbf{k}$
$= -32{,}000\,\mathbf{k} + 6{,}259.29\,\mathbf{k} + 178.61\,\mathbf{k} + 5{,}071.42\,\mathbf{k} + 5{,}000\,\mathbf{k}$
⇒ $\mathbf{M}_A = -15{,}490.73\,\mathbf{k}$ N-m

Locating the line-of-action of **R** relative to point A shows

a x **R** = **M**$_A$
a **i** x (1,390.00 **i** - 6,248.46 **j**) = -15,490.73 **k**
-6,248.46a **k** = -15,490.73 **k**
a = 2.48 m
⇒ **a** = 2.48 **i** m

Problems

5.1 The two-force system below creates a moment at point O equal to 600 **k** N-m. Determine vector representations for the resultant force **R** (through point O) and force **F**.
(Ans. **R** = 728.57 **j** N, **F** = 1,028.57 **j** N)

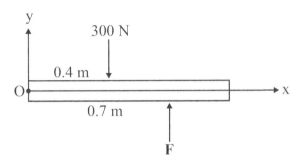

5.2 In Problem 5.1, if F = 700 N, replace the two forces with a resultant force **R** and a moment **M** at point O.
(Ans. **R** = 400 **j** N, **M**$_O$ = 370 **k** N-m)

5.3 For the case of F = 140 lb, determine the resultant force and moment about point O of the system of forces shown.
(Ans. **R** = -252.29 **i** + 193.90 **j** lb, **M**$_O$ = 997.72 **k** lb-in)

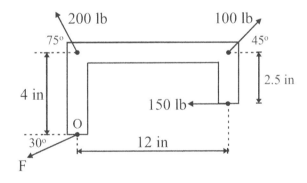

5.4 For the system of forces and the moment applied to the beam below, determine a single resultant force and locate this force relative to point O.
(Ans. **R** = -300 **j** N, **a** = 4.67 **i** m)

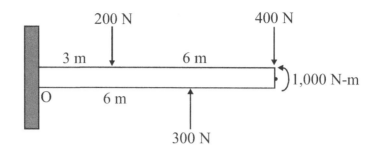

5.5 Determine the resultant force of the force-couple system acting on the beam and locate this force relative to the wall.
(Ans. **R** = 2 **j** kN, **a** = 3.0 **i** m)

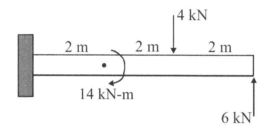

5.6 For the pulley system shown below, the resultant moment about point O is zero. Determine the tension T in the upper cable, the magnitude of the resultant force **R** acting through O, and the angle **R** makes with the positive x axis for the case where F = 295 N.
(Ans. T = 290.68 N, R = 273.15 N, θ = 116.08° CCW from the x-axis)

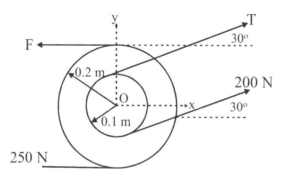

5.7 Consider Problem 5.3 for the case of F = 195 lb. Replace the system of forces with a single resultant force and locate this resultant relative to point O.
(Ans. **R** = -299.93 **i** + 166.40 **j** lb, x = 6.0 in)

5.8 Solve Problem 5.6 for F, R, and θ in the case of T = 325 N.
(Ans. F = 875.0 N, R = 719.9 N, θ = 158.62°)

MODULE 6: Equilibrium of Coplanar Force Systems

When a body is in equilibrium, the resultant of all forces and all moments acting on the body are equal to zero. Specific equilibrium conditions for two-dimensional problems are specified below.

Conditions of Equilibrium

Equilibrium of a body can be ensured by satisfying any one of the following three sets of conditions:

I. Summing the forces in both directions to zero and summing the moments about <u>any</u> point A, on or off the body, to zero.

$$\Sigma F_x = 0 \quad , \quad \Sigma F_y = 0 \quad , \quad \Sigma M_A = 0$$

II. Summing the forces in one direction to zero and summing the moments about <u>any</u> two points on the body to zero, where points A and B must not line on a line perpendicular to the direction of the summed forces.

$$\Sigma F_x = 0 \text{ or } \Sigma F_y = 0 \quad , \quad \Sigma M_A = 0 \quad , \quad \Sigma M_B = 0$$

III. Summing the moments about <u>any</u> three points on the body to zero.

$$\Sigma M_A = 0 \quad , \quad \Sigma M_B = 0 \quad , \quad \Sigma M_C = 0$$

where points A, B, and C cannot lie on a straight line.

Each set of conditions can be used to solve for three unknowns in any problem. Fewer than three unknowns in a problem require fewer than three equations in each condition. Satisfying any of the three conditions above will guarantee that equilibrium exists in the problem being addressed.

Free-Body Diagrams

A free-body diagram (FBD) is a sketch of a body showing all of the external forces and moments acting upon it. Drawing the free-body diagram is the single most important step in the solution of mechanics problems and is essential to correctly analyzing and solving problems.

External forces and moments to be shown on free-body diagrams include those applied from external loading conditions as well as those supplied by any supports or constraints attached to the body. Supports or constraints can take the form of cables or ropes, smooth or rough surfaces, roller supports, pinned connections which allow rotation, pinned connections which do not allow rotation, built-in or fixed supports, or free-sliding guides. These supports and constraints and their associated free-body diagrams are provided in Table 6.1. Before attempting to solve equilibrium problems, some additional definitions are important in understanding possible solution methods. These definitions include statically determinate structures, statically indeterminate structures, and redundant supports. 'Statically determinate' structures are those that are supported by the minimum number of constraints necessary to maintain equilibrium.

Table 6.1 Two-Dimensional Supports

Condition	Free-Body Diagram

1. Flexible cable or rope.

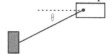   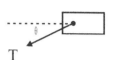

2. Smooth surface.

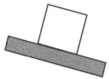

3. Rough surface.

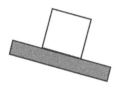

4. Simple and roller support.

5. Pinned connection (free to rotate).

6. Pinned connection (no rotation).

7. Built-in or fixed support.

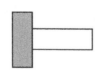   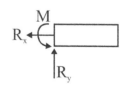

8. Free-sliding guide.

Problems involving these types of structures are generally solvable by standard solution methods. 'Statically indeterminate' structures are those that possess more external supports or constraints than are necessary to maintain equilibrium. Problems involving these types of structures are generally not solvable by standard solution methods. 'Redundant supports' are supports that can be removed without destroying the equilibrium conditions of a body. The existence of redundant supports in a structure usually makes that structure statically indeterminate.

Example 6.1

For the simple supported beam shown below, calculate the reaction forces at supports A and B.

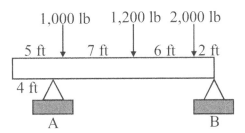

Solution: The free-body diagram for this beam is

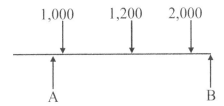

There are only two unknowns in this problem, the reaction forces in the upward direction at supports A and B. Therefore, the equilibrium of this beam can be shown by summing the forces in the y direction to zero and by summing the moments about any point on the beam to zero. Since there are no x direction forces involved, summing the forces in the x direction will not be useful.

$\Sigma F_y = 0$
$A - 1,000 - 1,200 - 2,000 + B = 0$
$\Rightarrow$ $A + B = 4,200$ lb

It is often advantageous to sum the moments about a point that will eliminate one of the unknowns from the moment equation. In this problem, summing the moments about either point A or B would result in an equation having only one unknown.

$\Sigma M_A = 0$
$1\,\mathbf{i} \times (-1,000\,\mathbf{j}) + 8\,\mathbf{i} \times (-1,200\,\mathbf{j}) + 14\,\mathbf{i} \times (-2,000\,\mathbf{j}) + 16\,\mathbf{i} \times B\,\mathbf{j} = 0$
$-38,600\,\mathbf{k} + 16B\,\mathbf{k} = 0$
$\Rightarrow$ $A = 1,787.5$ lb and $B = 2,412.5$ lb

Example 6.2

In the figure below, block A weighs 300 N and is connected to rod OB by a cable. If all surfaces are smooth, calculate the magnitude of the force **P** applied at point B on the rod maintain equilibrium.

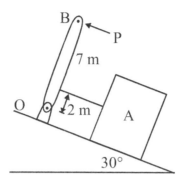

Solution: In drawing the free-body diagrams for block A and rod OB, the coordinate system is chosen such that the x axis is up the inclined plane and the y axis is perpendicular to the plane.

Block A: Rod OB:

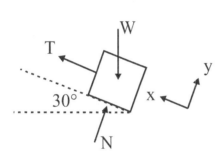   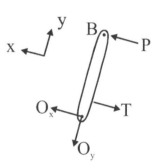

For block A, summing the forces in the x direction gives

$\Sigma F_x = 0$
T - W sin 30° = 0
T = W sin 30° = 300(0.5)
T = 150 N
$\Rightarrow$ **T** = 150 **i** N

For rod OB, if the moments are summed about point O an equation having only one unknown will be obtained.

$\Sigma M_O = 0$
9 **j** x P **i** + (2 **j**) x (-150 **i**) = 0
-9P **k** + 300 **k** = 0
$\Rightarrow$ P = 33.3 N

36

Therefore, a force of P = 33.3 N will be required to maintain equilibrium. If P has a value less than 33.3 N, the block will slide down the plane and the rod will rotate clockwise. If P has a value greater than 33.3 N, the rod will rotate counterclockwise and pull the block up the plane.

Example 6.3

Determine the tension in cable BC and the angle θ if the resultant of the applied forces at B is zero. Assume that member AB does not carry any load.

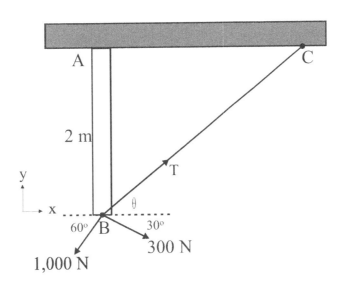

Solution: Summing the applied forces at point B shows

$$\mathbf{R} = -1{,}000 \cos 60° \,\mathbf{i} - 1{,}000 \sin 60° \,\mathbf{j} + 300 \cos 30° \,\mathbf{i} - 300 \sin 30° \,\mathbf{j}$$
$$+ T \cos \theta \,\mathbf{i} + T \sin \theta \,\mathbf{j} = 0$$
$$\Rightarrow -500.0 \,\mathbf{i} - 866.0 \,\mathbf{j} + 259.8 \,\mathbf{i} - 150.0 \,\mathbf{j} + T \cos \theta \,\mathbf{i} + T \sin \theta \,\mathbf{j} = 0$$

Separating this equation into vector components gives

i dir: $-240.2 + T \cos \theta = 0$, **j** dir: $-1{,}016.0 + T \sin \theta = 0$

Solving these equations simultaneously for T and θ gives T = 1,044.0 N and $\theta = 76.7°$.

Problems

6.1 The 15 ft long ladder shown in the figure below weighs 50 lb. Considering that all surfaces are smooth, determine the force P necessary for the ladder not to slide.
(Ans. P = 13.53 lb)

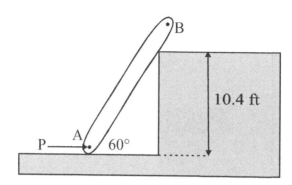

6.2 In Example 6.3, determine the reaction forces and moment at A for the case if T = 500 N and $\theta = 50°$. Consider the rod AB to have a mass of 20 kg.
(Ans. A_x = -81.20 N, A_y = 829.21 N, **M** = -162.40 **k** N-m)

6.3 For a weight of 500 N, determine the reaction forces at A and D and the tension in cable BC. Consider all surfaces to be smooth.
(Ans. A = 166.67 N, D = 166.67 N, T_{BC} = 500 N)

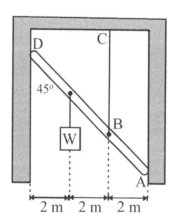

6.4 For the cable system below, calculate the tension in cables AC and BC.
(Ans. T_{AC} = 261.0 lb, T_{BC} = 351.8 lb)

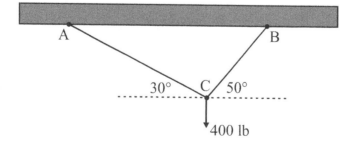

6.5 Calculate the force **P** that is necessary to begin pulling the wheel over the step. Consider the wheel to weigh 100 lb and have a diameter of 32 in.
(Ans. **P** = 124.90 **i** lb)

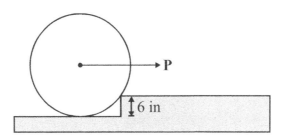

6.6 Compute the reaction forces at points A and B for the given structure. Consider the pin at A to be free to rotate.
(Ans. A_x = 2,000 N, A_y = 2,000 N, B = 2,000 N)

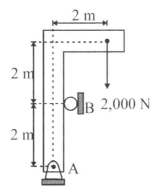

6.7 Find the weight of the block and the tension in cable BC in Problem 6.3 if the reaction forces at A and D each equal 227 N.
(Ans. W 683.0 N, T_{BC} = 683.0 N)

6.8 Solve Problem 6.5 for the case where force **P** is applied at the top of the wheel and the step is 8 in high.
(Ans. **P** = 200.0 **i** lb)

MODULE 7: Equilibrium of Coplanar Force Systems (cont.)

This module presents additional material on the subject of equilibrium of coplanar force systems.

Two-Force Members

The analysis of many structures can be simplified by recognizing the existence of two-force members. A two-force member is one in which forces are only applied at the ends of the member and those two forces are equal, opposite, and collinear. In this case, the force transmitted through the member must act along an axis connecting the end points. This situation is depicted in Figure 7.1.

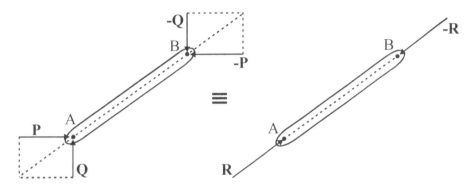

Figure 7.1

In this case, link AB is a two-force member and the resultant force **R** will be directed along the axis AB. Therefore it holds that

$$R = P + Q$$
$$-R = -P - Q$$

In solving problems, the identification of any two-force members present will simplify the analysis.

Example 7.1

For the linkage below, determine the force within links AB and BC.

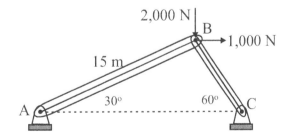

Solution: Since links AB and BC both have loads applied only at the ends, they are each two-force members. Therefore, the forces transmitted through these links F_{AB} must be directed along their longitudinal axes. The free-body diagrams for these links are

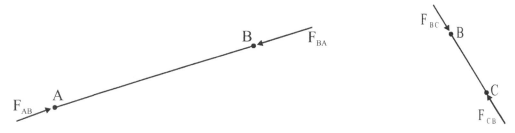

Both of these links are shown to be in compression. Drawing a free-body diagram of the pin B connecting links AB and BC shows

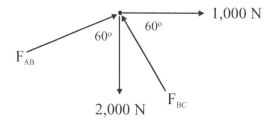

Summing the forces in both the x and y directions on the pin gives

$\Sigma F_x = 0$
$F_{AB} \cos 30° - F_{CB} \cos 60° + 1,000 = 0$
$\Rightarrow 0.866 F_{AB} - 0.5 F_{CB} + 1,000 = 0$

$\Sigma F_y = 0$
$F_{AB} \sin 30° + F_{CB} \sin 60° - 2,000 = 0$
$\Rightarrow 0.5 F_{AB} + 0.866 F_{CB} - 2,000 = 0$

Solving the two force equations simultaneously for F_{AB} and F_{CB} gives
$F_{AB} = 134.2$ N and $F_{CB} = 2,232.0$ N.

Example 7.2

In the pinned linkage shown below, determine the reaction forces at points A and C.

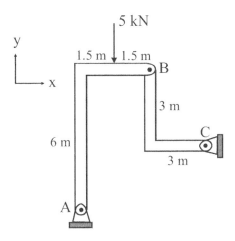

Solution: Since there are 4 unknown forces to be determined, A_x, A_y, C_x, and C_y, and only three equilibrium equations, the structure must be broken-up into two separate parts, link B and link BC. Also, since forces are only applied at the endpoints of link BC, BC is a two-force member. Therefore, the force carried by BC must be directed along the line connecting points B and C. The free-body diagrams for each part can be drawn as

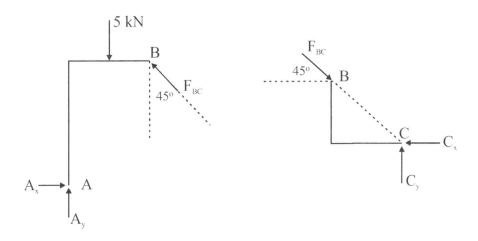

For link AB:

$\Sigma F_x = 0$
$A_x - F_{BC} \cos 45° = 0$
$\Rightarrow A_x - 0.707 F_{BC} = 0$

$\Sigma F_y = 0$
$A_y + F_{BC} \sin 45° - 5 = 0$
$\Rightarrow A_y = 5 - 0.707 F_{BC}$

$\Sigma \mathbf{M}_B = 0$
$(-1.5 \mathbf{i} \times (-5 \mathbf{j})) \times (-6 \mathbf{j} \times A_x \mathbf{i}) + (-3 \mathbf{i} \times A_y \mathbf{j}) = 0$
$7.5 \mathbf{k} + 6A_x \mathbf{k} - 3A_y \mathbf{k} = 0$
$\Rightarrow A_y = 2A_x + 2.5$

Solving these three equilibrium equations gives $A_x = 0.83$ kN, $A_y = 4.17$ kN, and $F_{BC} = 1.18$ kN.

For link BC:

$\Sigma F_x = 0$
$F_{BC} \cos 45° - C_x = 0$
$C_x = 0.707 F_{BC} = 0.707(1.18)$
$\Rightarrow C_x = 0.83$ kN

$\Sigma F_y = 0$
$F_{BC} \sin 45° + C_y = 0$
$C_y = 0.707 F_{BC} = 0.707(1.18)$
$\Rightarrow C_y = 0.83$ kN

If a negative sign would have been calculated for any force, the sense initially assumed for that force would have been incorrect.

Problems

7.1 A mass of 10 kg is supported by the structure as shown. Determine the force in member BC and the reaction forces at pin A.
(Ans. F_{BC} = 245.64 N, A_x = 167.53 N, A_y = -81.67 N)

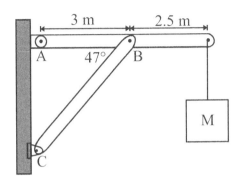

7.2 For the structure below, determine the reaction forces at C and the tension in cable AB if P = 50 N.
(Ans. T_{AB} = 100 N, C_x = 100 N, C_y = 50 N)

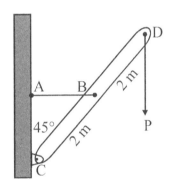

7.3 The beam below weighs 200 N and is pinned at point O. Determine the tension in cable AB and the reaction forces at O for the loading shown.
(Ans. T_{AB} = 472.81 N, O_x = 428.37 N, O_y = 100 N)

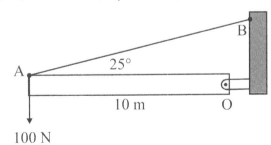

7.4 Solve Problem 7.2 considering that P = 65 N and the weight of member CD is 150 N and acting at point B.
(Ans. T_{AB} = 280 N, , C_x = 280 N, C_y = 215 N)

7.5 For the structure loaded as shown below, calculate the tension in cable AB and the reaction forces at pin C for the case where L = 8 ft.
(Ans. T_{AB} = 6,212.90 lb, C_x = 5,840.13 lb, C_y = 875.0 lb)

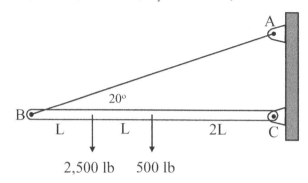

7.6 Calculate the reaction forces at point A and the tension in cable BC for the given structure.
(Ans. T = 2,121.32 N, A_x = 1,500 N, A_y = 3,500 N)

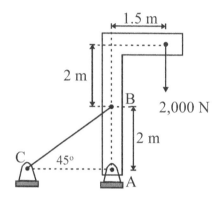

7.7 Find the mass of the block in Problem 7.1 which will create a force of 400 N in member BC.
(Ans. M = 16.31 kg)

7.8 Solve Problem 7.2 for the case where the load applied at point D is 125 N, the weight of member CD is 210 N, and cable AB is replaced with a cable from A to D.
(Ans. T_{AD} = 230 N, C_x = 230 N, C_y = 335 N)

MODULE 8: Trusses

Some of the most important structural units used in engineering are trusses. Trusses are structures composed of individual rigid elements connected together to form one or more triangular sections, with the individual elements being pinned together at joints. The rigid elements which form a truss generally lie in the same plane, therefore only coplanar force systems are involved. The weight of the members is neglected initially and all external forces are applied at the joints. Furthermore, all of the elements composing a truss are two-force members and are therefore loaded in either tension or compression. If a truss is loaded in tension, the force within the member will pull on the joint, and if a truss is loaded in compression, the force within the member will push on the joint. Examples of simple trusses are shown in Figure 8.1.

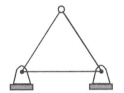 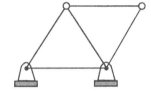 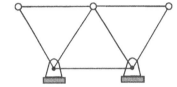

Figure 8.1

Since trusses are formed using triangular sections, it is often not necessary to know the lengths of the members or the overall dimensions of the truss. In analyzing trusses it is important to determine the axial forces in each member of the truss. There are two methods generally used in truss analysis, the method of joints and the method of sections.

The method of joints considers free-body diagrams of each joint and solves two-dimensional force equilibrium equations to determine the force in each member. This method is useful in determining the forces that must be carried by the pinned connections.

The method of sections cuts the truss through certain members to form smaller sections of the truss. Two-dimensional equilibrium equations are then solved in order to determine the forces being carried through the members that are cut. This method is useful in determining the internal forces of selected members. The method of sections will only be addressed in this text.

Method of Sections

The general procedure for the application of the method of sections is as follows:

1. Draw a free-body diagram of the complete structure.
2. Use force and moment equilibrium equations to determine the support reaction forces.
3. Identify the particular members whose internal forces need to be determined.
4. Cut a section through the truss, cutting through the members to be analyzed up to a maximum of three members.
5. Draw a free-body diagram of one portion of the sectioned truss, showing all externally applied loads, support loads, and the internal loads carried by the members cut. Assume either a tension or compression for the unknown loads in these members.

6. Using two-dimensional equilibrium equations for the section being considered, calculate the loads being carried by the cut members. If a force is calculated to be positive, the assumed direction (tension or compression) was correct. If a force is calculated to be negative, the assumed direction was incorrect.

Examples of the use of the method of sections are provided below.

Example 8.1

For the truss shown, determine the forces in members BC, FC, and FG.

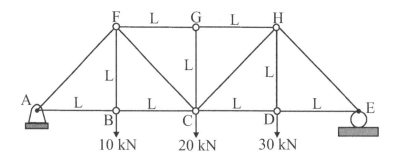

Solution: Drawing a FBD of the complete truss shows

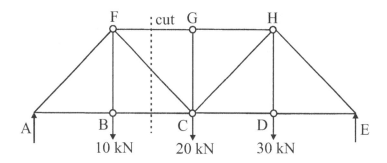

The reaction forces at the supports are found by equilibrium equations to be A = 25.0 kN and E = 35.0 kN.

In order to determine the forces in members BC, FC, and FG, the truss must be cut through those three members as shown above, creating two portions of the truss. Either of the two potions can be analyzed in order to determine the forces in members BC, CF, and FG. Considering the left portion of the truss shows

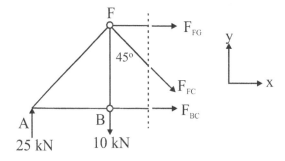

All of the members are assumed to be in tension and the length of each horizontal and vertical member is assumed to be L. The unknown forces F_{BC}, F_{FC}, and F_{FG} can be determined by solving the equilibrium conditions as follows:

$\Sigma F_y = 0$
$25.0 - 10.0 - F_{FC} \cos 45° = 0$
$\Rightarrow F_{FC} = 21.2$ kN $= 21.2$ kN T

$\Sigma M_A = 0$
$L\,\mathbf{i} \times (-10.0\,\mathbf{j}) + (L\,\mathbf{i} + L\,\mathbf{j}) \times F_{FG}\,\mathbf{i} + (L\,\mathbf{i} + L\,\mathbf{j}) \times (F_{FC} \sin 45°\,\mathbf{i} - F_{FC} \cos 45°\,\mathbf{j}) = 0$
$-10.0L\,\mathbf{k} - F_{FG}L\,\mathbf{k} - (0.707)\,F_{FC}L\,\mathbf{k} - (0.707)\,F_{FC}L\,\mathbf{k} = 0$
$-10.0 - F_{FG} - (0.707)(21.2) - (0.707)(21.2) = 0$
$\Rightarrow F_{FG} = -40.0$ kN $= 40.0$ kN C

$\Sigma F_x = 0$
$F_{BC} + F_{FC} \cos 45° + F_{FG} = 0$
$F_{BC} + 21.2(0.707) + (-40.0) = 0$
$\Rightarrow F_{BC} = 25.0$ kN $= 25.0$ kN T

From these results, members FC and BC will be in tension (T) and member FG will be in compression (C).

Example 8.2

For the truss shown below, determine the forces in members AB, BC, and CD. All members have a length equal to d.

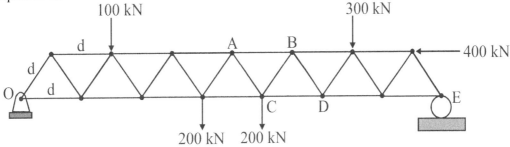

Solution: FBD:

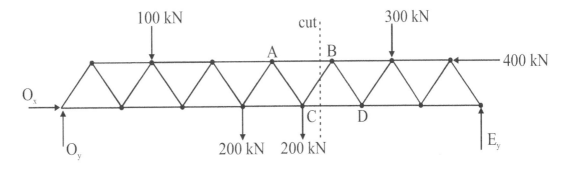

49

The reaction forces at the supports are

$O_x = 400.0$ kN , $O_y = 392.3$ kN , $E_y = 407.7$ kN

Cutting the truss as shown will give the right portion as

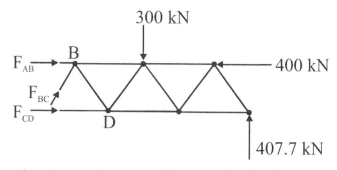

The three members in question are each assumed to be in compression. Solving for the unknown forces shows

$\Sigma F_y = 0$
$407.7 - 300.0 + F_{BC} \sin 60° = 0$
$\Rightarrow F_{BC} = -124.4$ kN $= 124.4$ kN T

$\Sigma M_B = 0$
$d\,\mathbf{i} \times (-300.0\,\mathbf{j}) + 2.5d\,\mathbf{i} \times 407.7\,\mathbf{j} + (-d \cos 30°)\,\mathbf{j} \times F_{CD}\,\mathbf{i} = 0$
$-300d\,\mathbf{k} + 1{,}019.3d\,\mathbf{k} + 0.866dF_{CD}\,\mathbf{k} = 0$
$\Rightarrow F_{CD} = -830.6$ kN $= 830.6$ kN T

$\Sigma F_x = 0$
$F_{CD} + F_{AB} + F_{BC} \cos 60° - 400.0 = 0$
$-830.6 + F_{AB} + (-124.4)(0.5) - 400.0 = 0$
$\Rightarrow F_{AB} = 1{,}292.8$ kN $= 1{,}292.8$ kN C

This indicates that AB is in compression (C) and BC and CD are in tension (T).

Problems

8.1 Determine the forces in members CD, CG, and FG of the truss below if $P = 1{,}000$ lb.
(Ans. $F_{CD} = 630.3$ lb T, $F_{CG} = 394.6$ lb T, $F_{FG} = 827.6$ lb C)

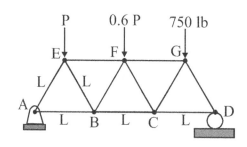

8.2 In Example 8.1, determine the forces in members CD, CH, and GH.
(Ans. F_{CD} = 35.0 kN T, F_{CH} = 7.07 kN T, F_{GH} = 40.0 kN C)

8.3 Calculate the forces in members BC, CE, and EF for the condition of P = 500 N.
(Ans. F_{BC} = 1,722.2 N T, F_{CE} = 637.4 N C, F_{EF} = 3,166.7 N C)

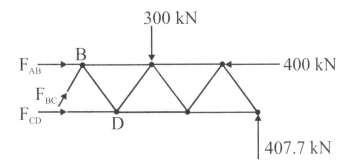

8.4 In the truss shown below, determine the forces in members FG, BG, and BC.
(Ans. F_{FG} = 26.7 kN C, F_{BG} = 24.0 kN C, F_{BC} = 40.0 kN T)

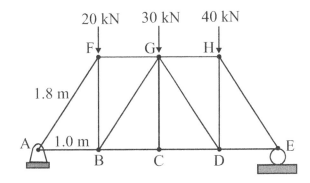

8.5 Calculate the forces in members AD, BC, and BD when P = 50 kN.
(Ans. F_{AD} = 62.5 kN T, F_{BC} = 0 kN, F_{BD} = 0 kN)

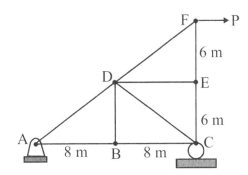

8.6 Determine the forces in members CD, CG, and FG in the truss below.
(Ans. F_{CD} = 17,754.0 N T, F_{CG} = 6,929.2 N C, F_{FG} = 16,500.4 N C)

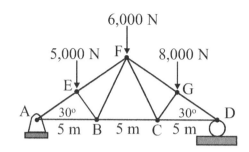

8.7 In Problem 8.1, calculate the value of P which would create a force of 1,000 lb in member FG.
(Ans. P = 1,317.24 lb)

8.8 In Problem 8.6, determine the forces in members BC, BF, and EF.
(Ans. F_{BC} = 10,825.3 N, F_{BF} = 4,330,1 N, F_{EF} = -15,000.0 N)

MODULE 9: Friction

Friction forces result when two surfaces that possess some degree of roughness, i.e., not smooth, move or attempt to move relative to each other. Two types of friction forces exist, static friction forces and kinetic friction forces. Static friction is the tangential force that opposes the sliding of one body relative to another. Kinetic friction is the tangential force between two bodies after motion begins. The magnitudes of these two types of friction forces are given as

$$f_s \leq \mu_s N \quad , \quad f_k = \mu_k N$$

where

μ_s = coefficient of static friction
μ_k = coefficient of kinetic friction

Since μ_k is usually smaller than μ_s, the magnitude of the kinetic friction force is generally less than the magnitude of the static friction force. The coefficients of friction are functions of the materials of the two bodies and the degree of roughness of the surfaces. The relationship between static friction and kinetic friction can be seen in Figure 9.1, where F is applied to a block resting on a surface.

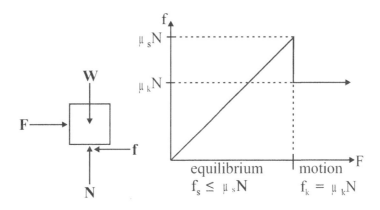

Figure 9.1

This figure indicates that as the applied force **F** increases from zero, the static friction force resisting the motion between the block and the surface increases during the equilibrium (or no-slipping) phase. When motion of the block is impending, i.e., motion ready to begin, the magnitude of the maximum static friction force is achieved and is equal to

$$f_{max} = \mu_s N$$

When motion (or slipping) of the block begins, the magnitude of the friction force drops to a value equal to the kinetic friction force, which will be constant as along as the block remains in motion.

Example 9.1

Consider a block of mass m positioned on a plane inclined at an angle θ. Determine the maximum value of θ for equilibrium.

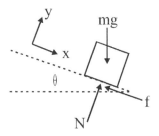

Solution: Assuming the x axis to be parallel to the inclined plane and the y axis to be perpendicular to the inclined plane, the free-body diagram of the block will be

Since motion will be impending at the maximum value of θ, the static friction force will also be a maximum at this point. Summing the force equations to zero gives

$\Sigma F_x = 0$
$W \sin \theta - f_{max} = 0$
$W \sin \theta = \mu_s N$
$\Rightarrow N = (W \sin \theta) / \mu_s$

$\Sigma F_y = 0$
$-W \cos \theta + N = 0$
$\Rightarrow N = W \cos \theta$

$(W \sin \theta) / \mu_s = W \cos \theta$
$\Rightarrow \theta = \tan^{-1} \mu_s$

Therefore the critical angle of the incline is a function only of μ_s and not the mass of the block.

Example 9.2

For the two block system shown below, calculate the magnitude of the force **P** for impending motion up the plane. Block A weighs 20 N and block B weighs 15 N. Assume that the pulley is frictionless and the coefficient of static friction between all other surfaces is 0.25.

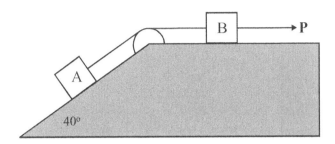

Solution: Drawing the free-body diagrams for each block shows

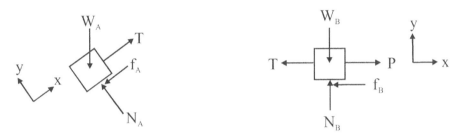

Since motion is impending, the static friction forces will be maximized. Evaluating the equilibrium conditions for each bock gives

Block A:

$\Sigma F_x = 0$
$T - f_A - W_A \sin \theta = 0$
$T - \mu_s N_A - W_A \sin \theta = 0$
$T = 0.25 N_A + 20 \sin 40°$
$\Rightarrow T = 0.25 N_A + 12.86$

$\Sigma F_y = 0$
$N_A - W_A \cos \theta = 0$
$N_A = 20 \cos 40°$
$\Rightarrow N_A = 15.3$ N

Block B:

$\Sigma F_x = 0$
$P - T - f_B = 0$
$P - T - \mu_s N_B = 0$
$\Rightarrow P = T + 0.25 N_B$

$\Sigma F_y = 0$
$N_B - W_B = 0$
$\Rightarrow N_B = 15.0$ N

Substituting and solving the x-direction force equations for T and P gives

$T = 0.25(15.32) + 12.86$
$\Rightarrow T = 16.69$ N
$P = 16.69 + 0.25(15.0)$
$\Rightarrow P = 20.45$ N

Problems

9.1 Block A has a mass of 20 kg and block B has a mass of 60 kg. Determine the magnitude of force **P** in order to move block B and determine the force in the cable attached at C. The coefficient of friction between all surfaces is 0.35.
(Ans. P = 307.79 N, T_{AC} = 71.98 N)

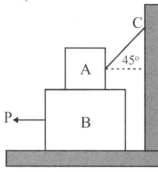

9.2 In Example 9.2, determine the mass of block A for impending motion down the plane for the case of P = 0.
(Ans. m_A = 0.847 kg)

9.3 The ladder shown in the figure below weighs 250 lb. Considering that μ_s = 0.15, determine the force P necessary for the ladder not to slide.
(Ans. P = 34.37 lb)

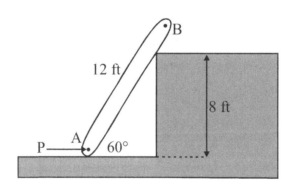

9.4 In the figure below, block A weighs 100 N and block B weighs 150 N. If μ_s = 0.3, determine the maximum value P can have before slipping occurs.
(Ans. P = 31.68 N)

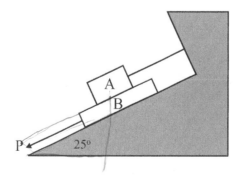

9.5 Determine the minimum value of P necessary to start motion in the two-block system shown. The coefficient of static friction between all surfaces is 0.3 and M = 10 kg.
(Ans. P = 218.40 N)

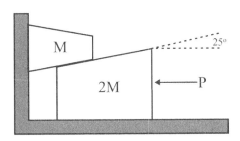

9.6 For the system shown, determine the range of values of W for block A to maintain equilibrium. The weight of block A is 125 lb and the coefficient of friction between the blocks and the inclined surfaces is 0.4. Assume that the pulley is frictionless.
(Ans. 18.01 lb < W < 158.86 lb)

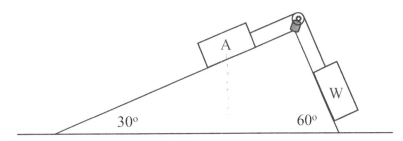

9.7 Solve Problem 9.4 for the case where **P** acts up the plane rather than down the plane.
(Ans. P = 158.58 N)

9.8 Solve Problem 9.5 for the case where P acts to the right and the top block has a mass equal to 3M.
(Ans. P = 140.64 lb)

MODULE 10: Friction (cont.)

The previous module addressed friction problems in which motion was either occurring or impending. In those cases the friction forces can be easily calculated. If motion is occurring, the friction force is equal to the kinetic friction force, and if motion is impending, the friction force is equal to the maximum possible static friction force. Problems of a more challenging nature are ones in which the analysis must determine the magnitude of the friction force present and whether or not motion is occurring or impending. The following examples demonstrate those types of friction problems.

Example 10.1

In the two block system shown, block A has a mass of 4 kg and block B has a mass of 3 kg. The coefficient of static friction between blocks A and B is 0.35, and the coefficient of static friction between block B and the surface is 0.25. Determine the value of the applied force P for impending motion of block A and determine if block B is slipping.

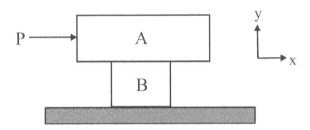

Solution: Drawing free-body diagrams for each block shows

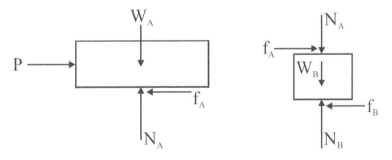

Since motion of A is impending, f_A will be a maximum. Evaluating the equilibrium conditions for each block gives

Block A:

$\Sigma F_y = 0$
$N_A - m_A g = 0$
$N_A = 4(9.81)$
$\Rightarrow N_A = 39.24$ N

Block B:

$\Sigma F_y = 0$
$N_B - N_A - m_B g = 0$
$N_B = 39.240 + 3(9.81)$
$\Rightarrow N_B = 68.67$ N

59

$\Sigma F_x = 0$
P - f_A = 0
P = $\mu_A N_A$ = 0.35(39.24)
⇒ P = 13.73 N

$\Sigma F_x = 0$
$f_A - f_B$ = 0
⇒ $f_B = \mu_A N_A$ = 13.73 N

At this point, the actual friction force between block B and the surface must be compared to the maximum possible friction force, computed by

$f_{B\text{-max}} = \mu_B N_B$ = 0.25(68.67)
⇒ $f_{B\text{-max}}$ = 17.17 N

Since the actual friction force is less than the maximum possible friction force, there will not be any slipping between block B and the surface.

Example 10.2

The block below has a weight of 75 lb. The coefficients of friction between the block and the inclined plane are μ_s = 0.30 and μ_k = 0.25.

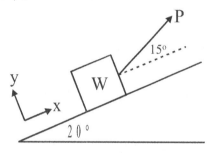

Determine the friction force for the following cases: (a) P = 0, (b) P = 35 lb, (c) P = 70 lb, and (d) find P for impending motion of the block up the plane.

Solution: The free-body diagram for the block is drawn below. Note that the direction of the friction force can actually be either up or down the plane, depending on the direction of motion or impending motion. It will be assumed that the friction force will be acting in the upward direction on the block. If the friction force is calculated to be a negative number, the sense will be opposite to this assumed direction.

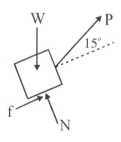

In analyzing problems of this type, it is often necessary to assume that either equilibrium exists or that slipping occurs. Whichever assumption is made can then be proven to be valid or invalid based upon the results of the calculations. Therefore, in solving this problem it will be assumed that equilibrium conditions exist. Summing the forces acting on the block to zero gives

$\Sigma F_x = 0$
P cos 15° + f - W sin 20° = 0
$\Rightarrow$ f = 25.65 - 0.966P

$\Sigma F_y = 0$
N + P sin 15° - W cos 20° = 0
$\Rightarrow$ N = 70.48 - 0.259P

(a) For P = 0:   f = 25.65 lb ,   N = 70.48 lb

The maximum possible friction force will be

$f_{max} = \mu_s N = 0.30(70.48)$
$\Rightarrow$ $f_{max} = 21.14$ lb

Since f > f_{max}, the original assumption of equilibrium is invalid. Therefore the block will be slipping and the friction force will be equal to the kinetic friction force calculated by

$f = \mu_k N = 0.25(70.48)$
$\Rightarrow$ f = 17.62 lb

(b) For P = 35 lb: f = -8.16 lb ,   N = 61.52 lb

Since f is negative, the friction force will be equal to 8.16 lb acting downward on the block instead of upward. The maximum friction force is

$f_{max} = \mu_s N = 0.30(61.52)$
$\Rightarrow$ $f_{max} = 18.46$ lb

Since f < f_{max} in the case, the original assumption of equilibrium is valid.

(c) For P = 70 lb: f = -41.97 ,   N = 52.35 lb

Again, the negative sign on the friction force indicates the direction is upward with a magnitude of 41.968 lb and the maximum friction force is

$f_{max} = \mu_s N = 0.30(52.35)$
$\Rightarrow$ $f_{max} = 15.70$ lb

Since $f > f_{max}$, the original assumption of equilibrium is again invalid and

$f = \mu_k N = 0.25(52.35)$
⇒ $f = 13.09$ lb

(d) For impending motion up the plane:

$f = f_{max} = \mu_s N = 0.30(70.48 - 0.259P)$
⇒ $f = 21.14 - 0.08P$ lb (downward)

$\Sigma F_x = 0$
$f = 0.97P - 25.65$
$21.14 - 0.08P = 0.97P - 25.65$
⇒ $P = 44.56$ lb

Problems

10.1 Force of $P = 200$ N is acting on a block weighing 600 N as shown. For the case where $\mu_s = 0.30$ and $\mu_k = 0.25$, determine if the block is in equilibrium, sliding up the plane, or sliding down the plane. Also calculate the value of the friction force.
(Ans. Block is sliding down the plane, $f = 114.91$ N)

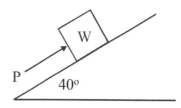

10.2 Two blocks on an inclined plane are connected by a rope as shown. Block B weighs 30 lb and has a coefficient of static friction with the plane of 0.5. Block A has a coefficient of static friction with the plane of 0.25. Determine the minimum weight of block A so that motion of the two blocks is impending and determine the tension in the rope.
(Ans. $W = 35.84$ lb, $T = 3.83$ lb)

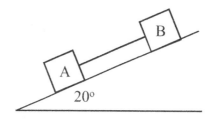

10.3 In the figure below the weight of the block is 500 lb and the coefficients of static and kinetic friction are 0.35 and 0.30, respectively. If P = 100 lb, determine if the block is in equilibrium and calculate the magnitude and direction of the friction force.
(Ans. The block is in equilibrium, f = 120.68 lb up the plane)

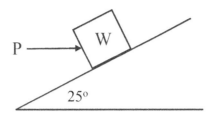

10.4 In Problem 10.3, consider the block to weigh 400 lb. Calculate the coefficient of static friction if a force of P = 80 lb is required to keep the block in equilibrium.
(Ans. μ = 0.244)

10.5 Blocks A, B, and C below have masses of 30kg, 25 kg, and 20 kg, respectively. The coefficients of static friction are 0.40 between blocks A and B, 0.35 between blocks B and C, and 0.30 between block C and the surface. As θ is slowly increased from 0°, determine which block will begin to slide first and the value of θ at which this sliding first occurs.
(Ans. Block C slides first when θ = 16.70°)

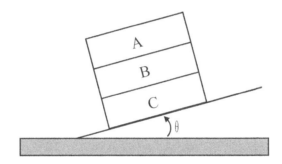

10.6 Blocks A, B, and C have masses of 20 kg, 25 kg, and 30 kg, respectively. The coefficients of static friction are 0.4 between A and B, 0.3 between B and C, and 0.2 between C and the floor. Calculate the smallest value of P that will cause one of the blocks to move and determine which block will move.
(Ans. P = 210.70 N, block B will move)

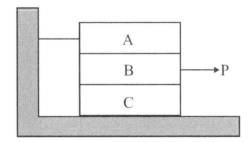

10.7 Solve Problem 10.5 for the case where the coefficients of static friction are 0.30 between blocks A and B, 0.35 between blocks B and C, and 0.40 between block C and the surface.
(Ans. Block A slides first when $\theta = 16.70°$)

10.8 Solve Problem 10.6 for the value of P for the case where both blocks A and C are attached to the vertical wall.
(Ans. P = 210.7 N)

MODULE 11: Centroids

A centroid is defined as the geometrical center of a body. If the body is homogeneous, i.e., the same density throughout, the centroid coincides with the center-of-gravity of the body. If the body is not homogeneous, these points do not coincide. Centroids are used to determine the center-of-gravity of a body and the point within a distributed load where the total load can be considered to act.

Consider a thin, flat plate having uniform thickness throughout to be a two-dimensional body. The centroid of such a body can be defined as the geometrical center of the two-dimensional area that defines the shape of this body. The location of the centroid, denoted by the coordinates x^* and y^*, is calculated using the principle of first moments of area as defined by the integral expressions

$$x^* = \int(xdA) / A \quad , \quad y^* = \int(ydA) / A$$

where A is the total area of the shape being considered. The quantities $\int xdA$ and $\int ydA$ are called the 'first moments of area'.

For common shapes, simple formulas for x^* and y^* can be used without the need for integration. Table 11.1 provides a summary of common shapes and their centroids.

Method of Composite Areas

When a body can be easily divided into several parts whose centroids are known or easily determined, the method of composite areas can be used to determine the centroid of the entire body. This is done by using the following formulas, along with the formulas presented in Table 11.1, for the computation of the coordinates of the centroid of the composite area, x^*_C and y^*_C.

$$x^*_C = \Sigma x^* A / \Sigma A \quad , \quad y^*_C = \Sigma y^* A / \Sigma A$$

where the terms x^*A and y^*A represent the product of the individual centroid components and areas. This method is demonstrated in the examples that follow Table 11.1.

Table 11.1 Centroids of Common Shapes

Rectangular Area:

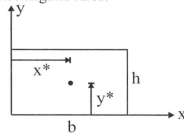

$x^* = b/2$ $y^* = h/2$

Triangular Area:

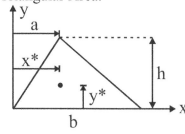

$x^* = (a+b)/3$ $y^* = h/3$

Circular Area:

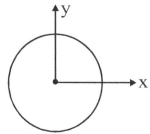

$x^* = 0$ $y^* = 0$

Semi-Circular Area:

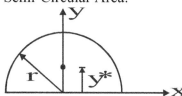

$x^* = 0$ $y^* = 4r/3\pi$

Quarter-Circular Area:

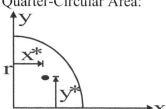

$x^* = 4r/3\pi$ $y^* = 4r/3\pi$

Example 11.1

Locate the centroid of the body shown below.

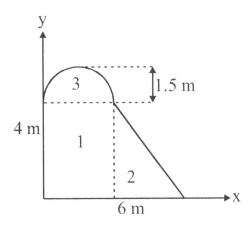

Solution: This body can easily be broken into three commonly-shaped areas; a rectangular area, a triangular area, and a semicircular area. These areas are designated as areas 1, 2, and 3, respectively. The table below provides the quantities x^*, y^*, A, x^*A, and y^*A for each area, where x^* and y^* are calculated using the formulas provided in Table 11.1. Note that these values are adjusted to provide the coordinates of the centroid of each area in the coordinate system specified for the entire composite area. The columns for A, x^*A, and y^*A are then added and the results are used to compute x^*_C and y^*_C from the formulas provided above.

Area	x^* (m)	y^* (m)	A (m²)	x^*A (m³)	y^*A (m³)
1	1.50	2.00	12.00	18.00	24.00
2	4.00	1.33	6.00	24.00	8.00
3	1.50	4.64	3.53	5.30	16.38
Totals:			21.53 m²	47.30 m³	48.38 m³

For the composite body then

$x^*_C = \Sigma x^* A / \Sigma A = 47.30 / 21.53$
$\Rightarrow x^*_C = 2.20$ m

$y^*_C = \Sigma y^* A / \Sigma A = 48.38 / 21.53$
$\Rightarrow y^*_C = 2.25$ m

Example 11.2

The body below contains a circular cutout having a radius of 1.0 in. Compute the centroid of the composite body shown.

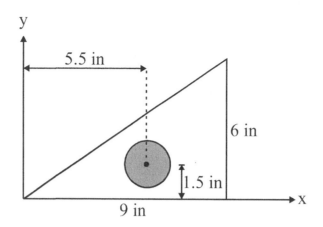

Solution: The method of composite areas can also be used for a problem containing cutouts. However, the cutout sections must be considered to have a negative area when computing the tabular quantities used in the solution. Considering the triangular area to be area 1 and the circular cutout to be area 2, the following table of values can be constructed using the formulas for common shapes.

Area	x^* (m)	y^* (m)	A (m²)	x^*A (m³)	y^*A (m³)
1	6.00	2.00	27.00	162.00	54.00
2	5.50	1.50	-3.14	-17.27	-4.71
Totals:			23.86 in²	144.73 in³	49.29 in³

For the composite body then

$x^*_C = \Sigma x^*A / \Sigma A = 144.73 / 23.86$
⇒ $x^*_C = 6.07$ in

$y^*_C = \Sigma y^*A / \Sigma A = 49.29 / 23.86$
⇒ $y^*_C = 2.07$ in

Problems

11.1 Compute the centroid of the area below if a = 2.0 ft.
(Ans. $x^*_C = 1.09$ ft, $y^*_C = 1.04$ ft)

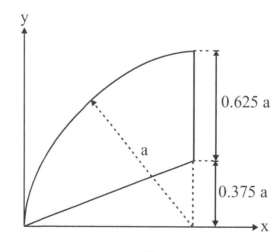

11.2 Compute the centroid of the area shown for the case of L = 6 in.
(Ans. x^*_C = 8.82 in, y^*_C = 5.41 in)

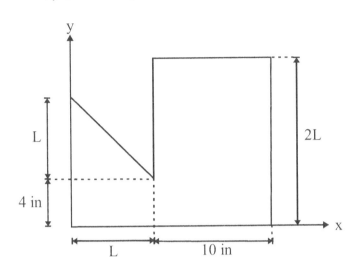

11.3 Compute the x coordinate of the centroid for the triangular area and cutout below. The units of h are meters.
(Ans. x^*_C = 0.412h m)

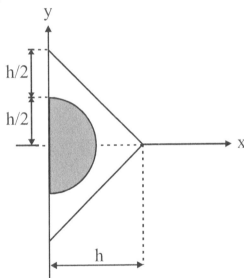

11.4 Compute the centroid of the area shown. The radius of the cutout is 2.2 m.
(Ans. x^*_C = 5.57 m, y^*_C = 2.97 m)

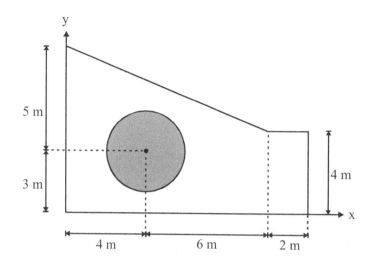

11.5 The plate shown below includes a set of 2.0 in diameter cutouts. Compute both the x and y coordinates of the centroid of this plate.
(Ans. $x^*_C = 7.80$ in, $y^*_C = 5.40$ in)

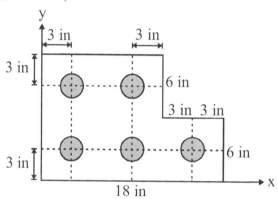

11.6 Compute the centroid of the area below with respect to the given coordinate system.
(Ans. $x^*_C = 0.010$ m, $y^*_C = 0.013$ m)

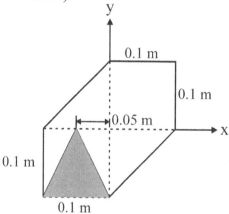

11.7 Solve Problem 11.1 in terms of the unknown dimension a.
(Ans. $x^*_C = 0.548a$ in, $y^*_C = 0.518a$ in)

11.8 Solve Problem 11.5 for the case where the diameter of the cutouts is 3.0 in.
(Ans. $x^*_C = 7.82$ in, $y^*_C = 5.40$ in)

MODULE 12: Distributed Loads on Beams

Beams

Beams are structural members that provide a resistance to bending due to applied loads. Beams are generally long prismatic bars and loads are most often applied normal to the longitudinal axis of the bar. These applied loads can be couples, concentrated loads, or various types of distributed loads. Modules 12 and 13 address methods of analyzing beams in cases of distributed loads.

Prior to the study of distributed loadings on beams, however, it is important to understand the two different types of beams. Beams that are supported in a manner that the external support reactions can be calculated by the methods addressed in statics are called 'statically determinate' beams. Beams that are supported by more external supports than are necessary for equilibrium are called 'statically indeterminate' beams. More advanced analysis methods are required in order to determine the support reactions in beams that are statically indeterminate. Figure 12.1 gives examples of both statically determinate and statically indeterminate beams.

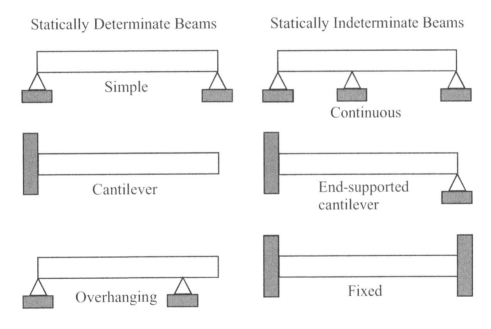

Figure 12.1

Types of Loading

Distributed loads are loads that are applied over a portion of the beam's length with a given intensity. This intensity, w, is expressed as a force per unit length of beam and can be uniform or variable, and can be continuous or discontinuous. Loadings that are uniformly distributed, i.e., constant, or distributed as a linear function of the beams length, are easily handled. Examples of uniformly and linearly varying distributed loads are shown in Figure 12.2.

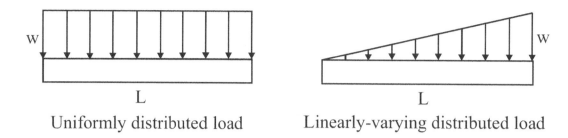

Figure 12.2

The effects of distributed loads are analyzed by replacing the distributed load with a concentrated load having a magnitude equal to the total load, i.e., area under the curve of w, and placed at the centroid of the area representing the load distribution. For a uniform load, the concentrated load would be equal to R = wL, and placed at the center of the load's span. For a linearly distributed load, the concentrated load would be equal to R = 0.5wL, and placed at a distance of L/3 from the non-zero side of the load distribution. Figure 12.3 shows how distributed loads can be replaced with concentrated loads at the centroid of each load distribution.

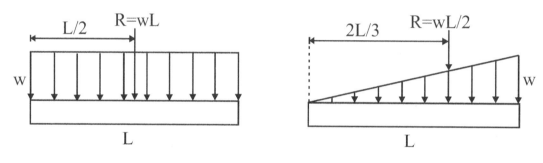

Figure 12.3

Distributed loads can also consist of a combination of a uniformly and a linearly varying distribution. An example of this condition is shown in Figure 12.4.

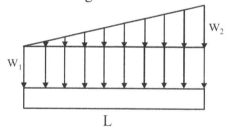

Figure 12.4

In this case, the distributed loads can be replaced with concentrated loads by one of two methods. One method is to place a concentrated load for each distributed load at the centroid of each area, as was done in Figure 12.3. Another method is to place a single concentrated load at the centroid of the combined areas representing the uniform load distribution and the linearly varying load distribution. In this case, the centroid must first be determined by the method of composite areas, as described in Module 4, and will therefore require additional calculations.

Example 12.1

For the simple beam shown below, determine the reactions at the supports.

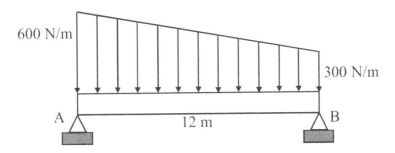

Solution: The distributed loads for this beam consist of a uniform load of $w_1 = 300$ N/m, and a linearly varying load $w_2 = 300$ N/m at the left support and decreasing to zero at the right support. These distributed loads can be replaced with two concentrated loads where

$R_1 = w_1 L = 300(12.0)$
$\Rightarrow R_1 = 3{,}600$ N

$R_2 = w_2 L / 2 = 300(12.0) / 2$
$\Rightarrow R_2 = 1{,}800$ N

These concentrated loads will be placed at the centroids of the rectangular area (for the constant load) and the triangular area (for the linearly varying load) as shown on the free-body diagram below.

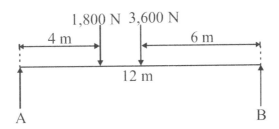

$\Sigma F_y = 0$
$A + B = 5{,}400$
$\Rightarrow A = 5{,}400 - B$

$\Sigma M_A = 0$
$4\,\mathbf{i} \times (-1{,}800\,\mathbf{j}) + 6\,\mathbf{i} \times (-3{,}600\,\mathbf{j}) + 12\,\mathbf{i} \times B\,\mathbf{j} = 0$
$-7{,}200\,\mathbf{k} - 21{,}600\,\mathbf{k} + 12B\,\mathbf{k} = 0$
$12B = 28{,}800$
$\Rightarrow B = 2{,}400$ N and $A = 3{,}000$ N

Example 12.2

For the cantilever beam, determine the reactions at the wall.

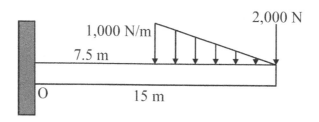

Solution: The linearly varying distributed load can be replaced by a concentrated load of 1000(7.5) / 2 = 3,750 N, at the centroid of the triangular area, which is a distance of 5 m from the end of the beam. The free-body diagram can then be drawn as

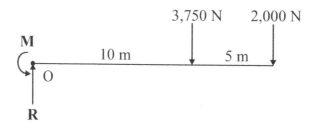

$\Sigma F_y = 0$
R - 3,750 - 2,000 = 0
$\Rightarrow$ R = 5,750 N

$\Sigma M_O = 0$
10 **i** x (-3,750 **j**) + 15 **i** x (-2,000 **j**) + **M** = 0
-37,500 **k** - 30,000 **k** + M **k** = 0
$\Rightarrow$ M = 67,500 N-m

Problems

12.1 Determine the reactions at the supports for the beam shown and the case of w = 600 lb/ft.
(Ans. A = 4,401 lb, B = 2,799 lb)

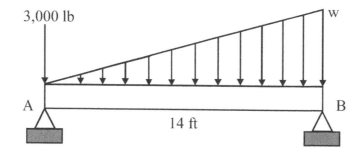

12.2 Determine the reactions at the supports for the loading conditions shown.
(Ans. A = 300 N, B = 650 N)

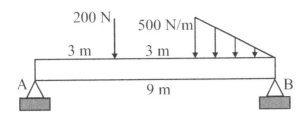

12.3 Determine the reactions at the supports for the loading conditions shown.
(Ans. A. = 2,150 N, B = 650 N)

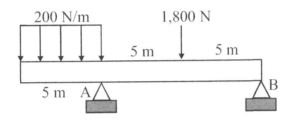

12.4 Determine the reaction forces at the supports for the simple beam shown below if w = 700 lb/ft.
(Ans. A = 1,816.7 lb, B = 1,383.3 lb)

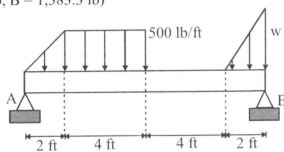

12.5 Determine the reactions at the wall of the cantilever beam shown. The intensity of the distributed load at the wall is 300 lb/ft and L = 12 ft.
(Ans. R = 7,200 lb, M = 50,400 lb-ft)

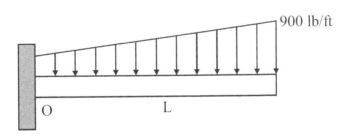

12.6 If L = 10 m, find the distance d so that the reaction forces at the supports are equal.
(Ans. d = 3.21 m)

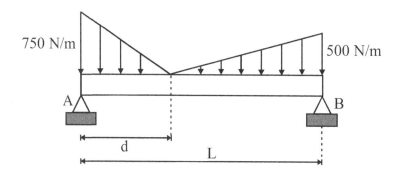

12.7 Solve Problem 12.4 in terms of the unknown distributed load w.
(Ans. A = 1,777.79 – 0.056w lb, B = 722.21 + 0.944w lb)

12.8 Solve Problem 12.6 for the case where support A carries 60% of the total applied load.
(Ans. d = 6.206 m)

MODULE 13: Distributed Loads on Beams (cont.)

In addition to uniformly and linearly varying distributed loads, it is common for beams to be loaded with distributed loads that are a function of the beam's length in a nonlinear manner. This distribution could be sinusoidal, parabolic, elliptic, cubic, some combination of these functions, or a more complicated function of the distance along the beam on which the loading is applied. Whatever the case, the loading distribution is generally given, or easily determined, as a function a distance x along the beam. In this case the same general procedure will be used to analyze the loading effects on the beam as was described in Module 12. First, the total load provided by the distributed load will be determined, and second, the centroid of the area representing the loading pattern will be located so the total load can be applied at this point. The difference between these types of loads and loads having a uniformly or linearly varying distribution however, is that it is slightly more difficult to determine the centroid and total load in nonlinear loading patterns. In the general case, a distributed load has the form of $w = w(x)$, where x is the distance measured from the starting or initial point, e.g., left side (generally), of the applied load. The total load represented by this loading pattern over the application span can be calculated by the integral expression

$$W = \int w \, dx$$

Since w is most often a simple function of x, this integral is generally not difficult to evaluate over the length of the loading span. Once this total load is obtained, the centroid of the area representing the loading pattern can be found using the integral expression for the first moment of the load given by

$$x^* = (\int xw \, dx) / W$$

Finding the x coordinate of the centroid in this manner is similar to the method presented in Module 11. Once again, this integral is generally not difficult to evaluate over the loading span. However the functional form of w often involves constants that must be evaluated using the load values at the initial point and/or final point of the loading pattern. Once both the load and the centroid are determined, the beam support reactions are evaluated using the standard methods previously discussed. Of course, nonlinear distributed loads can also be applied in combination with uniformly, linearly varying, or concentrated loads.

Example 13.1

For the simple beam shown below, the loading distribution is given by the function, $w = w_0 + kx^2$. Determine the reactions at the supports due to this loading condition.

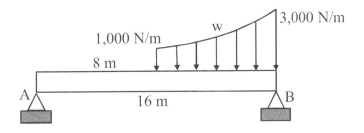

Solution: The first step in the analysis of the given loading condition is to determine the constants w_0 and k in the loading function. This is done by using the values of the load at both the initial point of load application ($x = 0$) and the final point of load application ($x = 8$ m). The initial and final values of the load will then be

at $x = 0$ m: $w = 1,000$ N/m , at $x = 8$ m: $w = 3,000$ N/m

Using this information to evaluate w_0 and k shows

$1,000 = w_0 + k(0)^2$
$\Rightarrow w_0 = 1,000$ N/m
$3,000 = 1,000 + k(8)^2$
$\Rightarrow k = 31.25$ N/m^3

The loading function can then be expressed as

$w = 1,000 + 31.25x^2$ N/m

Determining the total load provided by w over the span of 8 m gives

$W = \int w \, dx = \int (1,000 + 31.25x^2) \, dx$ N
$= [1,000x + 31.25x^3 / 3]$, evaluated from $x = 0$ to $x = 8$
$= 1,000(8) + 31.25(8)^3 / 3$
$\Rightarrow W = 13,333.3$ N

Evaluation of the centroid location shows

$x^* = (\int xw \, dx) / W = [\int x(1,000 + 31.25x^2) \, dx] / W$ m
$= [\int (1,000x + 31.25x^3) \, dx] / W$
$= [500x^2 + 31.2 x^4 / 4] / 13,333.3$, evaluated from $x = 0$ to $x = 8$
$= [500(8)^2 + 31.25(8)^4 / 4] / 13,333.3$
$\Rightarrow x^* = 4.8$ m

This result indicates that the centroid of the loaded area will be 4.8 m to the right of the start of the loading pattern, or a total distance of 12.8 m from point A on the beam. The free-body diagram is

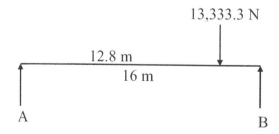

Solving for the reaction forces at A and B by summing the y forces and summing the moments about point A or point B, gives the solution as

$A = 2{,}666.7 \text{ N}$, $\quad B = 10{,}666.7 \text{ N}$

Example 13.2

Determine the reactions at the wall for the beam shown below. The applied load is given as $w = kx^{1/2}$.

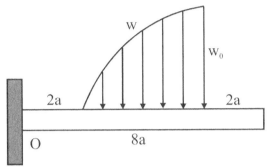

Solution: The end conditions of the load are, at $x = 0$: $w = 0$, and at $x = 4a$: $w = w_0$.

$w_0 = 2ka^{1/2}$
$k = w_0 / 2a^{1/2}$
$\Rightarrow w = (w_0 / 2)(x / a)^{1/2}$

The total load and centroid are found by

$W = \int (w_0 / 2a^{1/2}) x^{1/2} \, dx$
$\quad = [w_0 x^{3/2} / 3a^{1/2}]$, evaluated from $x = 0$ to $x = 4a$
$\Rightarrow W = 8 w_0 a / 3$

$x^* = (\int xw \, dx) / W = [\int x(w_0 / 2a^{1/2}) x^{1/2} \, dx] / W$
$\quad = [\int (w_0 / 2a^{1/2}) x^{3/2} \, dx] / W$
$\quad = [w_0 x^{5/2} / 5a^{1/2}] / (8 w_0 / 3a)$, evaluated from $x = 0$ to $x = 4a$
$\Rightarrow x^* = 2.4 \, a$

Therefore, a concentrated load equal to W can be applied at a point a distance of 2.4a to the right of the left side of the distributed load, or a distance of 4.4a from the wall. The free-body diagram then becomes

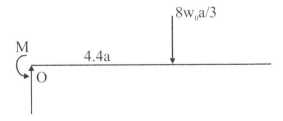

Solving the equilibrium equations gives

$$O = 8w_0a/3 \quad , \quad M = 11.73w_0a^2$$

Problems

13.1 Determine the reactions at supports A and B below for the loading pattern of $w = 10x^2$ N/m.
(Ans. A = 104.17 N, B = 312.50 N)

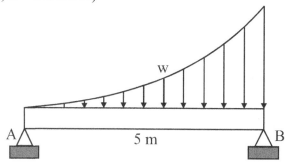

13.2 In Example 13.2, calculate the reaction forces at the supports if the beam has simple supports, A and B, and each end, respectively.
(Ans. A = $1.20w_oa$, B = $1.47w_oa$)

13.3 The figure below shows an overhanging simple beam supporting a distributed load given by $w = x + kx^2$. The value of this load at the right side of the distribution is 500 lb/ft. Determine the reactions at the supports.
(Ans. A = 897.26 lb, B = 1,469.14 lb)

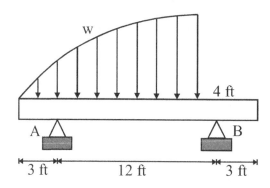

13.4 For the beam shown, the distributed load is given as $w = 20 \sin(\pi x / L)$ lb. Determine the reactions at the wall of the beam in terms of L ft.
(Ans. R = 12.73L lb, M = 6.37L² lb-ft)

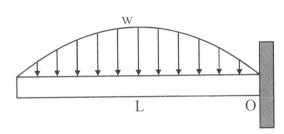

13.5 For the distributed loading shown, $w_1 = k_1 x^2$ N/m and $w_2 = k_2 + k_3 x^2$ N/m, and the values of the loads at points B and C are 200 N/m and 300 N/m, respectively. Calculate the reaction forces at supports A and D.
(Ans. A = 482.25 N, D = 744.42 N)

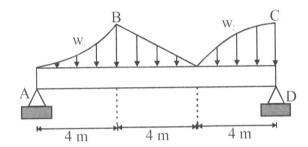

13.6 The beam in the figure below is subjected to a distributed load given by $w = 300 x^{1/2}$ N/m. Determine the reactions at the supports for this loading condition.
(Ans. A = 3,840 N, B = 8,960 N)

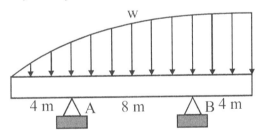

13.7 Solve Problem 13.1 for the case where $w = 10x^3$ N/m.
(Ans. A = 312.5 N, B = 1,250.0 N)

13.8 Determine the reactions at the supports in Problem 13.6 for the distributed load given by $w = 300 x^{1/3}$ N/m.
(Ans. A = 3,239.6 N, B = 5,831.8 N)

PART II - MECHANICS OF MATERIALS

MODULE 14: Stress and Strain

The study of statics presented the methods and techniques used to determine the forces and moments transmitted through rigid members and bodies. The study of mechanics of materials addresses the internal effects of these loads on bodies. However, it can no longer be assumed that the bodies being affected are rigid as they will deform under the application of all external loads.

External loads applied to a body are resisted by internal loads within the body. Stress is a measure of the intensity of the body's resistance to the externally applied loads and stress is generally determined by averaging the internal force in a body over the area through which it acts. The units of stress are therefore lb/in^2 (psi), or N/m^2 (Pascals).

The deformation of a body resulting from stress is called strain. Strain is defined as the change in length per unit length of the body, as in/in or m/m, therefore strain is actually a dimensionless quantity.

Consider a structural member of length L to which an external force **P** is applied along its longitudinal axis. If the member is being stretched, **P** is defined as a positive force and the member is said to be in 'tension'. If the member is being compressed, **P** is defined as a negative force and the member is said to be in 'compression', as shown in Figure 14.1.

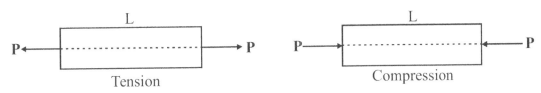

Figure 14.1

The case of tension is further depicted in Figure 14.2. If the member is cut at section O-O, the internal force distribution resisting **P** can be seen acting through the cross-sectional area A of the member as shown.

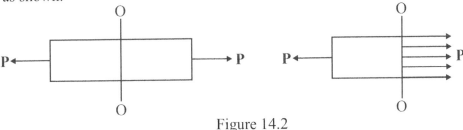

Figure 14.2

In the cases of both tension and compression, the 'normal' stress σ acts in a direction normal (or perpendicular) to the cross-sectional area within the member. The normal stress is found by dividing the magnitude of the applied force over the cross-sectional area as

$$\sigma = P / A$$

Consistent with the sense of **P**, the normal stress in tension, called the tensile stress, is considered to be positive, while the normal stress in compression, called the compressive stress, is considered to be negative. The deformation resulting from tension in the member is shown in Figure 14.3, where Δ is the elongation of the member due to **P**.

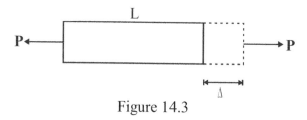

Figure 14.3

The normal strain ε is defined as

$$\varepsilon = \Delta / L$$

Consistent with the sign convention of stress, a positive strain indicates tension of the member, while a negative strain indicates compression of the member.

Relationship Between Stress and Strain

The relationship between the stress and strain in a member is a function of the material from which the member is constructed. This relationship can best be shown by a stress-strain diagram for the specific material, similar to the one depicted in Figure 14.4.

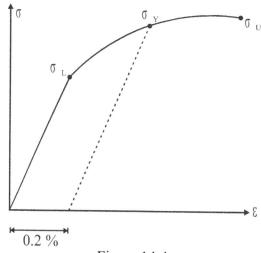

Figure 14.4

In this diagram, σ_L is the 'proportional limit' of the material, σ_Y is the material's 'yield strength', and σ_U is the material's 'ultimate strength'. The portion of the diagram up to the proportional limit defines the elastic range of the material, which means any corresponding strain will be completely reversed when the stress is removed. Loading the material beyond the proportional limit will result in a level of strain that will not be completely reversed upon removal of the stress, therefore a small amount of permanent deformation will remain in the member. A level of stress reaching the yield strength σ_Y will result in a permanent strain of approximately 0.2%. A member in which the stress level reaches the ultimate strength of the material σ_U will fail completely, either by fracturing or by excessive deformation. The values of σ_L, σ_Y, and σ_U for materials are generally determined through testing. Materials that elongate more than 5% before failure are considered to be ductile, and those that elongate less than 5% before failure are considered to be brittle. The analytical relationship between stress and strain is given by Hooke's Law as

$$\sigma = E\varepsilon$$

where E is the modulus of elasticity of the material. However, when a member elongates in the axial direction under a tensile loading condition, it also undergoes a strain similar to a compressive strain in the lateral direction (perpendicular to the loading direction). This effect is shown in Figure 14.5 below.

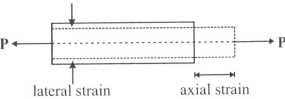

Figure 14.5

The ratio of the lateral strain to the axial strain is also a function of the material and is defined by Poisson's Ratio μ as

$$\mu = \text{lateral strain} / \text{axial strain}$$

Poisson's Ratio can be used in calculating the three-dimensional strains that a member undergoes during various types of loading conditions. These strains are determined using Generalized Hooke's Law as

$$\varepsilon_x = [\sigma_x - \mu(\sigma_y + \sigma_z)] / E$$
$$\varepsilon_y = [\sigma_y - \mu(\sigma_x + \sigma_z)] / E$$
$$\varepsilon_z = [\sigma_z - \mu(\sigma_x + \sigma_y)] / E$$

Table 14.1 provides the properties of some common materials in SI Units and Table 14.2 provides those properties in U.S. Customary Units. G is the modulus of rigidity of the specified material in both tables.

Table 14.1 Material Properties (SI Units)

Material	E (GPa)	G (Gpa)	μ	σ_Y (MPa)	σ_U (MPa)
Aluminum (cast)	76	27	0.35	160	250
Brass (red, annealed)	100	38	0.35	73	236
Cast iron (gray)	67	27	0.28	40	177
Stainless steel (annealed)	190	76	0.27	208	521
Steel (structural)	207	76	0.32	250	395
ABS plastic	2.3	0.98	0.41	43.2	35.8
Polyester (PET)	3.45	1.70	0.39	176	72.8
Nylon (PA-6)	1.69	0.12	0.37	72.7	45.0
Polystyrene	2.76	1.30	0.22	33.1	40.2
Polycarbonate	2.34	0.80	0.36	63.3	64.5
S-Glass	86.2	35	0.22	NA	4590
E-Glass	72.4	30	0.22	NA	3620

Table 14.2 Material Properties (U.S. Customary Units)

Material	E (x 10^6 psi)	G (x 10^6 psi)	μ	σ_Y (10^3 psi)	σ_U (10^3 psi)
Aluminum (cast)	11	3.9	0.35	24	36
Brass (red, annealed)	15	5.4	0.35	11	35
Cast iron (gray)	10	3.9	0.28	6	26
Stainless steel (annealed)	28	11.0	0.27	30	75
Steel (structural)	30	11.0	0.32	36	58
ABS plastic	0.33	0.14	0.41	6.20	5.19
Polyester (PET)	0.50	0.25	0.39	25.5	10.6
Nylon (PA-6)	0.25	0.02	0.37	10.5	6.53
Polystyrene	0.40	0.19	0.22	4.80	5.83
Polycarbonate	0.34	0.10	0.36	9.18	9.35
S-Glass	12.5	5.10	0.22	NA	666
E-Glass	10.5	4.00	0.22	NA	525

Conversions between U.S. Customary and SI units are given as

1 psi = 6895 Pa
1000 psi = 6.895 MPa (1 MPa = 10^6 Pa)
10^6 psi = 6.895 GPa (1 GPa = 10^9 Pa)
1 Pa = 1 N/m^2

Example 14.1

The structure shown below is composed of a steel section and a brass section and is loaded by a tensile load of 20,000 lb. Determine the maximum normal stress and axial strain in each section. Use the following properties for each section: $W_s = 540$ lb, $A_s = 8$ in^2, $W_b = 345$ lb, and $A_b = 6$ in^2.

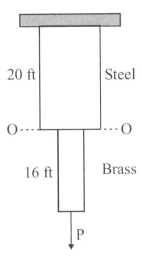

Solution: The free-body diagrams of each section show

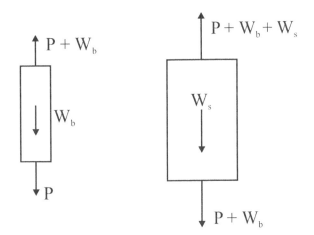

The maximum normal stress will occur where the maximum loads are transmitted through each section. For the brass section, the maximum load will occur just below line O-O, while for the steel section, the maximum load will occur just below where the structure is attached to the support.

Brass: $\sigma_b = P_b / A_b = (20{,}000 + 345) / 6.0$
$\Rightarrow \sigma_b = 3{,}391$ psi

$\varepsilon_b = \sigma_b / E_b = 3{,}391 / (15 \times 10^6)$
$\Rightarrow \varepsilon_b = 2.261 \times 10^{-4}$ in/in

Steel: $\sigma_s = P_s / A_s = (20{,}000 + 345 + 540) / 8.0$
⇒ $\sigma_s = 2{,}611$ psi

$\varepsilon_s = \sigma_s / E_s = 2{,}611 / (30 \times 10^6)$
⇒ $\varepsilon_b = 8.703 \times 10^{-5}$ in/in

Example 14.2

Two cylindrical cast iron columns are being compressed by a load of 30,000 lb as shown. Determine the normal stress and strain in each section and the total shortening of the structure due to the applied load. Neglect the weight of the columns.

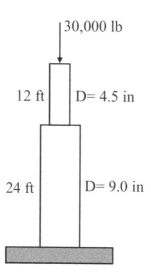

Solution: Top: $\sigma_t = P / A_t = 30{,}000 / [\pi(4.5)^2 / 4]$
⇒ $\sigma_t = 1{,}886$ psi

$\varepsilon_t = \sigma_t / E_{ci} = 1{,}886 / (10 \times 10^6)$
⇒ $\varepsilon_t = 1.886 \times 10^{-4}$ in/in

$\Delta_t = \varepsilon_t L_t = (1.886 \times 10^{-4})(12)(12)$
⇒ $\Delta_t = 0.027$ in

Bottom: $\sigma_b = P / A_b = 30{,}000 / [\pi(9.0)^2 / 4]$
⇒ $\sigma_b = 472$ psi

$\varepsilon_b = \sigma_b / E_{ci} = 472 / (10 \times 10^6)$
⇒ $\varepsilon_b = 4.720 \times 10^{-5}$ in/in

$\Delta_b = \varepsilon_b L_b = (4.720 \times 10^{-5})(24)(12)$
⇒ $\Delta_b = 0.014$ in

The total shortening of the structure will be the sum of the compressions of the two sections, calculated by

$$\Delta = \Delta_t + \Delta_b = 0.027 + 0.014$$
$$\Rightarrow \Delta = 0.041 \text{ in}$$

Example 14.3

A rectangular steel rod having dimensions 0.1 m x 0.2 m x 10 m is subjected to a three-dimensional loading condition that creates the following stresses

$$\sigma_x = 96.530 \text{ MPa} \quad , \quad \sigma_y = -41.370 \text{ MPa} \quad , \quad \sigma_z = 27.580 \text{ MPa}$$

If σ_x is the stress in the longitudinal direction of the rod, calculate the three-dimensional strains and the deformation in each direction.

Solution: The strains can be determined by the use of Generalized Hooke's Law.

$$\varepsilon_x = [\sigma_x - \mu(\sigma_y + \sigma_z)] / E$$
$$= [96.530 - 0.32(-41.370 + 27.580)] / (207 \times 10^3)$$
$$\Rightarrow \varepsilon_x = 5.051 \times 10^{-4} \text{ m/m}$$

$$\varepsilon_y = [\sigma_y - \mu(\sigma_x + \sigma_z)] / E$$
$$= [-41.370 - 0.32(96.530 + 27.580)] / (207 \times 10^3)$$
$$\Rightarrow \varepsilon_y = -4.196 \times 10^{-4} \text{ m/m}$$

$$\varepsilon_z = [\sigma_z - \mu(\sigma_x + \sigma_y)] / E$$
$$= [27.580 - 0.32(96.530 - 41.370)] / (207 \times 10^3)$$
$$\Rightarrow \varepsilon_z = 5.138 \times 10^{-5} \text{ m/m}$$

These results indicate that the member will elongate in the x and z directions but will contract in the y-direction. The amount of deformation in each direction can be calculate as

$$\Delta_x = \varepsilon_x L_x = (5.051 \times 10^{-4})(10)$$
$$\Rightarrow \Delta_x = 5.051 \times 10^{-3} \text{ m}$$

$$\Delta_y = \varepsilon_y L_y = (-4.196 \times 10^{-4})(0.2)$$
$$\Rightarrow \Delta_y = -8.392 \times 10^{-5} \text{ m}$$

$$\Delta_z = \varepsilon_z L_z = (5.138 \times 10^{-5})(0.1)$$
$$\Rightarrow \Delta_z = 5.138 \times 10^{-6} \text{ m}$$

Problems

14.1 A 10 ft long aluminum bar has a cross-sectional area of 2.5 in². If this bar is subjected to a tensile loading which causes the stress level to reach the material's yield strength, determine the amount of permanent deformation in the bar when the loading is removed.
(Ans. Δ = 0.240 in)

14.2 The steel and cast iron structure loaded in compression as shown. If the maximum allowable deformation of the entire structure is 0.01 in, determine the maximum applied load P.
(Ans. P = 9,308.4 lb)

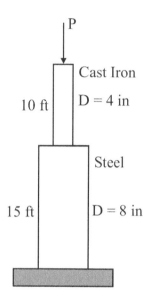

14.3 The composite steel and aluminum rod below has a diameter of 0.2 m. If the normal stress in the rod is 41.370 MPa, calculate the magnitude of the applied load P and the total elongation of the composite rod.
(Ans. P = 1,299,845.4 N, Δ = 2.777 x 10⁻³ m)

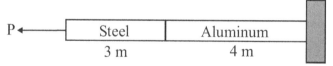

14.4 If the rod in Problem 14.3 has a diameter of 0.2 m, determine the applied load and normal stress in the rod if the total elongation of the rod is 0.0025 m.
(Ans. P = 1,170,216.5 N, σ = 37.244 MPa)

14.5 A steel member is subjected to a three-dimensional stress condition as

$$\sigma_x = 20{,}000 \text{ psi}, \quad \sigma_y = -14{,}000 \text{ psi}, \quad \sigma_z = -9{,}000 \text{ psi}$$

If the dimensions of this member are 18 ft x 6 in x 8 in, determine the deformation in each direction.
(Ans. Δ_x = 0.197 in, Δ_y = -3.50 x 10⁻³ in, Δ_z = -2.91 x 10⁻³ in)

14.6 A test member 0.2 m long with a 0.05 m x 0.05 m cross-section, deforms 0.0015 m under a compressive load while each lateral dimension increases by 1.0×10^{-4} m. Calculate Poisson's ratio for this material assuming the deformations are elastic.
(Ans. $\mu = 0.267$)

14.7 Consider the structure in Problem 14.2 where the cast iron section is replaced with a section of unknown material with the same dimensions. Calculate the load P and the modulus of elasticity E of the unknown material if each section deforms 0.005 in.
(Ans. $E = 80 \times 10^6$ psi)

14.8 In Problem 14.3, calculate the total deformation Δ if the steel section is replaced by a brass section having a length of 5 m.
(Ans. $\Delta = 4.25 \times 10^{-3}$ m)

MODULE 15: Stress and Strain (cont.)

Design Stress

When structural members are designed, factors of safety are generally used to reduce the allowable stress that the member may experience during loading conditions. Factors of safety based upon a material's yield strength, designated N_Y, are used for ductile materials, while factors of safety based upon a material's ultimate strength, designated N_U, are used for brittle materials. Values for N_Y commonly range between 1.5 and 4.0, and values for N_U commonly range between 3 and 20. The allowable stress for a particular material can be calculated using the relationships

$$\text{Ductile material:} \quad \sigma_{all} = \sigma_Y / N_Y \qquad\qquad \text{Brittle material:} \quad \sigma_{all} = \sigma_U / N_U$$

In general, lower factors of safety are used for steady loads, higher factors of safety are used for varying loads, and the highest factors of safety are used for shock or vibration loads.

Thermal Expansion

Materials expand when they're heated and contract when they're cooled. The amount of expansion or contraction is a function of the change in temperature, the length of the member, and the material of construction. The change in the original length L of a member during thermal expansion is given by the expression

$$\Delta L = \alpha L \Delta T$$

where α is a property of the material called the 'coefficient of thermal expansion' and ΔT is the change in temperature. Table 15.1 provides average coefficients of thermal expansion for a variety of materials in U.S. Customary Units.

Table 15.1 Coefficients of Thermal Expansion

Material	α (x 10^{-6} in/in/°F)	α (x 10^{-6} m/m/°C)
Aluminum (cast)	13	23
Brass (red, annealed)	10	18
Cast iron (gray)	6.2	11
Stainless steel (annealed)	9.6	17
Steel (structural)	7	13
ABS plastic	44	79
Polyester (PET)	32	57
Nylon (PA-6)	44	80
Polystyrene	42	76
Polycarbonate	37	66
S-Glass	3	5.4
E-Glass	2.8	5

Thermal Stresses

If a member is allowed to expand freely during a change in temperature, no stresses are created within the member. If a member is heated and is not allowed to expand freely, thermal stresses are induced in the member. These thermal stresses are functions of the modulus of elasticity, the coefficient of thermal expansion, and the change in temperature. Thermal stresses can be calculated using the relationship

$$\sigma = E\alpha\Delta T$$

Stress in Compound Bars

Compound bars are made up of two or more bars of different materials that are parallel to each other and rigidly connected at their ends. Consider the compound bar shown in Figure 15.1, where individual bars A, B, and C are rigidly attached at each end and the unit is loaded by a tensile force **P** as shown.

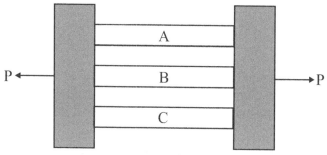

Figure 15.1

Each individual bar must share the total applied load. Therefore, each of the bars will only carry a portion of **P** such that the sum of the magnitudes of the forces carried by bars A, B, and C is equal to the total magnitude of **P**, as

$$P = P_A + P_B + P_C$$

Since the lengths of the individual bars will be equal before and after the load is applied, their individual strains must also be equal. Therefore

$$\varepsilon_A = \varepsilon_B = \varepsilon_C$$

Writing this relationship in terms of the σ and E for each bar gives

$$\sigma_A / E_A = \sigma_B / E_B = \sigma_C / E_C$$

These relationships can be used for the cases of both tensile and compressive loads. Determining the stresses induced in each bar for the prescribed strains allows for the calculation of the forces carried by each member.

Example 15.1

A cast iron circular column must carry a maximum load of 30,000 lb and have a factor of safety based on yield strength of 2.25. Determine the required diameter of the column.

Solution: The maximum allowable stress will be

$$\sigma_{all} = \sigma_Y / N_Y = 6,000 / 2.25$$
$$\Rightarrow \sigma_{all} = 2,667 \text{ psi}$$

$$A = P / \sigma_{all} = 30,000 / 2,667$$
$$\Rightarrow A = 11.25 \text{ in}^2$$

$$D = [4A / \pi]^{1/2} = [4(11.25) / \pi]^{1/2}$$
$$\Rightarrow D = 3.78 \text{ in}$$

Example 15.2

Determine the change in length of an aluminum bar 3 m long due to a temperature change of 40° C. If the ends of the bar are fixed and the elongation along the longitudinal axis is constrained, determine the thermal stress resulting in the bar.

Solution:
$$\Delta L = \alpha L \Delta T = (23 \times 10^{-6})(3)(40)$$
$$\Rightarrow \Delta L = 0.00276 \text{ m}$$

$$\sigma = E \alpha \Delta T = (76 \times 10^9)(23 \times 10^{-6})(40)$$
$$\Rightarrow \sigma = 69.92 \text{ MPa}$$

Example 15.3

A solid circular plate is attached to the top of two hollow concentric cylinders 10 ft in length as shown below. The steel cylinder has an outside diameter of 6 in and an inside diameter of 5 in, and the aluminum cylinder has an outside diameter of 4 in and an inside diameter of 3 in. If each of the cylinders is compressed a total of 0.15 in, determine the magnitude of the applied load P.

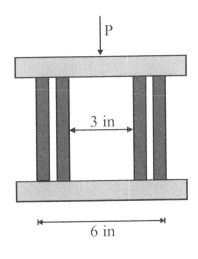

Solution: $\varepsilon_s = \varepsilon_a = \Delta L / L$
$= 0.15 / [(10)(12)]$
$\Rightarrow \varepsilon_s = \varepsilon_a = 1.250 \times 10^{-3}$ in/in

Steel: $\sigma_s = E_s \varepsilon_s$
$= (30 \times 10^6)(1.250 \times 10^{-3})$
$\Rightarrow \sigma_s = 37,500$ psi

$P_s = \sigma_s A_s$
$= 37,500 \, \pi[(6.0)^2 - (5.0)^2] / 4$
$\Rightarrow P_s = 323,977$ lb

Aluminum: $\sigma_a = E_a \varepsilon_a$
$= (11 \times 10^6)(1.250 \times 10^{-3})$
$\Rightarrow \sigma_a = 13,750$ psi

$P_a = \sigma_a A_a$
$= 13,750 \, \pi[(4.0)^2 - (3.0)^2] / 4$
$\Rightarrow P_a = 75,590$ lb

$P = P_s + P_a$
$= 323,977 + 75,590$
$\Rightarrow P = 399,567$ lb

Problems

15.1 An aluminum aircraft part has a cross-sectional area of 2.0 in². If $N_Y = 1.50$, determine the maximum tensile load this part may carry.
(Ans. P = 32,000.0 lb)

15.2 A block is hanging from the end of a 20 ft long bar as shown below. The bar is firmly welded to the top support leaving a gap of 0.1 in between the block and the floor. If a temperature change of 30° F will cause the bar to close the gap, determine the coefficient of thermal expansion of the bar.
(Ans. $\alpha = 1.389 \times 10^{-5}$ in/in/°F)

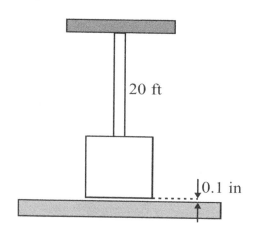

15.3 In the composite bar below, bar A is made of brass and bar B is made of steel. Each bar is circular with a diameter of 0.03 m. If a load of P = 50,000 N is applied at cross-section CD as shown, determine the reaction forces at each wall and the displacement of plane CD.
(Ans. P_A = 19,588.2 N, P_B = 30,411.8 N, Δ = 0.08313 x 10^{-3} m)

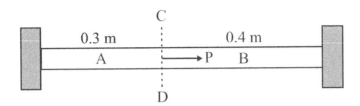

15.4 In Example 15.3, consider the inside diameter of the steel cylinder to be 4.5 in and the outside diameter of the aluminum cylinder to be 3.5 in. Determine the normal stress in each cylinder and the amount that the cylinders are compressed under a total load of 225,000 lb.
(Ans. σ_S = 16,910 psi, σ_A = 6,200 psi, Δ = 0.0676 in)

15.5 A very stiff bar of negligible weight is suspended horizontally by two vertical rods as shown below. One of the rods is made of steel, has a diameter of 0.015 m and is 1.5 m long, while the other rod is made of brass, has a diameter of 0.025 m and is 3 m long. If a vertical load of 25,000 N is applied to the bar, determine the value of x in order that the stiff bar will remain horizontal.
(Ans. x = 1.406 m)

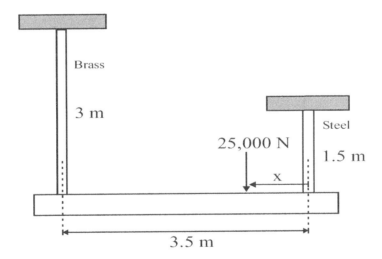

15.6 Rods A and C are made of aluminum and rod B is made of stainless steel. Each rod has a cross-sectional area of 4 in². Determine the magnitude of the load P that will cause the normal stress in the stainless steel to be four times larger than the normal stress in the aluminum.
(Ans. P = 76,990.1 lb)

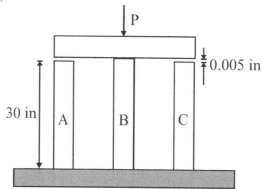

15.7 In Problem 15.3, calculate the diameter of the bars if the displacement of plane CD is 0.2×10^{-3} m.
(Ans. D = 0.0193 m)

15.8 Determine the elongation in each rod in Problem 15.5 for the case where x = 2.5 m. Neglect the effects of the rotation of the stiff horizontal bar.
(Ans. $\Delta_S = 0.293 \times 10^{-3}$ m, $\Delta_B = 1.09 \times 10^{-3}$ m)

MODULE 16: Direct Shear Stress

The stress in a member that acts in a direction tangent to the cross-sectional area is called the shear stress and is denoted by τ. The units of shear stress will also be force/area, as psi or N/m^2. The formation of shear stress is depicted in Figure 16.1, which shows a rigidly supported bar being subjected to a large force P.

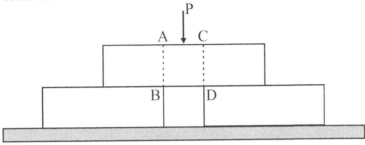

Figure 16.1

The force will cause the material of the bar to deform along the cross-sectional areas defined by planes AB and CD, i.e., the applied force will tend to 'slice through' the bar along planes AB and CD. A free-body diagram of that rectangular section is shown in Figure 16.2.

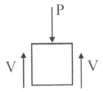

Figure 16.2

This figure indicates that the internal force, $V = P / 2$, must be applied by each side of the rectangular section for equilibrium. If this 'shear' force is averaged over the cross-sectional area of the member, A, the 'average shear stress' through the cross-section is defined by

$$\tau = V / A$$

This loading condition is an example of 'direct' shear, sometimes referred to 'simple' or 'pure' shear and often occurs in simple connection devices such as rivets, pins, bolts, or welds.

Single Shear

A single shear connection, or 'lap joint', is shown in Figure 16.3, where the bonding surface between the members is subjected to a single shear force V = P.

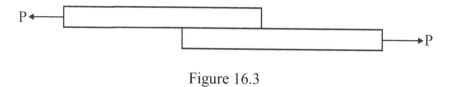

Figure 16.3

Double Shear

A double shear connection, or 'double lap joint', is shown in Figure 16.4.

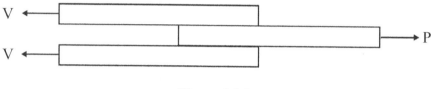

Figure 16.4

In this case the bonding between the members occurs on two surfaces, therefore each bonding surface is only subjected to a shear force of: V = P / 2, which is the force used in the calculation of the average shear force. In all cases of direct shear, the shear stress is determined by applying the shear force V over the area resisting the force. This can be seen in the case of rivets, etc., where the applied shear force is attempting to shear through the cross-sectional area of the rivet.

Fillet Weld

Fillet welds are often used to fasten two objects together as shown in Figure 16.5

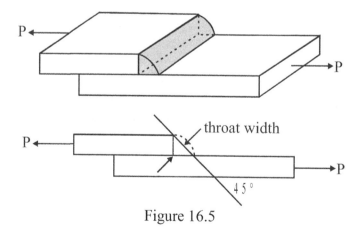

Figure 16.5

In welds of this type, the entire area of the throat of the fillet weld resists the shearing forces created by the applied load P. This throat area is determined by multiplying the throat width shown above, by the length of the weld. The throat area is then used in the calculation of the average shear stress.

Example 16.1

Two plates are fastened together using three 0.5 in diameter rivets and are subjected to a load of P = 1,000 lb as shown below. Determine the shear stress in the rivets.

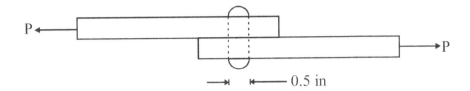

Solution: $\tau = V / A$
         $= P / 3A_r$
         $= 1,000 / [3\pi(0.25)^2]$
    $\Rightarrow$ $\tau = 1,698$ psi

Example 16.2

Two metal plates are fastened together using a double shear connection as depicted in Figure 16.4. If the adhesive bonding the plates together can withstand a shear stress of 5 MPa and the contact area on each side of the center plate is 0.02 m^2, determine the maximum load that this connection can withstand.

Solution: $\tau = V / A$
         $= P / 2A$
         $P = 2\tau A$
         $= 2(5 \times 10^6)(0.02)$
    $\Rightarrow$ $P = 200,000$ N

Example 16.3

The welded unit shown below must withstand a load of P = 6,500 lb. If the maximum shear stress must not exceed 2,000 psi, determine the size of the fillet weld, b.

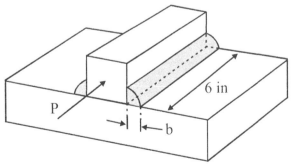

Solution: $\tau = V / A$
         $= P / [2(6)b \cos 45°]$
         $b = P / [12(0.707)\tau]$
         $= 6,500 / [(8.49)(2,000)]$
    $\Rightarrow$ $b = 0.38$ in

Problems

16.1 In Example 16.1, determine the number of rivets that would be necessary if the total load was 30,000 lb and the maximum allowable shear stress was 2,500 psi.
(N = 62 rivets)

16.2 In Example 16.2, determine the factor of safety in the double shear connection for a load of 70,000 N and a contact area of 0.03 m².
(N = 4.286)

16.3 In the figure below, block A is a solid cylinder having a 9 in diameter and weighing 1,000 lb. Block B is a rectangular solid 28 in by 28 in having a thickness of 8.5 in and a weight of 4,000 lb. Determine the maximum shear stress in block B.
(τ_{max} = 10.5 psi)

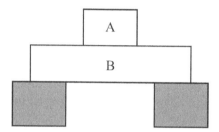

16.4 In Example 16.3, if b = 0.4 in, determine the maximum load the welded joint could withstand if the maximum allowable shear stress was 5,000 psi.
(Ans. P = 16, 970.6 lb)

16.5 Beam A is subjected to a distributed load where w_1 = 10,000 N/m and w_2 = 12,500 N/m. If A has a cross-sectional area of 0.04 m², calculate the shear stress at each end beam A.
(Ans. τ_L = 135,405 Pa, τ_R = 145,845 Pa)

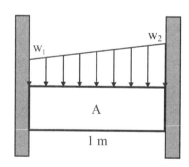

16.6 In the figure below, a bolt passes through a frame and is subjected to a tensile load of P = 12,500 lb. Calculate the shear stress through the bolt head and through the frame due to this loading condition.
(Ans. τ_h = 15,915 psi, τ_f = 1,989 psi)

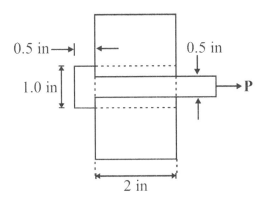

16.7 Solve Problem 16.5 for the distributed loads w_1 and w_2 if the resulting shear stresses at the ends of beam A are τ_1 = 125,000 Pa and τ_2 = 140,000 Pa.
(Ans. w_1 = 8,792.8 N/m, w_2 = 12,407.2 N/m)

16.8 Solve Problem 16.6 for the case where the diameter of the bolt is 0.4 in. and the applied load is 12,000 lb.
(Ans. τ_h = 19,099 psi, τ_f = 1,910 psi)

MODULE 17: Area Moments of Inertia

When forces are distributed over a cross-sectional area, it is often necessary to calculate the moment created by these forces about an axis that is either in the plane of the area or perpendicular to the plane of the area. The area moment of inertia, also called the 'second moment of area', is used for this purpose. This quantity is primarily used in the study of mechanics of materials. The area moment of inertia is purely a mathematical quantity of an area that has no physical meaning. Consider the arbitrarily shaped body shown in Figure 17.1.

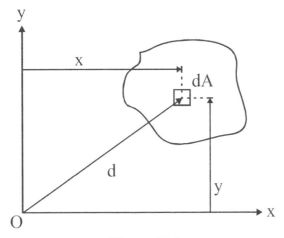

Figure 17.1

The rectangular area moments of inertia, I_x and I_y, and the polar moment of inertia, I_z are defined by

$$I_x = \int y^2 \, dA \quad , \quad I_y = \int x^2 \, dA \quad , \quad I_z = \int d^2 \, dA$$

It can be shown the these quantities are related by the expression

$$I_z = I_x + I_y$$

The radius of gyration k is a measure of the distribution of the body's area from a particular axis, i.e., if all of the area of the body is concentrated at a distance k from an axis. In Cartesian coordinates, these quantities are defined as

$$k_x = [I_x / A]^{1/2} \quad , \quad k_y = [I_y / A]^{1/2} \quad , \quad k_z = [I_z / A]^{1/2}$$

and

$$k_z^2 = k_x^2 + k_y^2$$

When the area moments of inertia and radii of gyration are taken about the body's centroidal axes, the terms I^*_x, I^*_y, I^*_z, k^*_x, k^*_y, and k^*_z are used.

Parallel-Axis Theorem

The area moments of inertia about a body's centroidal axes are often the most important in solving mechanics of materials problems. However, when the area moments of inertia about non-centroidal axes are required, the parallel-axis theorem is used for their computation. Consider an arbitrarily shaped body of area A, whose centroidal axes are designated as x^* and y^* as shown in Figure 17.2.

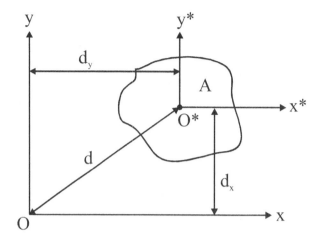

Figure 17.2

The quantities d_x, d_y, and d are defined as the distances between the x and x^* axes, the y and y^* axes, and point O and O^*, respectively. The parallel axis theorem provides formulas for the calculation of the area moments of inertia about the x and y axes as

$$I_x = I^*_x + Ad_x^2 \quad , \quad I_y = I^*_y + Ad_y^2 \quad , \quad I_z = I^*_z + Ad^2$$

Here, the terms Ad_x^2, Ad_y^2, Ad^2 are known as the transfer terms. For the radius of gyration terms, the formulas are

$$k_x^2 = k^{*2}_x + d_x^2 \quad , \quad k_y^2 = k^{*2}_y + d_y^2 \quad , \quad k_z^2 = k^{*2}_z + d^2$$

For common shapes, simple formulas for I^*_x and I^*_y are provided in Table 17.1, while formulas for I_x and/or I_y are also provided for selected shapes.

Table 17.1 Area Moments of Inertia of Common Shapes

Rectangular Area:

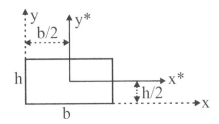

$I^*_x = bh^3 / 12$ $\qquad I^*_y = hb^3 / 12$
$I^*_z = (bh^3 + hb^3) / 12$
$I_x = bh^3 / 3$ $\qquad I_y = hb^3 / 3$
$I_z = (bh^3 + hb^3) / 3$

Triangular Area:

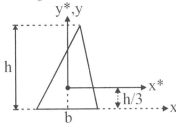

$I^*_x = bh^3 / 36$ $\qquad I^*_y = hb^3 / 36$
$I_x = bh^3 / 12$ $\qquad I_y = hb^3 / 12$

Circular Area:

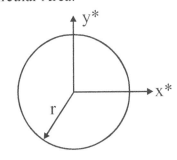

$I^*_x = I^*_y = \pi r^4 / 4$
$I^*_z = \pi r^4 / 2$

Semi-Circular Area:

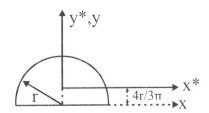

$I^*_x = (\pi / 8 - 8 / 9\pi) r^4$ $\qquad I^*_y = \pi r^4 / 8$
$I^*_z = (\pi / 4 - 8 / 9\pi) r^4$
$I_x = \pi r^4 / 8$ $\qquad I_y = \pi r^4 / 8$
$I_z = \pi r^4 / 4$

Quarter-Circular Area:

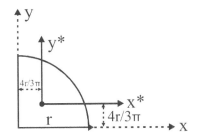

$I^*_x = I^*_y = (\pi / 16 - 4 / 9\pi) r^4$
$I^*_z = (\pi / 8 - 8 / 9\pi) r^4$
$I_x = I_y = \pi r^4 / 16$
$I_z = \pi r^4 / 8$

Method of Composite Areas

Similar to the methods presented for the computation of centroids of areas in Module 11, the method of composite areas can be used to determine the area moments of inertia of a body that can be divided into the commonly shaped areas. This is done by using the following formulas, along with the formulas presented in Table 17.1, for the computation of area moments of inertia about x and y axes.

$$I_x = \Sigma I^*_x + \Sigma A d_x^2 \quad , \quad I_y = \Sigma I^*_y + \Sigma A d_y^2 \quad , \quad I_z = I_x + I_y$$

The terms I^*_x, $A d_x^2$, I^*_y, and $A d_y^2$ represent the area moments of inertia of each common shape and the associated transfer terms.

Example 17.1

The area shown below contains a cutout having a diameter of 0.6 m. Determine the area moments of inertia about the x and y axes provided.

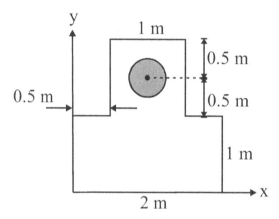

Solution: This body can easily be broken into three commonly shaped areas, a rectangular area, a square area, and a circular area, which are designated as areas 1, 2, and 3, respectively. The table below provides the quantities A, I^*_x, I^*_y, d_x, d_y, $I^*_x + A d_x^2$, and $I^*_y + A d_y^2$ for each area, where I^*_x and I^*_y are calculated from the formulas provided in Table 17.1. The quantities calculated in the columns for $I^*_x + A d_x^2$ and $I^*_y + A d_y^2$ are then added and the results are used to compute I_x and I_y from the formulas provided above. Note that the cutout section is treated as having a negative area and negative area moments of inertia.

Area	A (m²)	I^*_x (m⁴)	I^*_y (m⁴)	d_x (m)	d_y (m)	$I^*_x + Ad_x^2$ (m⁴)	$I^*_y + Ad_y^2$ (m⁴)
1	2.00	0.167	0.667	0.50	1.00	0.67	2.67
2	1.00	0.083	0.083	1.50	1.00	2.33	1.08
3	-0.28	-0.006	-0.006	1.50	1.00	-0.64	-0.29
Totals:						2.36 m⁴	3.46 m⁴

Therefore, for the entire body

$I_x = 2.36$ m⁴ , $I_y = 3.46$ m⁴ , $I_z = 5.80$ m⁴

Example 17.2

For the body shown, compute the polar moment of inertia I^*_z about the centroid.

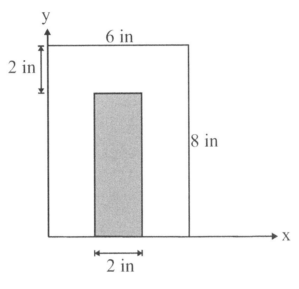

Solution: Before the moments of inertia terms can be calculated, the centroid of the body must be determined since it is not given. Designating the solid area as area 1 and the cutout area to be area 2, the method of composite areas can be used to construct the following table in order to determine the centroid.

Area	x^* (in)	y^* (in)	A (in²)	x^*A (in³)	y^*A (in³)
1	3.00	4.00	48.00	144.00	192.00
2	3.00	3.00	-12.00	-36.00	-36.00
Totals:			36.00 in²	108.00 in³	156.00 in³

The centroid of the composite body is then calculated by

$$x_C = \Sigma x^* A / \Sigma A = 108.00 / 36.00$$
$\Rightarrow$ $x_C = 3.00$ in

$$y_C = \Sigma y^* A / \Sigma A = 156.00 / 36.00$$
$\Rightarrow$ $y_C = 4.33$ in

Using these values for the body's centroid, the following table can be constructed and used to calculate the area moments of inertia. Note that the distances d_x and d_y are the distances from each area's centroidal axes to the centroidal axes of the composite body determined above.

Area	A (in²)	I_x^* (in⁴)	I_y^* (in⁴)	d_x (in)	d_y (in)	$I_x^* + A d_x^2$ (in⁴)	$I_y^* + A d_y^2$ (in⁴)
1	48.00	256.0	144.0	0.33	0.00	261.23	144.00
2	-12.00	-36.0	-4.0	1.33	0.00	-57.32	-4.00
Totals:						203.91 in⁴	140.00 in⁴

Therefore, the area moments of inertia about the centroid of the composite body are

$$I_x^* = 203.91 \text{ in}^4 \quad , \quad I_y^* = 140.00 \text{ in}^4$$

The polar moment of inertia is then calculated as

$$I_z^* = I_x^* + I_y^*$$
$$= 203.91 + 140.00$$
$\Rightarrow$ $I_z^* = 343.91$ in⁴

Problems

17.1 Calculate the moments of inertia about the x and y-axes for the case of L = 8.0 m. (Ans. $I_x = 401.25$ m⁴, $I_y = 810.38$ m⁴)

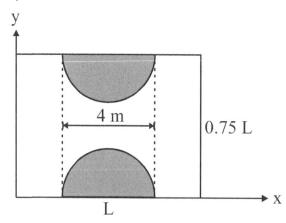

17.2 Compute the polar moments of inertia for the figure in Example 17.1 with respect to the given coordinate system.
(Ans. $I_z = 5.82$ in^4)

17.3 In the area below, calculate the area moments of inertia about the axes provided.
(Ans. $I_x = 281.61$ m^4, $I_y = 1,557.35$ m^4)

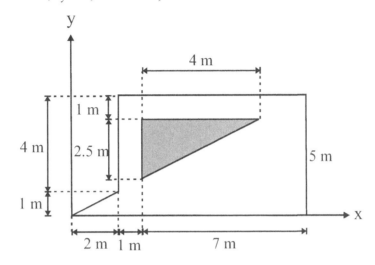

17.4 Calculate the area moments of inertia about the centroidal axes for the area shown.
(Ans. $I^*_x = 231.81$ in^4, $I^*_y = 422.53$ in^4)

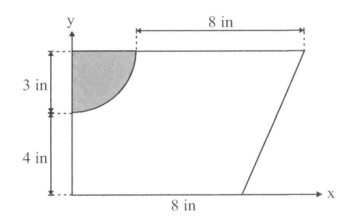

113

17.5 Find the area moments of inertia about both its centroidal axes and the given x and y-axes for the case where h = 8 m.
(Ans. I^*_x = 415.33 m^4, I^*_y = 777.83 m^4, I_x = 1,535.33 m^4, I_y = 2,895.33 m^4)

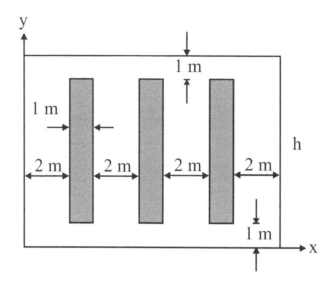

17.6 In Problem 17.4, calculate the polar moment of inertia about the given x and y-axes.
(Ans. I_z = 2966.70 in^4)

17.7 Solve Problem 17.1 in terms of the unknown dimension L.
(Ans. I_x = 0.140L^4 - 3.537L^2 + 8.005L – 12.571 in^4, I_y = 0.250L^4 – 3.142L^2 – 12.566 in^4)

17.8 In Problem 17.7, for what value of L will I^*_x = I^*_y.
(Ans. L = 4.267 in)

MODULE 18: Torsion

In addition to the case of direct shear stress, shear stress is also created by the twisting of a bar or rod. This twisting action is known as 'torsion', and the applied load T is called the torque. The sense of the torque vector, as in the case of a moment, is governed by the right-hand rule. The case of torsion is depicted in Figure 18.1 below.

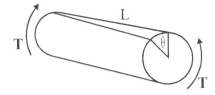

Figure 18.1

If a torque is applied at one end of a bar, twisting the bar through angle θ, an equal and opposite torque must be applied at the other end in order to maintain equilibrium.

Shear Stress

The shear stress in the bar resulting from the applied torque is a function of the distance from the centroid of the cross-sectional area, where the shear stress is zero, to the outer surface of the rod, where the shear stress is a maximum. This shear stress distribution can be calculated by the equation

$$\tau = T\rho / J$$

where ρ is the distance from the centroid of the cross-section to the location of interest, and J is the polar moment of inertia of the cross-section about the centroidal axis and is equivalent to I^*_z, as was described in Module 17. The maximum shear stress at the outer surface is calculated by

$$\tau_{max} = Tc / J$$

where c is the distance from the centroid to the farthest point on the outer surface. Shear stresses due to torsion are easily determined for members having circular cross-sections. The polar moments of inertia for two common torsional members are given as follows.

Solid Round Section: $\quad J = \pi D^4 / 32 = \pi r^4 / 2$

Hollow Round Section: $\quad J = \pi(D^4 - D_i^4) / 32 = \pi(r^4 - r_i^4) / 2$

where D is the outside diameter, D_i is the inside diameter, r the outside radius, and r_i the inside diameter of the cross-section.

Determining the shear stress in non-circular cross-sectional areas is more difficult and beyond the scope of this text.

Shear Strain

The shear stress resulting from an applied torque will create 'shear strain' in the member in the direction of the applied torque. The shear strain γ is given by the relationship

$$\gamma = \tau / G$$

where G is the modulus of rigidity of the material, also called the shear modulus. The relationship between G, E, and μ is given as

$$G = E / [2(1 + \mu)]$$

The resulting angular displacement θ resulting from the shear strain is given by the expression

$$\theta = TL / GJ$$

where θ is the twist angle in radians. Tables 14.1 and 14.2 provide values of the modulus of rigidity for several common materials.

Example 18.1

Compare the maximum shear stresses in two members having circular cross-sections, one solid and one hollow, having the same length, same material, same torque, and same outside diameter of 4 in. The hollow member has an inside diameter of 3 in.

Solution: For the solid cross-section

$$(\tau_{max})_s = Tc / J$$
$$= T(D/2) / (\pi D^4 / 32)$$
$$= 16T / [\pi(4)^3]$$
$\Rightarrow \quad (\tau_{max})_s = 0.08T \text{ psi}$

For the hollow cross-section

$$(\tau_{max})_h = Tc / J$$
$$= T(D/2) / [\pi(D^4 - D_i^4) / 32]$$
$$= T(64) / [\pi((4)^4 - (3)^4)]$$
$\Rightarrow \quad (\tau_{max})_h = 0.12T \text{ psi}$

Therefore, the maximum shear stress in the hollow section is

$$(\tau_{max})_h = (0.12 / 0.08) (\tau_{max})_s$$
$\Rightarrow \quad (\tau_{max})_h = 1.50 (\tau_{max})_s$

Example 18.2

For the stepped shaft shown below, determine how much the right end of the shaft will twist relative to the fixed left end. The diameter of the brass section is 4.0 in and the diameter of the steel section is 2.0 in.

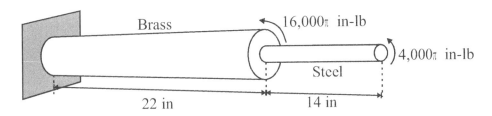

Solution: $\theta = \theta_B + \theta_S$
$= T_B L_B / G_B J_B + T_S L_S / G_S J_S$
$= 20,000\pi(22) / [(5.4 \times 10^6)\pi(4)^4 / 32] + 4,000\pi(14) / [(11 \times 10^6)\pi(2)^4 / 32]$
$= 0.0102 + 0.0102$
$\Rightarrow \theta = 0.0204$ rad $= 1.17°$

Problems

18.1 Find the diameter of a solid circular shaft that is to transmit a torque of 3,500 in-lb if the shear stress in the shaft is not to exceed 10,000 psi.
(Ans. D = 1.213 in)

18.2 What torque will a 1.25 in diameter solid circular steel shaft transmit if a shear stress of 12,000 psi is allowed? If the shaft is 36 in long, determine the angular displacement during transmission of this torque.
(Ans. T = 4,601.9 in-lb, θ = 0.063 rad)

18.3 In the figure below, determine the amount of twist at the right end of the shaft for the load specified. The outside diameter is 3 in.
(Ans. θ = 0.0166 rad)

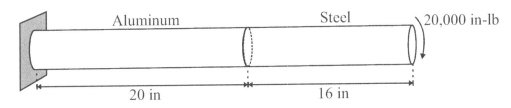

18.4 Consider a single torque T applied at the end of the stepped shaft in Example 18.2. If the maximum twist is 0.0065 rad, calculate the applied torque and the maximum shear stress in each material.
(Ans. T = 6,684.9 in-lb, τ_S = 4,256 psi, τ_B = 532 psi)

18.5 Shaft AE is made of stainless steel and has a diameter of 2.0 in. It is loaded by the following torques in the directions indicated: $T_B = 1{,}200$ in-lb, $T_C = 1{,}600$ in-lb, and $T_D = 750$ in-lb. If the shaft is fixed at point A but free to rotate at point E, compute the shear stress developed in each of the four sections of the shaft.
(Ans. $\tau_{DE} = 0$ psi, $\tau_{CD} = 477$ psi, $\tau_{BC} = 1{,}496$ psi $\tau_{AB} = 2{,}258$ psi)

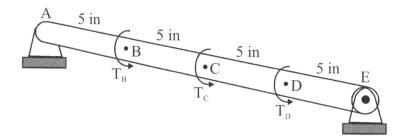

18.6 For the stepped shaft shown in Example 18.2, consider both ends to be fixed at a wall. If a torque of 16,000 in-lb is applied at the point where the two materials are joined, calculate the maximum amount of twist in the shaft and the shear stress in both materials.
(Ans. $\theta = 0.00216$ rad, $\tau_S = 1{,}698$ psi, $\tau_B = 1{,}061$ psi)

18.7 Find the required diameter of the shaft in Problem 18.2 if $T = 12{,}000$ in-lb.
(Ans. $D = 1.72$ in)

18.8 In Problem 18.3, consider the case where the aluminum section is replaced with a section of unknown material having the same dimensions. Calculate the modulus of rigidity G for the unknown material if the total amount of twist at the right end is $\theta = 0.02$ rad.
(Ans. $G = 3.078 \times 10^6$ psi)

MODULE 19: Shear Forces and Bending Moments in Beams

Beams are generally long, straight members that are used to support loads that are usually applied perpendicular along their length. They are one of the most widely used structural members in engineering and are subjected to a wide range of loading conditions. Beams are most often used to support loads that will create both shear loads and bending moments within the beams. The shear stresses and bending stresses created within beams must be evaluated to ensure unacceptable stress levels are not reached as a result of the applied loads. Prior to analyzing these stresses, however, the shear loads and bending moments along the length of a beam must be determined. While this can be accomplished using both analytical and graphical methods, this text will rely primarily on the use of graphical techniques in the form of shear force and vending moment diagrams. As discussed in Module 12, there are three types of beams that are statically determinate: simply supported beams, cantilever beams, and overhanging beams as shown in Figure 19.1.

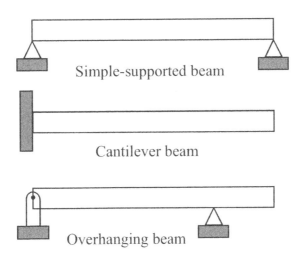

Figure 19.1

Shear and moment diagrams of beams provide a profile of the distribution of the shear forces and the bending moments along the length of the beam. Once the locations of the maximum shear force and maximum bending moment are determined, the stress corresponding to these loads at these locations can be calculated. In general, the profiles of shear and bending moments or their slopes will be discontinuous along the beam's length at locations where concentrated loads or moments are applied, or where distributed loads change. As a result, the values of the shear force and bending moments must be determined for sections of beam length between any such discontinuities. In constructing shear and bending moment diagrams, it is most convenient to define a coordinate system centered at the centroid of the left end of the beam. Therefore, x will be positive to the right and y will be positive upward. An upward shear force and a moment in the clockwise direction will be considered to be positive. With this definition of a coordinate system, a general procedure for the construction of shear and moment diagrams can now be stated.

Procedure for Constructing Shear Force and Bending Moment Diagrams

1. Draw the free-body diagram of the beam and determine all reaction forces and moments at the supports. Resolve all forces into x and y components.

2. Plot all y direction forces shown on the free-body diagram of the beam on a set of xy axes. The x dimension will represent the distance along the longitudinal axis of the beam and the y dimension will represent the magnitude of the shear forces. Positive forces are shown as vertical lines upward, negative forces are shown as vertical lines downward, and sections where no forces act are shown as horizontal lines. Distributed shear loads are shown as either increasing or decreasing as a function of x. As the force profile is drawn, the cumulative sum of the magnitudes of the forces should be written at all points of discontinuity in the diagram. The drawing will be closed and always begin and end on the x-axis. Enclosed areas above and below the x-axis will be apparent. This is the shear diagram.

3. The moments along the beam are plotted on another set of xy axes. The x dimension will again represent the longitudinal axis of the beam while the y dimension will represent the magnitude of the moments. As the moment profile is drawn, the cumulative sum of the magnitudes of the moments should be written at all points of discontinuity in the diagram. The value of the moment to be added to the previous sum is equal to the area under the curve of the corresponding enclosed area of shear on the shear diagram. Areas of shear above the x-axis will indicate positive moments to be drawn in the upward direction, while areas of shear below the x-axis will indicate negative moments to be drawn in the downward direction. The drawing will be closed and begin and end on the x-axis. This is the moment diagram.

In implementing the above procedure, for constant values of shear on the shear diagram, the corresponding moment will be a linear function of x, the distance measured from the left end of the beam. For shear loads that are linear functions of x, e.g., uniformly distributed loads, the moments will be quadratic functions of x. And, for shear loads that are quadratic functions of x, the moments will be cubic functions of x. Thus, the moments will be a function of one power of x higher than the shear forces. Table 19.1 illustrates how shear and moment diagrams are constructed for various types of loading conditions.

Table 19.1 Shear Force and Bending Moment Diagram Construction

Loading Conditions	Shear Force Diagram	Bending Moment Diagram

Example 19.1

For the simple-supported beam below, draw the shear and moment diagrams and determine the maximum shear force and bending moment.

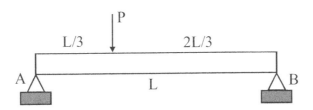

Solution: The support reaction forces are calculated to be: $A = 2P/3$ and $B = P/3$.

FBD:

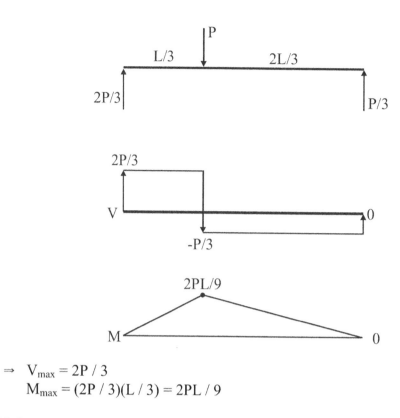

⇒ $V_{max} = 2P/3$
$M_{max} = (2P/3)(L/3) = 2PL/9$

Example 19.2

For the simple-supported beam below, draw the shear and moment diagrams and determine the maximum shear force and bending moment.

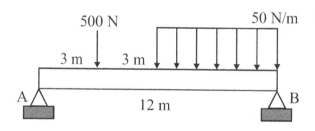

Solution: The support reaction forces are calculated to be A = 450 N and B = 350 N.

FBD:

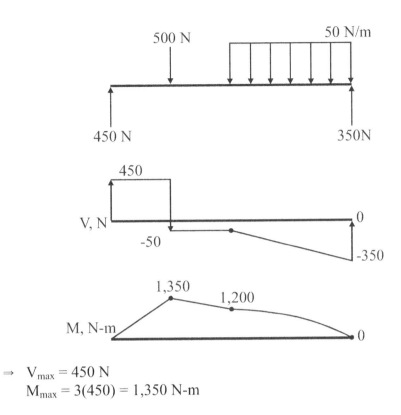

$\Rightarrow$ V_{max} = 450 N
M_{max} = 3(450) = 1,350 N-m

Problems

For the problems below, construct the shear and moment diagrams and determine the magnitude and location of the maximum shear force and maximum bending moment.

19.1

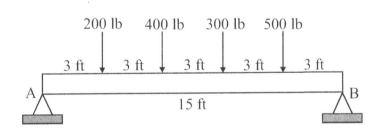

(Ans. V_{max} = -780 lb at: 12.0 ft $\leq$ x $\leq$ 15.0 ft, M_{max} = 3,180 lb-ft at: x = 9.0 ft)

19.2

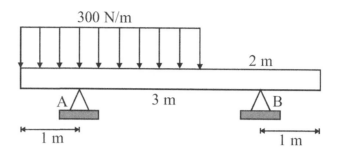

(Ans. V_{max} = 450 N at x = 1.0 m, M_{max} = 187.5 N-m at x = 2.5 m)

19.3

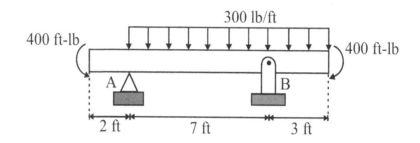

(Ans. V_{max} = -1,242.9 lb at x = 9.0 ft, M_{max} = -1,748.4 lb-ft at x = 9.0 ft)

19.4

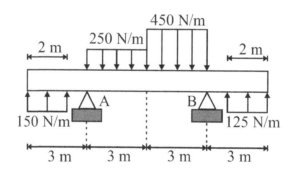

(Ans. V_{max} = -1,216.7 N at x = 9.0 m, M_{max} = 2,144.7 N-m at x = 6.30 m)

19.5

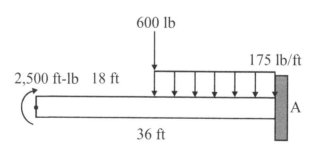

(Ans. V_{max} = -3,750 lb at x = 36.0 ft, M_{max} = -36,650 lb-ft at x = 36.0 ft)

19.6

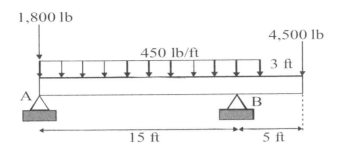

(Ans. V_{max} = 5,400 lb at x = 15.0 ft, M_{max} = -23,400 lb-ft at x = 15.0 ft)

19.7 In Problem 19.3, determine the value of the distributed load w so that M_B = -2,500 lb-ft.
(Ans. w = 467.7 lb/ft)

19.8 Solve Problem 19.6 including the weight of the uniform beam to be 1,000 lb.
(Ans. V_{max} = 5,601.7 lb at x = 15.0 ft, M_{max} = -23,400 lb-ft at x = 15.0 ft)

MODULE 20: Shear Forces and Bending Moments in Beams (cont.)

This module presents additional material on shear forces and bending moments in beams in the form of more example problems.

Example 20.1

For the cantilever beam below, draw the shear and moment diagrams and determine the maximum shear force and bending moment.

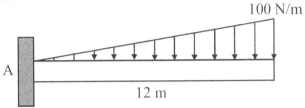

Solution: $A = 600$ N , $M_A = 4,800$ N-m

FBD :

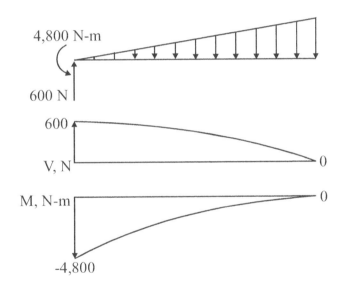

$\Rightarrow$ $V_{max} = 600$ N , $M_{max} = -4,800$ N-m

Example 20.2

For the simple-supported beam below, draw the shear and moment diagrams and determine the maximum shear force and bending moment.

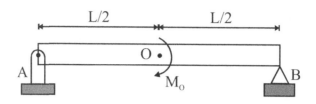

Solution: $A = -M_o / L$, $B = M_o / L$

FBD:

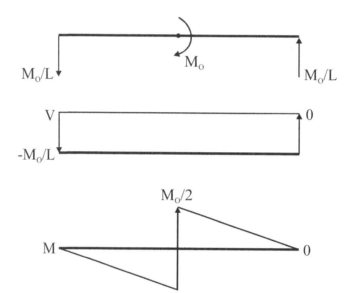

$\Rightarrow$ $V_{max} = -M_o / L$
$M_{max} = M_o / 2$

Example 20.3

For the overhanging beam below, draw the shear and bending moment diagrams and determine the maximum shear force and bending moment.

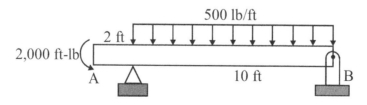

Solution: $A = 2{,}700 \text{ lb}$, $B = 2{,}300 \text{ lb}$

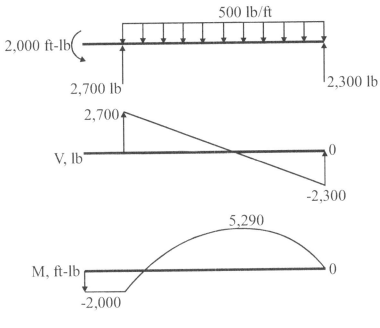

$\Rightarrow$ $V_{max} = 2{,}700$ lb
$M_{max} = 5{,}290$ ft-lb

Problems

For Problems 20.1-20.3 below, construct the shear and moment diagrams and determine the magnitude and location of the maximum shear force and maximum bending moment.

20.1 Consider the beam in Problem 19.5 to have simple supports at each end.
(Ans. $V_{max} = -2{,}732$ lb at $x = 36.0$ ft, $M_{max} = 21{,}325$ ft-lb at $x = 20.39$ ft)

20.2
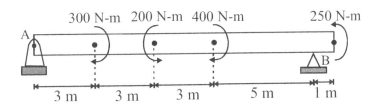

(Ans. $V_{max} = -17.9$ N for all x, $M_{max} = 339.3$ N-m at $x = 9.0$ m)

20.3
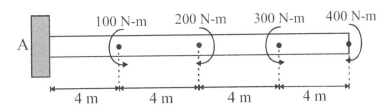

(Ans. $V_{max} = 0$ for all x, $M_{max} = -400$ N-m at: 12.0 m $\leq x \leq 16.0$ m)

For Problems 20.4-20.6 below, construct the shear diagram and determine the magnitude and location of the maximum shear force.

20.4

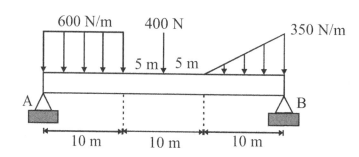

(Ans. V_{max} = 5,394.3 N at x = 0.0 m)

20.5

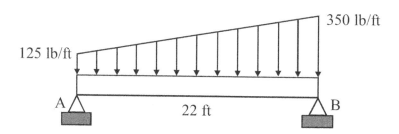

(Ans. V_{max} = -3,025.4 lb at x = 22.0 ft)

20.6

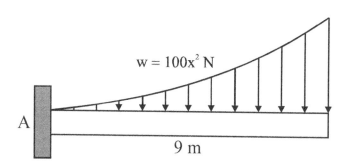

(Ans. V_{max} = 24,300 N at x = 0.0 m)

20.7 In Problem 20.5, consider the distributed load at the right end of the beam to have an intensity w, where w < 100 lb/ft. Determine the value of w so that the shear force within the beam at support A is 1,100 lb.
(Ans. w = 49.95 lb/ft)

20.8 Calculate the magnitudes of the maximum shear force and maximum bending moment in Problem 20.6 if $w = x^2/6$ N/m.
(Ans. V = 40.5 N at x = 0.0 m, M = 273.4 N-m at x = 0.0 m.

MODULE 21: Bending Stresses in Beams

The shear forces and bending moments along the length of a beam will produce both shear stresses and normal stresses within the beam. These stresses must be evaluated in order to determine a beam's capability to adequately support the applied loads.

Shear Stresses in Bending

Shear stresses that are formed during the bending of a beam are treated differently than direct shear stresses. Direct shear stresses were calculated by averaging the stress over the cross-sectional area through which the shear force acts. In the case of shear stresses created in bending, the stress values are a function of the shape of the cross-section and vary throughout the area. The shear stress will be zero on the top and bottom surfaces of the beam and will be a maximum at the neutral axis, i.e., centroid, of the cross-section. For example, a beam having a rectangular cross-sectional area has a corresponding shear stress profile due to bending as shown in Figure 21.1.

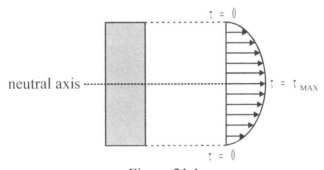

Figure 21.1

The maximum shear stress occurring at the neutral axis for commonly-used, symmetrical, cross-sectional areas can be calculated using the following formulas:

Rectangular Section: $\tau_{max} = 3V_{max} / 2A$
Solid Circular Section: $\tau_{max} = 4V_{max} / 3A$
Hollow Circular Section: $\tau_{max} = 2V_{max} / A$

Also, an approximation for wide-flange (WF) and I-beam sections, both commonly used in structural design, is given as

$$\tau_{max} = 2V_{max} / A_w$$

where A_w is the area of the web of the specific cross-section only.

Normal Stresses in Bending

If a simply supported beam bends due to a force acting at the center of the beam, the beam will be bent in a direction that is concave upward. This type of bending would create a normal stress in compression on the top surface of the beam and a normal stress in tension on the bottom surface of the beam. At the neutral axis, or centroid, of the cross-section the normal stress is zero. The profile of the normal stresses resulting from bending is shown through a rectangular cross-section in Figure 21.2.

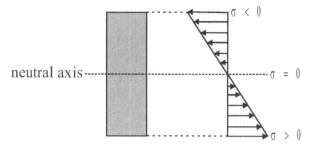

Figure 21.2

The negative value of σ and sense to the left indicates the top surface of the beam is in compression, while the positive value of σ and sense to the right indicates the bottom surface of the beam is in tension. The normal stress at any location within the beam is calculated using the formula

$$\sigma = -M_{max}\, y / I$$

where y is the distance from the neutral axis of the cross-section to the location of interest within the beam. The sign of y will be positive above the neutral axis and negative below, indicating that the top surface of the cross-section will be in compression and the bottom surface will be in tension. The negative sign in the formula above is necessary to be consistent with the established sign convention for the applied moments. The maximum normal stress within the beam is found by

$$\sigma_{max} = -M_{max}\, c / I = -M_{max} / Z$$

where c is the distance from the neutral axis to the point within the cross-section farthest from the neutral axis and Z is the 'section modulus' and equal to the quantity I/c.

Example 21.1

Consider the cantilever beam in Example 20.1 to have a circular cross-section with a diameter of 0.25 m. Determine the maximum normal and shear stresses in the beam due to bending.

Solution: From the results of Example 20.1, V_{max} = 600 N and M_{max} = -4,800 N-m.

The maximum moment occurs at the wall, therefore the maximum normal stress will also occur at the wall and is calculated by

$$\begin{aligned}\sigma_{max} &= -M_{max}\, c / I \\ &= -M_{max}\,(D/2) / [\pi r^4 / 4] \\ &= -32 M_{max} / \pi D^3 \\ &= -32(-4,800) / \pi (0.25)^3 \\ \Rightarrow \sigma_{max} &= 3.129 \times 10^6 \text{ N/m}^2\end{aligned}$$

These results indicate that the beam's top surface will be in tension and the bottom surface will be in compression. The maximum shear stress occurs at the center of the cross-section and is calculated by

$$\tau_{max} = 4V_{max} / 3A$$
$$= 4V_{max} / 3\pi(D^2/4)$$
$$= 16(600) / 3\pi(0.25)^2$$
$$\Rightarrow \tau_{max} = 16,297 \text{ N/m}^2$$

Example 21.2

Consider the simple-supported beam in Example 19.2 to have a rectangular cross-section with a width of 0.2 m and a height of 0.3 m. Determine the maximum normal and shear stresses due to bending.

Solution: The internal loads in this beam are determined as $V_{max} = 450$ N and $M_{max} = 1,350$ N-m.

The maximum moment occurs at the point of application of the 500 N force and the corresponding normal stress is calculated by

$$\sigma_{max} = -M_{max} c / I$$
$$= -M_{max} (h/2) / [bh^3/12]$$
$$= -6M_{max} / bh^2$$
$$= -6(1,350) / (0.2)(0.3)^2$$
$$\Rightarrow \sigma_{max} = -450,000 \text{ N/m}^2$$

This indicates that the top surface of the beam will be in compression and the bottom surface will be in tension. The maximum shear stress will occur at the neutral axis of the rectangular cross-section and is calculated by

$$\tau_{max} = 3V_{max} / 2A$$
$$= 3V_{max} / 2bh$$
$$= 3(450) / 2(0.2)(0.3)$$
$$\Rightarrow \tau_{max} = 11,250 \text{ N/m}^2$$

Example 21.3

Consider the simple supported beam in Example 20.2 to have a circular cross-section. Determine an expression for the required diameter if the maximum normal stress is to be limited to 18,000 psi.

Solution: As determined in Example 20.2, the maximum moment occurs at the center of the beam's span and is equal to $-M_o/2$.

$$\sigma_{max} = -M_{max} c / I$$
$$18,000 = -(-M_o/2)(D/2) / [\pi D^4/64]$$
$$= 16M_o / \pi D^3$$

$$D = [16M_o / \pi(18,000)]^{1/3}$$
$$\Rightarrow D = M_o^{1/3} / 15.23 \text{ in}$$

Problems

For the problems below, determine the maximum normal stress and maximum shear stress in the beam for each case described below.

21.1 A beam with a circular cross-section having a diameter of 4.2 in, carrying loads of V_{max} = -780 lb and M_{max} = 3,180 ft-lb.
(Ans. σ_{max} = -5,246 psi, τ_{max} = -75 psi)

21.2 A beam with a circular cross-section having a diameter of 7.5 in, carrying loads of V_{max} = -2,100 lb and M_{max} = -19,600 ft-lb.
(Ans. σ_{max} = 5,679 psi, τ_{max} = -63 psi)

21.3 A beam with a rectangular cross-section having a base of 6 in and a height of 10.8 in, carrying loads of V_{max} = -1,242.9 lb and M_{max} = -1,748.4 ft-lb.
(Ans. σ_{max} = 180 psi, τ_{max} = -29 psi)

21.4 A beam with a rectangular cross-section having a base of 0.25 m and a height of 0.6 m, carrying loads of V_{max} = -50 N and M_{max} = 480 N-m.
(Ans. σ_{max} = -32,000 N/m^2, τ_{max} = -500 N/m^2)

21.5 A beam with a circular cross-section having a diameter of 0.65 m, carrying only a load of M_{max} = -1,000 N-m.
(Ans. σ_{max} = 37,090 N/m^2, τ_{max} = 0 N/m^2)

21.6 A beam with a hollow circular cross-section having an outside diameter of 18 in, an inside diameter of 15 in, and carrying loads of V_{max} = -2,000 lb and M_{max} = 12,000 ft-lb.
(Ans. σ_{max} = -486 psi, τ_{max} = -51 psi)

21.7 Consider a beam having a rectangular cross-section with a base of x in and a height of 3x in. For the loads specified in Problem 21.2, determine the smallest value of x which will limit both the maximum normal stress to 5,000 psi and the maximum shear stress to -500 psi.
(Ans. x = 1.377 in)

21.8 Find the inside diameter of the beam in Problem 21.6 if τ_{max} = -100 psi.
(Ans. D_i = 16.525 in)

MODULE 22: Beam Deflections in Bending

A beam that is supported along its length at one or more points and is subjected to vertical loads will bend. This bending will create vertical displacements that vary along the length of the beam. The nature of the resulting normal stresses, i.e., tension or compression, can be more easily determined from a visualization of the beam bending. The amount of deflection of a beam can play a critical role in many engineering applications.

Generally it will be the case that any vertical deflections that result from shear stresses created during bending will be significantly smaller than the deflections resulting from the normal stresses and can be neglected. The mathematical analysis required to determine beam deflections along its length can be complicated and is beyond the scope of this text. However, a summary of beam deflection equations resulting from a variety of loading conditions for cantilever and simple-supported beams is presented in Table 22.1. These formulas can be used to compute the deflections at any point along the length of the beam under the assumption that the beam is not stressed beyond the proportional limit of the material. If this is not the case, beam deflections calculated using these formulas will be inaccurate.

In Table 22.1, the following notation is used.

y = beam deflection
y_{max} = maximum beam deflection
P = applied load
w = distributed load intensity
x = distance to deflection location measured from left edge of beam
E = modulus of elasticity
I = cross-sectional area moment of inertia
L = beam length
a, b = dimensions along beam's length

A computed negative value of deflection will indicate a downward displacement.

Principle of Superposition

The principle of superposition states that deflections in a beam due to two or more loads will equal the sum of the deflections for the individual loads. This means that the deflections due to the combination of different loading conditions described in Table 22.1 can be obtained by summing the deflections of each individual loading condition.

Table 22.1 Formulas for Beam Deflections In Bending

Bending Case	Deflection	Maximum Deflection
1. Cantilever, end load	$y = Px^2(x - 3L) / 6EI$	$y_{max} = -PL^3 / 3EI$

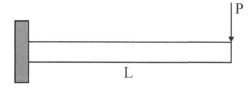

2. Cantilever, intermediate load	$y_{A \to B} = Px^2(x - 3a) / 6EI$ $y_{B \to C} = Pa^2(a - 3x) / 6EI$	$y_{max} = Pa^2(a - 3L) / 6EI$

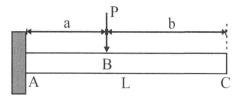

3. Cantilever, uniform load	$y = wx^2(4Lx - x^2 - 6L^2) / 24EI$	$y_{max} = -wL^4 / 8EI$

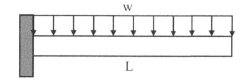

4. Cantilever, end moment load	$y = Mx^2 / 2EI$	$y_{max} = ML^2 / 2EI$

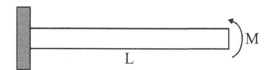

5. Simple supports, center load	$y_{A \to B} = Px(4x^2 - 3L^2) / 48EI$	$y_{max} = -PL^3 / 48EI$

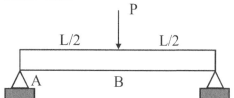

Table 22.1 Formulas for Beam Deflections In Bending (cont.)

Bending Case	Deflection	Maximum Deflection
6. Simple supports, intermediate load	$y_{A-B} = Pbx(x^2 + b^2 - L^2) / 6EIL$ $y_{B-C} = Pa(L - x)(x^2 + a^2 - 2Lx) / 6EIL$	$y_{max} = -Pa(L^2 - a^2)^{3/2} / 3^{5/2}LEI$

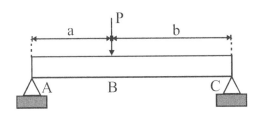

7. Simple supports, uniform load	$y = wx(2Lx^2 - x^3 - L^3) / 24EI$	$y_{max} = -5wL^4 / 384EI$

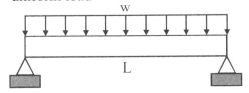

8. Simple supports, twin loads	$y_{A-B} = Px(x^2 + 3a^2 - 3aL) / 6EI$ $y_{B-C} = Pa(3x^2 + a^2 - 3Lx) / 6EI$	$y_{max} = Pa(4a^2 - 3L^2) / 24EI$

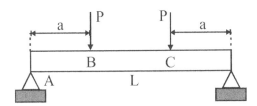

Example 22.1

The cantilever beam below has a square cross-section of 6 in x 6 in and is loaded with a uniform distributed load (which includes the beams weight). If the beam is constructed of steel, determine the deflection at both the midpoint and the end of the beam.

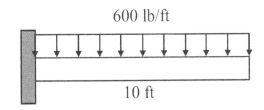

Solution: Using the formula for the beam deflection presented in Case 3 of Table 22.1 shows

$$y = wx^2(4Lx - x^2 - 6L^2) / 24EI$$

At the midpoint of the beam, $x = L/2$. Substitution shows

$$y = w(L/2)^2[4L(L/2) - (L/2)^2 - 6L^2] / 24EI$$
$$= wL^2/4[2L^2 - L^2/4 - 6L^2] / [24Ebh^3/12]$$
$$= -17(12)wL^4 / [16(24)Ebh^3]$$
$$= -0.531(50)(120)^4 / [(30 \times 10^6)(6)^4]$$
$\Rightarrow y = -0.142$ in

At the end of the beam, $x = L$, therefore

$$y_{max} = -wL^4/8EI$$
$$= -12(50)(120)^4 / [8(30 \times 10^6)(6)^4] \text{ in}$$
$\Rightarrow y_{max} = -0.400$ in

Example 22.2

The simple-supported beam below is loaded with a uniformly distributed load along its length and a concentrated load at its midpoint. Determine the maximum deflection of the beam if the beam is aluminum with a circular cross-section having a diameter of 6 in.

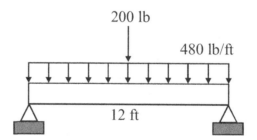

Solution: Using the principle of superposition, the maximum deflection of the beam will occur at the midpoint and will be equal to the sum of the deflections due to the uniformly distributed load (y_1) and the concentrated load (y_2). Therefore

$$y_{max} = y_1 + y_2$$
$$= (-5wL^4/384EI) + (-PL^3/48EI)$$
$$= (-5wL - 8P)L^3 / 384EI$$
$$= (-5wL - 8P)L^3 / (384E\pi D^4/64)$$
$$= (-5wL - 8P)L^3 / 6E\pi D^4$$
$$= [-5(40)(144) - 8(200)](144)^3 / [6(11 \times 10^6)\pi(6)^4]$$
$\Rightarrow y_{max} = -0.338$ in

Problems

22.1 In the figure below, determine the diameter of the circular steel beam so that the maximum deflection of the beam does not exceed 0.010 in.
(Ans. D = 13.26 in)

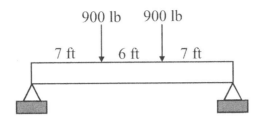

22.2 Determine the value of the load P in Case 1 in terms of the distributed load w in Case 3 so that the maximum deflections in each case are equal.
(Ans. P = 3wL / 8)

22.3 The cantilever beam shown below is constructed of stainless steel and has a rectangular cross-section with a base of 4 in and a height of 5 in. Determine the deflection at both the mid-point and end of the beam for the case where P = 300 lb and w = 10 lb/in.
(Ans. mid-point: y = -0.592 in; end: y = -1.646 in)

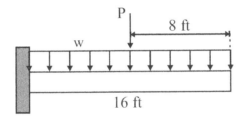

22.4 Show that for the case of simple-supported beam with an intermediate load (Case 6), $y_{A-B} = y_{B-C}$ at x = a, if a = L / 2.
(Ans. $y_{A-B} = y_{B-C} = -PL^3 / 48EI$)

22.5 The steel beam shown is subjected to two loads equal to P. If the beam has a circular cross-section of 5.0 in diameter, determine the maximum value of P so that the deflection at the center of the beam does not exceed 0.67 in.
(Ans. P = 2,478.3 lb)

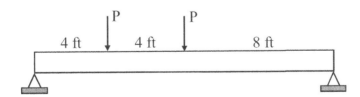

22.6 For the aluminum cantilever beam below, w = 250 lb/ft and M = 1,200 ft-lb. If the cross-section is a 6 in by 6 in square, determine the deflection at the end of the beam.
(Ans. y = -2.105 in)

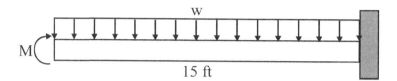

22.7 In Problem 22.3, consider the distributed load w to be unknown. Calculate the maximum value of w so the deflection at the mid-point of the beam is limited to 0.5 in.
(Ans. w = 8.226 lb/in)

22.8 If the length of the beam in Problem 22.6 is given as x ft, calculate the deflection of the end of the beam in terms of x.
(Ans. $y = (6{,}060.606\, x^2 - 2.192\, x^4) \times 10^{-9}$ in)

MODULE 23: Stresses Under Combined Loading Conditions

Thus far in the study of mechanics of materials, methods have been presented with which to analyze the internal effects of various types of loading conditions. These loading conditions are axial loads, direct shear loads, torsional loads, and bending loads which each create normal and/or shear stresses within the body being loaded. A summary of the stresses resulting from these different types of loading conditions follows below.

Normal Stresses

    axial loads: $\sigma = P / A$ (uniform through the cross-section)

    bending: $\sigma = -My / I$ (maximum at the surface of the cross-section where y = c; zero at the neutral axis)

Shear Stresses

    direct shear: $\tau = V / A$ (uniform through the cross-section)

    torsion: $\tau = Tr / J$ (maximum at the surface of the cross-section where r = c; zero at the neutral axis)

    bending: (shape dependent, as described below – the maximum occurs at the neutral axis; zero at the surface)

$$\tau_{max} = 3V_{max} / 2A \quad \text{(rectangle)}$$
$$\tau_{max} = 4V_{max} / 3A \quad \text{(solid circular)}$$
$$\tau_{max} = 2V_{max} / A \quad \text{(hollow circular)}$$

The cumulative effects of these different loading conditions can be determined using the principle of superposition. (Note: In general, direct shear isn't considered to occur with bending or torsion.)

Principle of Superposition

The principle of superposition, as described in Module 22 for beam deflections, is also applicable to stresses within a body. This means that the stresses resulting from two or more types of loading conditions will equal the sum of the stresses due to the individual types of loads. Virtually all types of possible loading scenarios on bodies can be modeled by the combination of the individual loads using the principle of superposition. Examples of this method are discussed below for the cases of bending combined with axial loads, and bending combined with torsion.

Bending Combined With Axial Loads

Consider a beam that is subjected to bending from a uniformly distributed load and tension from an axial load as shown in Figure 23.1. This figure shows both the loading conditions and the resulting normal stress profile through the cross-section.

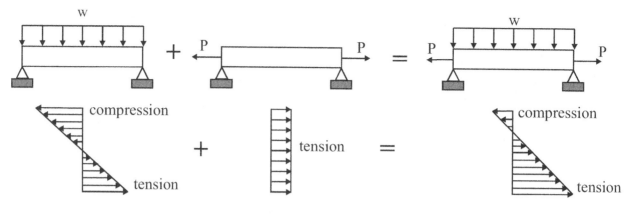

Figure 23.1

It can be seen from the stress profile that the magnitude of the normal stress on the bottom surface of the beam is much larger than the magnitude of the normal stress on the top surface due to the cumulative effects. This results in non-zero stress levels at the neutral axis of the beam. The combined normal stress throughout the cross-section is given by the expression

$$\sigma = P/A - My/I$$

The shear stresses from bending will be dependent upon the shape of the cross-section with the maximum shear stress occurring at the neutral axis and zero shear stress occurring at the surfaces as described in Module 21.

Bending Combined With Torsion

Consider a beam that is subjected to a bending from a uniformly distributed load and torsion as shown in Figure 23.2. This figure shows both the loading conditions and the resulting shear stress profile through the cross-section.

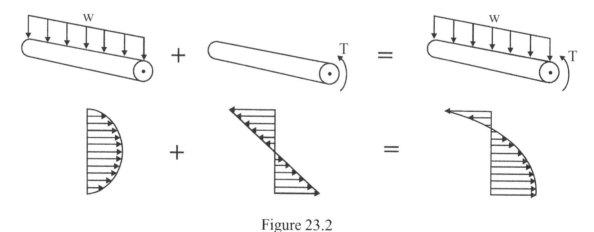

Figure 23.2

It can be seen that the cumulative effects of both loading conditions change the shear stress profile but the maximum shear stress on the bottom surface of the beam still results from torsion. The shear stress is again non-zero at the neutral axis.

Example 23.1

The beam shown is subjected to a compressive load and a concentrated bending load. Determine the maximum normal stresses on the top and bottom surfaces if the beam has a cross-sectional area of 19.11 in^2 and a section modulus of 88.0 in^3.

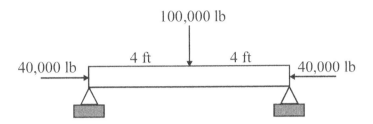

Solution: The maximum moment due to the 100,000 lb concentrated load is 200,000 lb-ft at the center of the beam and the corresponding maximum normal stress due to bending is

$\sigma_b = -M_{max} / Z$
$= -200,000(12) / 88.0$
⇒ $\sigma_b = -27,273$ psi

This indicates a compressive stress on the top surface of the beam and a tensile stress on the bottom surface. The 40,000 lb axial load will create a compressive stress throughout the cross-section equal to

$\sigma_a = -P / A$
$= -40,000 / 19.11$
⇒ $\sigma_a = -2,093$ psi

Therefore, the maximum normal stress at the top surface of the beam and have a magnitude of

$\sigma = \sigma_b + \sigma_a$
$= -27,273 + (-2,093)$
⇒ $\sigma = -29,366$ psi (compression)

The maximum normal stress at the beam's bottom surface and will have a magnitude of

$\sigma = -\sigma_b + \sigma_a$
$= 27,273 + (-2,093)$
⇒ $\sigma = 25,180$ psi (tension)

Example 23.2

The beam shown below has a cross-sectional area of 14.7 in² and a section modulus of 64.8 in³. For the loading condition shown, determine the maximum distributed load w that the beam can carry if the maximum allowable normal stress is 30,000 psi.

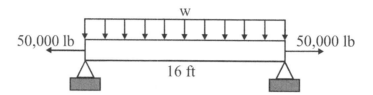

Solution: From construction of the shear and moment diagrams, the maximum moment can be calculated to be

$M_{max} = wL^2 / 8$
$= w(192)^2 / 8$ lb-in
$\Rightarrow M_{max} = 4{,}608w$ lb-in

The maximum normal stress will occur at the bottom surface and have a magnitude of

$\sigma_{max} = M_{max} / Z + P / A$
$= 4{,}608w / 64.8 + 50{,}000 / 14.7$
$\Rightarrow \sigma_{max} = 71.1w + 3{,}401$ psi

$\sigma_{all} = 71.1w + 3{,}401$
$30{,}000 = 71.1w + 3{,}401$
$w = (30{,}000 - 3{,}401) / 71.1$
$\Rightarrow w = 374$ lb/in

Problems

23.1 The beam below is subjected to axial load at the beam's center and bending loads as shown. Determine the maximum normal stresses on the top and bottom surfaces if the beam has a cross-sectional area of 15 in² and a section modulus of 60 in³.
(Ans. top: σ = -29,739 psi; bottom: σ = 24,405 psi)

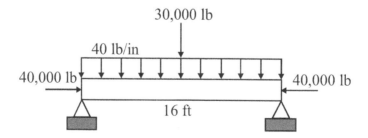

23.2 Determine the expressions for the maximum normal stress and the maximum shear stress at the wall for the loading condition shown below.
(Ans. $\sigma_{max} = -10.186PL/D^3$, $\tau_{max} = 5.093PL/D^3$)

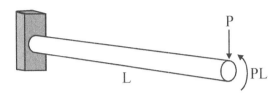

23.3 For the beam shown, A = 30 in^2 and Z = 90 in^3. Determine the maximum value of P such that the maximum normal stress is limited to 26,000 psi. Assume that wL = P.
(Ans. P = 41,052.6 lb)

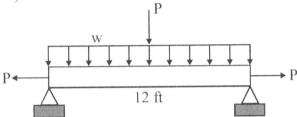

23.4 The cantilever beam below has a circular cross-section with a diameter of 3 inches and is subjected to a concentrated load and a torque as shown. Plot the value of the shear stress throughout the cross-section of the beam and determine the maximum shear stress within the cross-section.
(Ans. $\tau_{max} = 1,226$ psi)

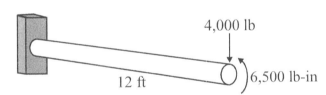

23.5 Consider the beam in Problem 23.4 to be loaded by a uniformly distributed load of 15 lb/ft downward, a concentrated load at the end of 1,000 lb downward, a tension load of 4,000 lb, and a counterclockwise torque of 6,500 lb-in. Determine the maximum normal stress and the maximum shear stress in the beam for this loading condition.
(Ans. $\sigma_{max} = 59,781$ psi, $\tau_{max} = 1,226$ psi)

23.6 For the cantilever beam shown, determine the maximum tensile force P if the maximum allowable normal stress in the beam is 15,000 psi. Consider the cross-section to have an area of 24 in^2 and a section modulus of 80 in^3.
(Ans. P = 289,440.0 lb)

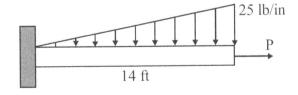

23.7 Calculate the maximum shear and normal stress in Problem 23.3 for the case of P = 20,000 lb and a beam length of 10 ft. Consider the beam to have a solid circular cross-section.
(Ans. τ_{max} = 888.9 psi, σ_{max} = 10,666.7 psi)

23.8 Solve Problem 23.5 for the case where the length of the beam is 8 ft.
(Ans. σ_{max} = 38,956 psi, τ_{max} = 1,226 psi)

MODULE 24: Principal Stresses

Normal and shear stresses created within a body vary by location. The stresses at any location can be analyzed by the construction of a 'stress element'. This stress element portrays a two-dimensional stress state, or 'plane stress', on a square element in the xy plane. Normal stresses in the x and y directions, and a shear stress perpendicular to the normal stresses are displayed in Figure 24.1.

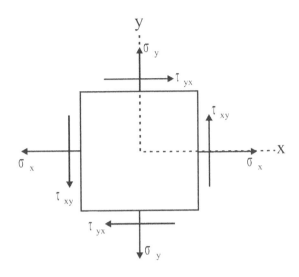

Figure 24.1

This figure defines positive stresses for the normal stresses σ_x and σ_y, and for the shear stress τ_{xy}. Stresses shown in the opposite direction to those in Figure 24.1 are defined as being negative. A positive normal stress indicates tension while a negative normal stress indicates compression. Note that this stress element represents a condition of equilibrium since the forces creating the stresses shown will be balanced. The normal and shear stresses shown on the stress element completely describe the stress state at one point within the body, however a stress element can be constructed at any point within or on the surface of the body. This concept is most convenient to study the maximum stresses within a body due to any particular loading condition. The state of stress depicted on a stress element is valid only for the particular orientation of the element shown. The stress state will change as the orientation of the element changes by a clockwise or counterclockwise rotation about the point at which the element is centered. This rotated orientation is shown in Figure 24.2.

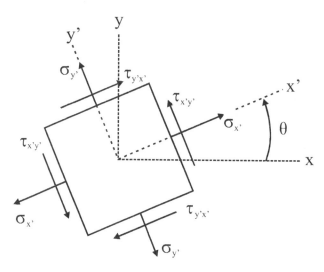

Figure 24.2

It can be seen that the original stress element is rotated counterclockwise through an angle θ, thereby creating a new stress state with normal stresses $\sigma_{x'}$ and $\sigma_{y'}$, and shear stress $\tau_{x'y'}$. These stress values are different from those in the original stress element due to the rotation. Writing force balance equations for this rotation gives the 'plane stress transformation equations' as

$$\sigma_{x'}, \sigma_{y'} = (\sigma_x + \sigma_y)/2 \pm [(\sigma_x - \sigma_y)/2]\cos 2\theta \pm \tau_{xy}\sin 2\theta$$

$$\tau_{x'y'} = -[(\sigma_x - \sigma_y)/2]\sin 2\theta + \tau_{xy}\cos 2\theta$$

For a certain rotation θ_p the shear stress will be zero and the normal stresses will represent the maximum and minimum normal stresses present at that point in the body. These maximum and minimum normal stresses are called 'principal' stresses and are designated as σ_1 and σ_2, respectively. This stress state is shown if Figure 24.3.

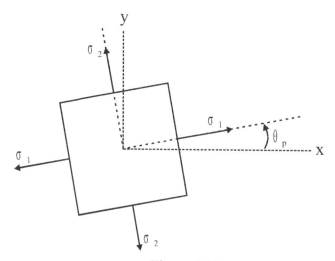

Figure 24.3

Performing a force balance on the rotated stress element can determine formulas for the principal stresses and the required angle of rotation as a function of the stresses of the original (nonrotated) element. Results of such a force balance gives

148

$$\sigma_1, \sigma_2 = (\sigma_x + \sigma_y)/2 \pm [(\sigma_x - \sigma_y)^2/4 + \tau_{xy}^2]^{1/2} \quad , \quad \theta_p = (\tan^{-1}[2\tau_{xy}/(\sigma_x - \sigma_y)])/2$$

Another angle of rotation θ_s exists for which the value of shear stress is a maximum and the normal stresses will be equal. This stress state is shown in Figure 24.4.

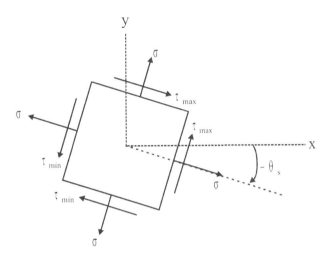

Figure 24.4

Performing a force balance on this rotated stress element can also determine formulas for the maximum (and minimum) shear stresses and the required angle of rotation as a function of the normal and shear stresses of the original (nonrotated) element. Results of such a force balance give

$$\tau_{max}, \tau_{min} = \pm [(\sigma_x - \sigma_y)^2/4 + \tau_{xy}^2]^{1/2} \quad , \quad \theta_s = (\tan^{-1}[-(\sigma_x - \sigma_y)/2\tau_{xy}])/2$$

Similar formulas for the principal stresses and maximum shear stress can be obtained for three-dimensional stress states, however that material is beyond the scope of this text.

Example 24.1

If $\sigma_x = -10,000$ psi, $\sigma_y = -2,000$ psi, and $\tau_{xy} = 4,000$ psi, find the magnitude and direction of the principal stresses.

Solution: Evaluating the formulas for principal stresses shows

$$\sigma_1, \sigma_2 = (\sigma_x + \sigma_y)/2 \pm [(\sigma_x - \sigma_y)^2/4 + \tau_{xy}^2]^{1/2}$$
$$= [-10,000 + (-2,000)]/2 \pm [(-10,000 - (-2,000))^2/4 + (4,000)^2]^{1/2}$$
$\Rightarrow \quad \sigma_1, \sigma_2 = -343$ psi, $-11,657$ psi

The direction of the principal stresses will be

$$\theta_p = (\tan^{-1}[2\tau_{xy}/(\sigma_x - \sigma_y)])/2$$
$$= (\tan^{-1}[2(4,000)/(-10,000 - (-2,000))])/2$$
$\Rightarrow \quad \theta_p = -22.50°$ (CW)

Example 24.2

Find the principal stresses, θ_p, and τ_{max}, for a bar having stresses $\sigma_x = 16,000$ psi and $\tau_{xy} = 6,000$ psi.

Solution:

$$\sigma_1, \sigma_2 = (\sigma_x + \sigma_y) / 2 \pm [(\sigma_x - \sigma_y)^2 / 4 + \tau_{xy}^2]^{1/2}$$
$$= (16,000 + 0) / 2 \pm [(16,000 - 0)^2 / 4 + (6,000)^2]^{1/2}$$
$\Rightarrow \quad \sigma_1, \sigma_2 = 18,000$ psi, $-2,000$ psi

$$\theta_p = (\tan^{-1} [2\tau_{xy} / (\sigma_x - \sigma_y)]) / 2$$
$$= (\tan^{-1} [2(6,000) / (16,000 - 0)]) / 2$$
$\Rightarrow \quad \theta_p = 18.43°$ (CCW)

$$\tau_{max} = [(\sigma_x - \sigma_y)^2 / 4 + \tau_{xy}^2]^{1/2}$$
$$= [(16,000 - 0)^2 / 4 + (6,000)^2]^{1/2}$$
$\Rightarrow \quad \tau_{max} = 10,000$ psi

Problems

24.1 If $\sigma_x = -7,000$ psi and $\tau_{xy} = -7,000$ psi, find the magnitude and direction of the principal stresses.
(Ans. $\sigma_1 = 4,326$ psi, $\sigma_2 = -11,326$ psi, $\theta_p = 31.72°$)

24.2 A beam is subject to a tensile stress σ_x and a compressive stress σ_y while $\tau_{xy} = 0$. Determine τ_{max} if $\sigma_x = -\sigma_y$.
(Ans. $\tau_{max} = \sigma_x$)

24.3 If $\sigma_x = 100$ psi, $\sigma_y = -60$ psi, and $\tau_{xy} = -80$ psi, calculate σ_1, σ_2, and τ_{max}.
(Ans. $\sigma_1 = 133$ psi, $\sigma_2 = -93$ psi, $\tau_{max} = 113$ psi)

24.4 Consider a stress state where $\sigma_x = 0$, $\sigma_y = -13,000$ psi, and $\tau_{xy} = -6,000$ psi. Calculate the magnitude and direction of the principal stresses and the maximum value of shear stress.
(Ans. $\sigma_1 = 2,346$ psi, $\sigma_2 = -15,346$ psi, $\theta_P = -21.36°$, $\tau_{max} = 8,846$ psi)

24.5 Given that $\sigma_x = -9,000$ psi, $\sigma_y = 5,000$ psi, and $\tau_{xy} = 1,000$ psi, determine θ_p and θ_s.
(Ans. $\theta_P = -4.07°$, $\theta_S = 40.93°$)

24.6 Consider a stress state where $\sigma_x = -10,000$ psi, $\sigma_y = 6,500$ psi, and $\tau_{xy} = 2,000$ psi. Calculate the magnitude and direction of the principal stresses and the maximum value of shear stress.
(Ans. $\sigma_1 = 6,739$ psi, $\sigma_2 = -10,239$ psi, $\theta_P = -6.81°$, $\tau_{max} = 8,489$ psi)

24.7 Solve Example 24.2 if $\sigma_x = 20,000$ psi, $\sigma_y = 6,000$ psi and $\tau_{xy} = -1,000$ psi.
(Ans. $\sigma_1 = 20,071.1$ psi, $\sigma_2 = 5,928.9$ psi, $\theta_p = -4.065°$, $\tau_{max} = 7,071.1$ psi)

24.8 Solve Problem 24.4 for the case of $\sigma_x = 2,000$ psi, $\sigma_y = -7,000$ psi, and $\tau_{xy} = 3,000$ psi.
(Ans. $\sigma_1 = 2,908.3$ psi, $\sigma_2 = -7,908.3$ psi, $\theta_p = 16.85°$, $\tau_{max} = 5,408.3$ psi)

MODULE 25: Mohr's Circle for Plane Stress

The plane stress transformation equations presented in the Module 24 have a graphical solution that makes it easier to visualize how the normal and shear stresses in a body change as the plane on which they act rotates. This graphical technique uses 'Mohr's Circle' to perform the stress transformation. Mohr's Circle is constructed by first establishing a coordinate axes where the normal stress σ is positive to the right and the shear stress τ is positive downward. For a stress state where σ_x, σ_y, and τ_{xy} are known, a circle is drawn having the center C located on the σ axis with a value of

$$\sigma_{avg} = (\sigma_x + \sigma_y) / 2$$

The radius R of the circle will be

$$R = [(\sigma_x - \sigma_y)^2 / 4 + \tau_{xy}^2]^{1/2}$$

Points A and B, which correspond to the coordinates (σ_x, τ_{xy}) and $(\sigma_y, -\tau_{xy})$, respectively, will lie on the circle as shown in Figure 25.1. Point A corresponds to a value of $\theta = 0°$ and point B corresponds to a value of $\theta = 180°$.

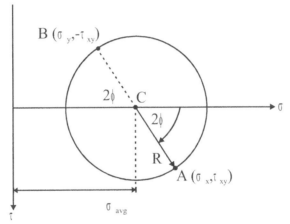

Figure 25.1

The angle between point A and the σ axis, designated 2ϕ, can be determined by the expression

$$2\phi = \tan^{-1} [\tau_{xy} / (\sigma_x - \sigma_{avg})]$$

Once Mohr's Circle is constructed it can be used to determine the normal and shear stress components acting on any arbitrary plane measured from reference point A or B. The plane of interest is located by moving through an angle of 2θ in either the counterclockwise (positive) or clockwise (negative) direction. This angular movement corresponds to a rotation of the stress element by angle θ in the same direction. Therefore a movement of $90°$ in the counterclockwise direction on Mohr's Circle corresponds to a rotation of the stress element by an angle of $45°$ in the counterclockwise direction. This geometrical relationship between point A and point P on the circle, which defines the new plane of interest, is shown in Figure 25.2. The coordinates corresponding to point P will be $(\sigma_{x'}, \tau_{x'y'})$ and will represent the stress state at the rotated orientation.

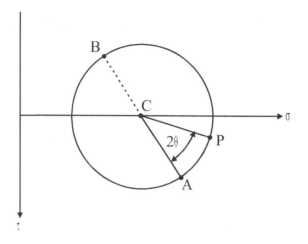

Figure 25.2

Principal Stresses

The principal stresses σ_1 and σ_2 can be determined from Mohr's Circle by rotating points A and B to lie on the σ axis, a location where the shear stress is zero. The larger value of the normal stress will be σ_1 and the smaller value of normal stress will be σ_2. Likewise, a rotation can be performed which locates the orientation where the normal stresses are equal and the shear stress is a maximum. These geometrical relationships are shown in Figure 25.3.

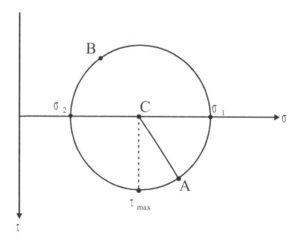

Figure 25.3

Failure Modes

The failure of members under combined stresses is generally based on one of two common failure theories: The Maximum-Normal-Stress Theory or the Maximum-Shear-Stress Theory. These two failure modes are described below.

Maximum-Normal-Stress Theory:

The maximum-normal-stress theory states that failure occurs whenever the largest principal stress equals the yield strength, or ultimate strength, of the material. Principal stresses can always be determined when the stress state at a point is given. If the largest of these principal stresses is designated as σ_1, then the maximum-normal-stress theory states that failure occurs whenever $\sigma_1 = \sigma_Y$ or $\sigma_1 = \sigma_U$, whichever is applicable. This theory also states that only the largest principal stress predicts failure and that the others may be neglected. But this theory also implies that in the case of pure torsion, failure would occur when $\tau_{max} = \sigma_1$, which does not agree with experimental data.

Maximum-Shear-Stress Theory:

The maximum-shear-stress theory states that a member will undergo a shear failure whenever $\tau_{max} = 0.5\,\sigma_Y$. That is, this theory predicts that the yield strength in shear is half the shear strength in tension. It has been shown experimentally that this shear limit is on the safe side and it has been used in many design codes.

Example 25.1

For the stress state shown on the element below, construct Mohr's circle and determine the stress state for a 15° counterclockwise rotation of the element.

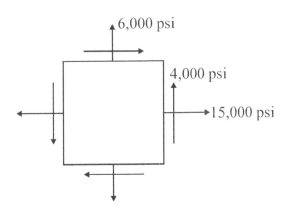

Solution: The center of the circle will be located at

$\sigma_{avg} = (\sigma_x + \sigma_y) / 2$
$= (15,000 + 6,000) / 2$
$\Rightarrow \sigma_{avg} = 10,500$ psi

The radius of the circle will be

$R = [(\sigma_x - \sigma_y)^2 / 4 + \tau_{xy}^2]^{1/2}$
$= [(15,000 - 6,000)^2 / 4 + (4,000)^2]^{1/2}$
$\Rightarrow R = 6,021$ psi

Drawing Mohr's Circle shows

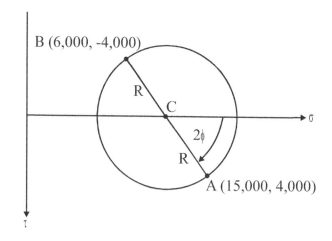

where σ_x = 15,000 psi, σ_y = 6,000 psi, and τ_{xy} = 4,000 psi. The angle between point A and the σ axis, represented by 2ϕ, can be determined by

$$2\phi = \tan^{-1}[\tau_{xy} / (\sigma_x - \sigma_{avg})]$$
$$= \tan^{-1}[4,000 / (15,000 - 10,500)]$$
$$\Rightarrow 2\phi = 41.63°$$

Therefore, with a counterclockwise rotation of the element of only 15°, i.e., $2\theta = 30°$, point A will still lie below the σ axis. The stress state through this plane can be determined from Mohr's Circle as

$$\sigma_{x'}, \sigma_{y'} = \sigma_{avg} \pm R \cos(2\phi - 2\theta)$$
$$= 10,500 \pm 6,021 \cos(41.63° - 30°)$$
$$\Rightarrow \sigma_{x'}, \sigma_{y'} = 16,397 \text{ psi}, 4,603 \text{ psi}$$

$$\tau_{x'y'} = R \sin(2\phi - 2\theta)$$
$$= 6,021 \sin(41.63° - 30°)$$
$$\Rightarrow \tau_{x'y'} = 1,214 \text{ psi}$$

Example 25.2

For the stress state defined below, determine the principal stresses, the maximum shear stress, and the orientation of the stress element in each case.

$$\sigma_x = -15,000 \text{ psi} \quad , \quad \sigma_y = 20,000 \text{ psi} \quad , \quad \tau_{xy} = 10,000 \text{ psi}$$

Solution: $\sigma_{avg} = (\sigma_x + \sigma_y) / 2$
$$= (-15,000 + 20,000) / 2$$
$$\Rightarrow \sigma_{avg} = 2,500 \text{ psi}$$

The radius of the circle will be

$$R = [(\sigma_x - \sigma_y)^2/4 + \tau_{xy}^2]^{1/2}$$
$$= [(-15{,}000 - 20{,}000)^2/4 + (10{,}000)^2]^{1/2}$$
$\Rightarrow$ R = 20,156 psi

and

$$2\phi = \tan^{-1}[\tau_{xy}/(\sigma_x - \sigma_{avg})]$$
$$= \tan^{-1}[10{,}000/(-15{,}000 - 2{,}500)]$$
$\Rightarrow$ $2\phi = -29.74°$ (CW)

It follows that

$$\sigma_1, \sigma_2 = \sigma_{avg} \pm R$$
$$= 2{,}500 \pm 20{,}156$$
$\Rightarrow$ $\sigma_1, \sigma_2 = 22{,}656, -17{,}656$ psi at $\theta = \phi = -14.87°$

$$\tau_{max} = R$$
$\Rightarrow$ $\tau_{max} = 20{,}156$ psi

The orientation at which τ_{max} acts will be in a plane 45° clockwise from the direction of the principal stress. The orientation of the stress element for τ_{max} will therefore be

$$\theta = -14.87° - 45°$$
$$= -59.87°$$
$\Rightarrow$ $\theta = 59.87°$ (CW)

Problems

25.1 For the state of stress given as $\sigma_x = 750$ psi, $\sigma_y = -800$ psi, and $\tau_{xy} = 450$ psi, determine the equivalent stress state if the stress element is rotated 55° in the counterclockwise direction from the original state.
(Ans. $\sigma_x = 133$ psi, $\sigma_y = -173$ psi, and $\tau_{xy} = -882$ psi)

25.2 For the state of stress given as $\sigma_x = -15{,}000$ psi, $\sigma_y = 10{,}000$ psi, and $\tau_{xy} = -8{,}000$ psi, determine the principal stresses, the maximum shear stress, and the orientation of the stress element in each case.
(Ans. $\sigma_1 = 12{,}341$ psi, $\sigma_2 = -17{,}341$ psi, $\theta_P = -16.31°$, $\tau_{max} = 14{,}841$ psi, $\theta_S = 28.69°$)

25.3 For the state of stress given as $\sigma_x = 300$ psi, $\sigma_y = 0$ psi, and $\tau_{xy} = 120$ psi, determine the principal stresses, the maximum shear stress, and the orientation of the stress element in each case.
(Ans. $\sigma_1 = 342$ psi, $\sigma_2 = -42$ psi, $\theta_P = -19.33°$, $\tau_{max} = 192$ psi, $\theta_S = 25.67°$)

25.4 Consider a stress state where $\sigma_x = 18,000$ psi, $\sigma_y = -4,000$ psi, and $\tau_{xy} = 8,000$ psi. Determine the principal stresses, the maximum shear stress, and the orientation of the stress element in each case.
(Ans. $\sigma_1 = 20,601$ psi, $\sigma_2 = -6,601$ psi, $\theta_P = 18.01°$, $\tau_{max} = 13,601$ psi, $\theta_S = -26.99°$)

25.5 An adhesive bond within a beam will fail if the tensile stress exceeds 2,400 psi. Determine the maximum allowable value of σ_y if $\sigma_x = 1,100$ psi and $\tau_{xy} = 800$ psi.
(Ans. $\sigma_y = 1,908$ psi)

25.6 A wooden block will crack along the wood grain if the shear stress exceeds 1,000 psi. If $\sigma_y = 700$ psi and $\tau_{xy} = 250$ psi, calculate the range of values that σ_x can have without the block cracking.
(Ans. $-1,236$ psi $< \sigma_x < 2,636$ psi)

25.7 Draw Mohr's Circle for the stress state of $\sigma_x = 14,000$ psi, $\sigma_y = -5,000$ psi, and $\tau_{xy} = 6,000$ psi, Graphically determine the values of σ_1, σ_2, τ_{max} and ϕ.
(Ans. $\sigma_1 = 15,736.1$ psi, $\sigma_2 = -6,736.1$ psi, $\tau_{max} = 11,236.1$ psi, $\phi = 16.85°$)

25.8 Solve Problem 25.5 for the maximum allowable σ_x if $\sigma_y = 1,200$ psi and $\tau_{xy} = -400$ psi.
(Ans. $\sigma_x = 2,266.7$ psi)

MODULE 26: Buckling

For certain types of structural members under compressive loads, failure may occur due to a means other than the compressive stress exceeding the material's yield or ultimate stress. Specifically, for long slender members under compressive loads, which are called 'columns', a lateral deflection termed 'buckling' can often lead to a sudden and dramatic failure of the member. This failure results from the instability in the column resulting from large lateral deflections. Therefore care must be taken in the design of columns to ensure they are able to support the intended loading conditions without buckling.

The 'critical load' of a column P_{cr} is defined as the maximum load a column can support before buckling. This critical load is independent of the column's compressive strength, but depends only on the column's length, area moment of inertial, modulus of elasticity, and the manner in which the ends are supported. Buckling will occur about the principal axis of the column's cross-section having the smallest area moment of inertia.

The general formula for the critical load of a column, often called the 'Euler formula', is given as

$$P_{cr} = \pi^2 EI / L_e^2$$

where L_e is the 'effective' length of the column when the support conditions of the ends are considered. The stress created by the application of P_{cr} must not exceed the proportional limit of the column's material. The 'critical stress' which corresponds to the application of P_{cr} is given by the expression

$$\sigma_{cr} = \pi^2 E / (L/k)^2$$

where k is the smallest radius of gyration of the column, determined from

$$k = [I/A]^{1/2}$$

The term L/k is known as the 'slenderness ratio' and is a measure of the column's flexibility.

Effective Column Length

The effective length of a column will depend on whether the column's ends pinned, fixed, or free. Four common types of columns are shown in Figure 26.1.

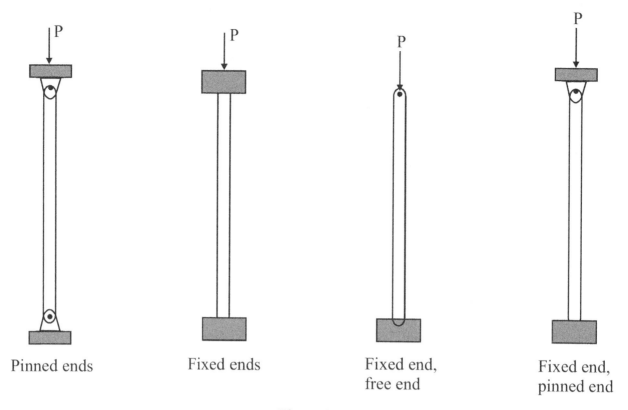

Figure 26.1

The effective column length for each condition is given in terms of the column length L as

    Pinned ends: $L_e = L$
    Fixed ends: $L_e = 0.5L$
    Fixed end, free end: $L_e = 2L$
    Fixed end, pinned end: $L_e = 0.7L$

Using these effective column lengths, the Euler formula and the formula for the critical column stress can be written for each particular end condition in terms of the column length L as:.

    Pinned ends: $P_{cr} = \pi^2 EI / L^2$ $\sigma_{cr} = \pi^2 E k^2 / L^2$
    Fixes ends: $P_{cr} = 4\pi^2 EI / L^2$ $\sigma_{cr} = 4\pi^2 E k^2 / L^2$
    Fixed end, free end: $P_{cr} = \pi^2 EI / 4L^2$ $\sigma_{cr} = \pi^2 E k^2 / 4L^2$
    Fixed end, pinned end: $P_{cr} = 2.04\pi^2 EI / L^2$ $\sigma_{cr} = 2.04\pi^2 E k^2 / L^2$

<u>Example 26.1</u>

Consider a 24 ft long steel column that has a cross-sectional area of 16 in² in which the smallest area moment of inertia of 21.33 in⁴. If both ends are pinned, determine the critical buckling load and critical stress of this column. Compare the critical stress with the normal yield stress for steel of 30,000 psi.

Solution: $P_{cr} = \pi^2 EI / L^2$
$= \pi^2 (30 \times 10^6)(21.33) / [24(12)]^2$
$\Rightarrow P_{cr} = 76{,}142$ lb

$\sigma_{cr} = \pi^2 E k^2 / L^2$
$= \pi^2 EI / AL^2$
$= \pi^2 (30 \times 10^6)(21.33) / (16)[24(12)]^2$
$\Rightarrow \sigma_{cr} = 4{,}759$ psi

The critical stress in this case is then only 13.22% of the yield stress of steel.

Example 26.2

A 10 ft long section of the column described in Example 26.1 is mounted such that one end is fixed and the other is free. Determine the largest axial load it can support if the factor of safety with respect to buckling is 2.0.

Solution: $\sigma_{cr} = \pi^2 EI / 4L^2 A$
$= \pi^2 (30 \times 10^6)(21.33) / \{(4)[10(12)]^2 (16)\}$
$\Rightarrow \sigma_{cr} = 6{,}853$ psi

$P_{cr} = \sigma_{cr} A$
$= 6{,}853(16)$
$\Rightarrow P_{cr} = 109{,}645$ lb

$P_{all} = P_{cr} / N$
$= 109{,}645 / 2.0$
$\Rightarrow P_{all} = 54{,}822$ lb

Problems

26.1 A 20 ft aluminum column with $A = 15$ in^2 and $I = 45$ in^4 is loaded in compression by a force of 30,000 lb. If both ends of the column are pinned, determine the factor of safety for a buckling application.
(Ans. N = 2.83)

26.2 Consider a 30 ft long aluminum column with a cross-sectional area of 9.23 in^2 and an area moment of inertia of 9.96 in^4. If both ends are pinned, calculate the maximum allowable axial load if a factor of safety of 3.0 is required.
(Ans. $P_{ALL} = 2{,}781.2$ lb)

26.3 An aluminum pipe has an outer diameter of 2.50 in, a wall thickness of 0.5 in, and is held in place by a wire as shown below and a horizontal force P is applied at the top of the pipe. Determine the largest force that can be applied before the pipe buckles.
(Ans. P = 7,478.2 lb)

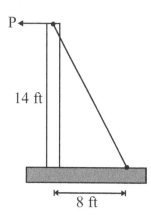

26.4 A 30 ft long stainless steel column with an area of 25 in^2 and a radius of gyration of 2.0 in has both ends pinned. Calculate the critical buckling load and critical stress for this column.
(Ans. P_{cr} = 213,232 lb, σ_{cr} = 8,529 psi)

26.5 Determine the minimum diameter required for a solid circular steel column, 100 in long with fixed ends, to support a compressive load of 8,000 lb with a factor of safety of 3.0.
(Ans. D = 1.425 in)

26.6 Calculate the maximum allowable load that a rectangular-shaped column (1.75 in x 0.75 in), made of aluminum, 10 ft in length, can withstand if both ends are pinned and a factor of safety of 2.25 is required.
(Ans. P_{cr} = 207.7 lb)

26.7 A steel column having one end fixed and one end free has a circular cross-section with an outside diameter of 2.0 in and an inside diameter of 1.5 in. If this column must support a load of 10,000 lb, calculate the maximum length of the column.
(Ans. L = 63.0 in)

26.8 Solve Problem 26.6 for the case of both ends being fixed.
(Ans. P_{cr} = 1,869.7 lb)

PART III - DYNAMICS

MODULE 27: Kinematics of Particles

Kinematics is the study of the motion of bodies without regard to the forces creating the motion. It focuses on the geometry of motion and the relationships between displacement, velocity, acceleration, and time.

Rectilinear Motion

The study of kinematics begins with the study of rectilinear, or straight-line motion. As a particle moves through a displacement Δs during the time interval Δt, the instantaneous velocity is defined (in the scalar sense) as the time derivative of the displacement as

$$v = ds/dt \quad \Rightarrow \quad ds = v\, dt$$

and the instantaneous acceleration is defined as the time derivative of the velocity as

$$a = dv/dt \quad \Rightarrow \quad dv = a\, dt$$

Solving the above equations for dt and setting the results equal gives the relationship

$$a\, ds = v\, dv$$

In solving rectilinear motion problems, the acceleration can be a function of time as: $a = f(t)$; a function of displacement as: $a = f(s)$; or a function of velocity as: $a = f(v)$. The particular form of the acceleration will indicate which of the integral forms should be used to solve the problem.

Constant Acceleration

For the case of constant acceleration, the formulas above can be integrated between the initial time ($t_0 = 0$, s_0, v_0) and the final time (t, s, v). Doing so yields the expressions

$$s = s_0 + v_0 t + at^2/2 \quad , \quad v = v_0 + at \quad , \quad v^2 = v_0^2 + 2a(s - s_0)$$

If the acceleration is not constant, the differential relationships provided above must be integrated using the given function of the acceleration. Accelerations can be expressed as functions of time, displacement, or velocity.

Curvilinear Motion

Curvilinear motion refers to motion on a curved path. If only two-dimensional motion is considered, it is referred to as plane curvilinear motion. Two coordinate systems will be used to describe plane curvilinear motion: the rectangular Cartesian (x-y) system, discussed in this module, and the normal and tangential (n-t) system, discussed in Module 28.

Rectangular Coordinates:

The position, velocity, and acceleration vectors of a particle in rectangular coordinates are written as

$$\mathbf{r} = x\,\mathbf{i} + y\,\mathbf{j}$$
$$\mathbf{v} = dx/dt\,\mathbf{i} + dy/dt\,\mathbf{j} = v_x\,\mathbf{i} + v_y\,\mathbf{j}$$
$$\mathbf{a} = d^2x/dt^2\,\mathbf{i} + d^2y/dt^2\,\mathbf{j} = a_x\,\mathbf{i} + a_y\,\mathbf{j}$$

where $\mathbf{i}$ and $\mathbf{j}$ are unit vectors in the x and y directions, respectively. The magnitudes of $\mathbf{r}$, $\mathbf{v}$, and $\mathbf{a}$ are

$$r = [x^2 + y^2]^{1/2} \quad , \quad v = [v_x^2 + v_y^2]^{1/2} \quad , \quad a = [a_x^2 + a_y^2]^{1/2}$$

The kinematic equations relating time, displacement, velocity, and acceleration presented earlier can now be written in both the x and y directions to solve curvilinear motion problems.

Example 27.1

An automobile is traveling at a speed of 60 mph along a straight road. If the driver applies the brakes such that the automobile decelerates at a constant rate of 10 ft/sec^2, determine both the time and the distance required for it to come to a stop.

Solution: Converting the initial speed from mph to ft/sec shows

v_o = 60 mph (5,280 ft / mile) (1 hr / 3,600 sec) = 88.0 ft/sec

Since the acceleration is constant, the time it takes for the automobile to stop can be found using the constant acceleration equations

$v = v_o + at$
$\Rightarrow\ t = (v - v_o)/a$
$\quad\quad = (0 - 88.0)/(-10.0)$
$\Rightarrow\ t = 8.80$ sec

The distance it will take for the automobile to stop will be

$v^2 - v_o^2 = 2as$
$\Rightarrow\ s = (v^2 - v_o^2)/2a$
$\quad\quad = [(0)^2 - (88.0)^2]/[2(-10.0)]$
$\Rightarrow\ s = 387.20$ ft

Example 27.2

A projectile is fired horizontally from a cliff (point A) which is 50 m high at a target (point B) which is a distance of 40 m away and 20 m below the cliff. Determine the initial speed of the projectile so it hits the target.

Solution: Defining the origin of the Cartesian coordinate system to be at the top of the cliff, the known kinematic quantities for this problem will be

$x_0 = 0$, $x = 40$ m , $(v_x)_0 = v$, $a_x = 0$
$y_0 = 0$, $y = -20$ m , $(v_y)_0 = 0$, $a_y = -9.81$ m/s^2

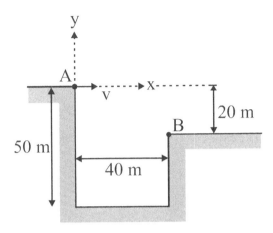

Writing the displacement equations for constant acceleration in the both the x and y directions gives

$x = x_0 + (v_x)_0 t + a_x t^2 / 2$
$40 = vt$
$\Rightarrow v = 40 / t$ m/s

$y = y_0 + (v_y)_0 t + a_y t^2 / 2$
$-20 = -4.905 t^2$
$\Rightarrow t = 2.02$ s

This result indicates that it will take a time of 2.02 sec for the projectile to hit the target. Substituting this value of t into the x displacement equation gives

$v = 40 / 2.02$
$\Rightarrow v = 19.81$ m/s

which is the required initial velocity in the x direction for the projectile to hit the target.

Example 27.3

A missile is fired with an initial velocity of 500 m/s at a target 6.25 km downrange and 2 km above the firing point. The missile's initial velocity makes an angle θ with the ground. Determine the possible values of θ for the missile to hit the target.

Solution: The known kinematic quantities for this problem will be

$$x_0 = 0, \quad x = 6{,}250 \text{ m}, \quad (v_x)_0 = 500 \cos\theta, \quad a_x = 0$$
$$y_0 = 0, \quad y = 2{,}000 \text{ m}, \quad (v_y)_0 = 500 \sin\theta, \quad a_y = -9.81 \text{ m/s}^2$$

Writing the displacement equations in the both the x and y directions gives

$$x = x_0 + (v_x)_0 t + a_x t^2 / 2$$
$$6{,}250 = (500 \cos\theta) t$$
$$\Rightarrow t = 12.50 / \cos\theta \text{ s}$$

$$y = y_0 + (v_y)_0 t + a_y t^2 / 2$$
$$2{,}000 = (500 \sin\theta)(12.50/\cos\theta) - 4.905(12.50/\cos\theta)^2$$
$$= 6{,}250 \tan\theta - 766.41 \sec^2\theta$$
$$2{,}000 = 6{,}250 \tan\theta - 766.41(1 + \tan^2\theta)$$
$$\Rightarrow \tan^2\theta - 8.15 \tan\theta + 3.61 = 0$$

Solving for θ gives two possible solutions as $\theta = 25.64°, 82.58°$.

Example 27.4

The acceleration of a particle is given as $a = t^3 + 3t^2 - t$ m/s². If the velocity is 4 m/s when t = 1 s, and the displacement is 10 m when t = 2 s, find the displacement, velocity, and acceleration when t = 3 s.

Solution: Since the acceleration is not constant the differential relationships for acceleration and velocity must be integrated.

$$a = dv/dt$$
$$dv = a\, dt$$
$$\int dv = \int a\, dt$$
$$v = \int(t^3 + 3t^2 - t)dt$$
$$\Rightarrow v = t^4/4 + t^3 - t^2/2 + C_1 \text{ m/s}$$

$$v = ds/dt$$
$$ds = v\, dt$$
$$\int ds = \int v\, dt$$
$$s = \int(t^4/4 + t^3 - t^2/2 + C_1)dt$$
$$\Rightarrow s = t^5/20 + t^4/4 - t^3/6 + C_1 t + C_2 \text{ m}$$

Evaluating the constants of integration at the initial conditions gives

$$C_1 = 3.25, \quad C_2 = -0.77$$

$$v = t^4/4 + t^3 - t^2/2 + 3.25 \text{ m/s}$$
$$s = t^5/20 + t^4/4 - t^3/6 + 3.25t - 0.77 \text{ m}$$

Evaluating s, v, and a for t = 3 s shows

s = 36.88 m , v = 46.00 m/s , a = 51.00 m/s²

Problems

27.1 A ball is thrown vertically upward with a speed of 30 m/s from the edge of a cliff which is 55 m above the ocean. Neglecting any resistance of the atmosphere, calculate the time it takes for the ball to hit the water and the velocity of the ball at impact.
(Ans. t = 7.60 s, V = -44.6 m/s)

27.2 A plane traveling in a horizontal direction at the rate of 450 km/h is at a position 500 m above the ground. If the pilot drops a bomb from the plane, determine how long it will take to impact the ground. Also calculate the horizontal distance the bomb will travel before impact. Neglect atmospheric resistance.
(Ans. t = 10.10 s, x = 1,262.50 m)

27.3 Boxes enter the chute below having a speed of 7 ft/sec at point A and an acceleration of 9 ft/sec² between points A and B. If the packages stop at point C, find the acceleration of the boxes between points B and C, and the time it takes the boxes to travel from A to C.
(Ans. a = -6.62 ft/sec², t = 3.49 sec)

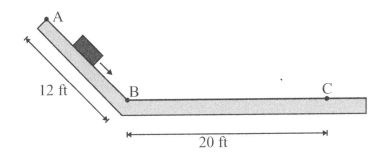

27.4 In Example 27.2, consider that the projectile has an initial velocity of 35 m/s at an angle of 35° upward from the x-axis. Determine how long it will take the projectile to impact the ground, the displacement in the x-direction when it does, and the speed of the projectile at impact.
(Ans. t = 4.92 s, x = 141.06 m, v = 40.21 m/s)

27.5 The deployment of a drag parachute creates an acceleration on a top fuel dragster of $a = -0.01\,v^2$ m/s². If the velocity is 85 m/s when the parachute is deployed, calculate the time required for the dragster to reach a speed of 30 m/s.
(Ans. t = 2.16 s)

27.6 The displacement of a particle is given as $s = 3t^3 + 15t + 6$ m. Determine the time required for the particle to reach a speed of 75 m/s from its initial speed of v = 15 m/s. Also calculate the acceleration of the particle when v = 40 m/s.
(Ans. t = 2.58 s, a = 30.06 m/s²)

167

27.7 A particle has a velocity component in the y-direction of $v_y = 8t$, and an acceleration component in the x-direction of $a_x = 4t^2$. When $t = 0$ s, $y = 2$ ft, $x = 0$, and $v_x = 0$. Calculate the magnitude of the velocity of the particle when $x = 18$ ft.
(Ans. $v = 34.28$ ft/sec)

27.8 In Problem 27.5, assume that the velocity of the dragster when the parachute is deployed is equal to v_o. Calculate the time required for the dragster to reach a speed of $0.5v_o$.
(Ans. $t = 100.0 / v_o$) s)

MODULE 28: Kinematics of Particles (cont.)

Curvilinear Motion

Normal and Tangential Coordinates:

When a particle moves on a curved path, a normal and tangential coordinate system can be defined with the origin located at the particle and moving with it. In this coordinate system the normal direction will point toward the center of curvature of the path and the tangential direction will point tangent to the path in the direction of travel. At any instant, unit vectors can be defined in the normal direction, e_n, and in the tangential direction, e_t, as shown in Figure 28.1.

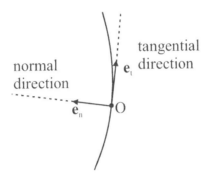

Figure 28.1

These unit vectors will have a constant magnitude equal to one but will change directions as the particle moves along its path. The radius of curvature of the path at any instant is defined as ρ. The velocity and acceleration vectors of a particle in normal and tangential coordinates can be written as

$$\mathbf{v} = v\, \mathbf{e_t}$$
$$\mathbf{a} = (v^2 / \rho)\, \mathbf{e_n} + (dv/dt)\, \mathbf{e_t}$$

where

$$a_n = v^2/\rho \quad , \quad a_t = dv/dt \quad , \quad a = |\mathbf{a}| = [a_n^2 + a_t^2]^{1/2}$$

The term v^2/ρ is called the normal acceleration component, a_n, and the term dv/dt is called the tangential acceleration component, a_t. These equations indicate that both the speed v and rate-of-change of the speed of the particle dv/dt will be tangent to the path of the particle. The normal acceleration component will keep the particle moving on the curved path but will not increase the speed of the particle. For a particle moving with constant speed, the tangential acceleration component will be zero while the normal acceleration will not be zero.

The most common case of curvilinear motion is that of circular motion, where $\rho = r =$ constant. In this case, the speed of the particle can be expressed as

$$v = r\omega$$

where ω is the angular velocity (rad/s), or the time-rate-of-change of the angular position θ of the particle on the circular path. The rate-of-change of the speed of the particle tangent to its path can be expressed as

$$dv/dt = r\alpha$$

where α is the angular acceleration (rad/s^2), or the time-rate-of-change of the angular velocity of the particle on the circular path. For circular motion, the velocity and acceleration vectors are written as

$$\mathbf{v} = r\omega \, \mathbf{e}_t$$
$$\mathbf{a} = (v^2/r) \, \mathbf{e}_n + r\alpha \, \mathbf{e}_t = r\omega^2 \, \mathbf{e}_n + r\alpha \, \mathbf{e}_t$$

where

$$a_n = v^2/r \quad , \quad a_t = r\alpha \quad , \quad a = |\mathbf{a}| = [a_n^2 + a_t^2]^{1/2}$$

Kinematic equations for angular motion exist, similar to those for rectilinear motion, relating angular position, angular velocity, and angular acceleration. For the case of circular motion having constant angular acceleration these equations can be written as

$$\theta = \theta_0 + \omega_0 t + \alpha t^2/2 \quad , \quad \omega = \omega_0 + \alpha t \quad , \quad \omega^2 = \omega_0^2 + 2\alpha(\theta - \theta_0)$$

Relative Motion: Translating Axes

Motion described in an inertial, or fixed coordinate system is called inertial or 'absolute' motion. It is sometimes simpler to describe or measure motion of a particle in a moving coordinate system, and to then describe the motion of the moving coordinate system in an inertial coordinate system. This type of motion description is referred to as 'relative-motion' analysis. Figure 28.2 below shows the motion of particle A in the translating (sliding) rectangular coordinate system, whose origin is point B.

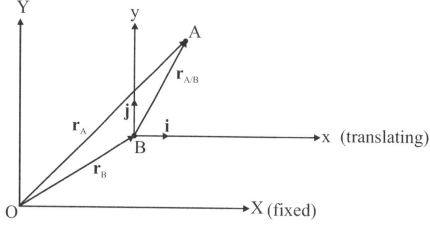

Figure 28.2

The absolute position of A (described in the fixed coordinate system) can be expressed as the sum of the absolute position of point B (which is moving relative to O, also described in the fixed coordinate system) and the position of A relative to B (described in the translating coordinate system) by the equation

$$r_A = r_B + r_{A/B}$$

This relative position equation reads: the absolute position of point A is equal to the absolute position of point B plus the position of point A relative to point B. Note that the position vector of point A relative to point B, $r_{A/B}$, indicates the position vector from B to A. Differentiating this expression twice gives similar relative velocity and relative acceleration as

$$v_A = v_B + v_{A/B} \quad , \quad a_A = a_B + a_{A/B}$$

Writing the relative vectors in terms of unit vectors **i** and **j** of the translating coordinate system shows

$$r_{A/B} = x\,\mathbf{i} + y\,\mathbf{j} \quad , \quad v_{A/B} = v_x\,\mathbf{i} + v_y\,\mathbf{j} \quad , \quad a_{A/B} = a_x\,\mathbf{i} + a_y\,\mathbf{j}$$

Relative motion can be explained more simply by considering the motion from different perspectives. Consider car A to be traveling east down a straight road at 50 mph. The absolute velocity of car A, i.e., relative to an observer standing in a fixed location on the side of the road, would be 50 mph east. If the observer was riding in car A, the velocity of car A relative to the observer would be zero since the observer was moving along with the car. Now, consider the observer to be riding in car B, which is traveling west down the same road and approaching car A at a speed of 30 mph. The velocity of car A relative to the observer in car B would be 80 mph east. Although the velocity of car A relative to the observer was different in each case, its absolute velocity was always the same, 50 mph east. Therefore, the relative motion of a particle is always dependent on the perspective of the observer.

Example 28.1

A circular disk having a diameter of 3 m accelerates uniformly from rest to 1,500 rpm (revolutions per minute) in 12 s. Determine the magnitudes of the velocity and acceleration of a point on the outer edge of the disk 2 s after it begins to accelerate.

Solution: ω = 1,500 rpm (1 min / 60 s)(2π rad / rev) = 157.08 rad/s

Since the angular acceleration is constant

$\omega = \omega_0 + \alpha t$
$\alpha = (\omega - \omega_0) / t$
   $= (157.08 - 0) / 12$
$\Rightarrow \alpha = 13.09$ rad/s^2

At t = 2 s:

$\omega = \omega_0 + \alpha t$
   $= 0 + 13.09(2)$
$\Rightarrow \omega = 26.18$ rad/s

At a point on the rim where r = 1.5 m:

$$v = r\omega$$
$$= 1.5(26.18)$$
$$\Rightarrow v = 39.27 \text{ m/s}$$

The components of acceleration will be

$$a_n = v^2 / r$$
$$= (39.27)^2 / 1.5$$
$$\Rightarrow a_n = 1,028.08 \text{ m/s}^2$$

$$a_t = r\alpha$$
$$= 1.5(13.09)$$
$$\Rightarrow a_t = 19.64 \text{ m/s}^2$$

$$a = [a_n^2 + a_t^2]^{1/2}$$
$$= [(1,028.08)^2 + (19.64)^2]^{1/2}$$
$$\Rightarrow a = 1,028.27 \text{ m/s}^2$$

Example 28.2

Consider train A traveling east with a constant speed of 75 km/h, and car B traveling north at a speed of 120 km/h (approaching the train tracks), which is decreasing at the rate of 5 km/h^2. Determine the velocity and acceleration vectors of train A relative to car B.

Solution: $\mathbf{v}_A = \mathbf{v}_B + \mathbf{v}_{A/B}$
$\mathbf{v}_{A/B} = \mathbf{v}_A - \mathbf{v}_B$
$\Rightarrow \mathbf{v}_{A/B} = 75\,\mathbf{i} - 120\,\mathbf{j}$ km/h

$\mathbf{a}_A = \mathbf{a}_B + \mathbf{a}_{A/B}$
$\mathbf{a}_{A/B} = \mathbf{a}_A - \mathbf{a}_B = 0 - (-5\,\mathbf{j})$
$\Rightarrow \mathbf{a}_{A/B} = 5\,\mathbf{j}$ km/h^2

Example 28.3

Particle A moves in a straight line and particle B moves on the curved path as shown below. Particle A has a speed of 50 ft/sec which is increasing at the rate of 15 ft/sec^2, while particle B has a constant speed of 30 ft/sec. Determine the velocity and acceleration of particle A relative to particle B.

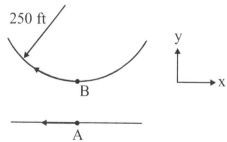

Solution: $\mathbf{v}_A = \mathbf{v}_B + \mathbf{v}_{A/B}$
$\mathbf{v}_{A/B} = \mathbf{v}_A - \mathbf{v}_B$
$= -50\,\mathbf{i} - (-30\,\mathbf{i})$
$\Rightarrow \mathbf{v}_{A/B} = -20\,\mathbf{i}$ ft/sec

$\mathbf{a}_A = \mathbf{a}_B + \mathbf{a}_{A/B}$
$\mathbf{a}_{A/B} = \mathbf{a}_A - \mathbf{a}_B$
$= -15\,\mathbf{i} - (v_B^2/r)\,\mathbf{j}$
$= 15\,\mathbf{i} - [(30)^2/250]\,\mathbf{j}$
$\Rightarrow \mathbf{a}_{A/B} = -15\,\mathbf{i} - 3.6\,\mathbf{j}$ ft/sec^2

Problems

28.1 A circular disk is rotating at a speed of 2,500 rpm. A brake is applied to the disk such that it slows down at a constant rate and stops in a period of 8 sec. Determine the angular acceleration of the disk after the brake is applied and the number of revolutions the disk makes before it stops.
(Ans. $\alpha = -32.72$ rad/s^2, n = 166.69 rev)

28.2 The disk shown below has a radius of 3.0 m and rotates in the counterclockwise direction. At the instant shown the acceleration of point P has a magnitude of 25 m/s^2. Determine the magnitudes of the angular velocity and the angular acceleration of the disk.
(Ans. $\alpha = 7.55$ rad/s^2, $\omega = 1.88$ rad/s)

28.3 Particle A has a speed of 35 km/h from east to west relative to particle B. Particle B has a speed of 20 km/h from southwest to northeast relative to particle C. Determine the velocity of particle A relative to particle C.
(Ans. $\mathbf{v}_{A/C} = -20.86\,\mathbf{i} + 14.14\,\mathbf{j}$ km/h)

28.4 In the figure below, automobile A has a speed of 75 km/h, which is decreasing at a rate 4 m/s². Automobile B has a speed of 60 km/h, which is increasing at the rate of 6 m/s². Determine the velocity and acceleration of car B relative to car A at the instant shown.
(Ans. $\mathbf{v}_{B/A}$ = -37.50 **i** m/s, $\mathbf{a}_{B/A}$ = -2.00 **i** + 0.93 **j** m/s²)

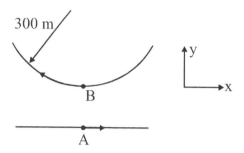

28.5 Particles A and B move on the circular paths as shown below. Particle A has a speed of 15 ft/sec that is decreasing at the rate of 3 ft/sec², and particle B has a speed of 12 ft/sec that is increasing at the rate of 5 ft/sec². Determine the velocity and acceleration of particle B relative to particle A.
(Ans. $\mathbf{v}_{B/A}$ = 12.00 **i** + 15.00 **j** ft/sec, $\mathbf{a}_{B/A}$ = 1.25 **i** - 5.40 **j** ft/sec²)

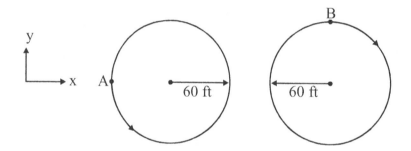

28.6 In Problem 28.5, particle B has a speed 30 ft/sec, which is increasing at the rate of 4 ft/sec². If the acceleration of particle A relative to particle B is 40 **i** + 64 **j** ft/sec², determine the speed of particle A and the rate at which it is changing.
(Ans. v_A = 51.38 ft/sec increasing at the rate of 49.00 ft/sec²)

28.7 The instantaneous velocity of a particle is given as **v** = 3 **i** + 4 **j** m/s. At this instant the radius of curvature of the particle's path is 6.0 m, and the speed of the particle is decreasing at the rate of 2 m/s². Write the expression for the particle's velocity and acceleration using unit vectors $\mathbf{e}_n$ and $\mathbf{e}_t$.
(Ans. **v** = 5.0 $\mathbf{e}_t$ m/s, **a** = 4.17 $\mathbf{e}_n$ -2.0 $\mathbf{e}_t$ m/s²)

28.8 In Problem 28.4, if the speed of automobile B is constant, determine the velocity and acceleration of automobile A relative to automobile B.
(Ans. $\mathbf{v}_{A/B}$ = 37.5 **i** m/s, **a** = -4 **i** m/s²)

MODULE 29: Constrained Motion of Connected Particles

Certain problems deal with particles (or bodies) whose motions are related due to the particles being connected. In these types of problems the constraints on the motion due to this connection must be accounted for in determining the motion of the particles. Consider the dynamical system of two masses connected by a cable running over pulleys as shown in Figure 29.1

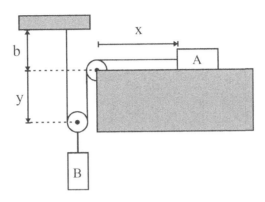

Figure 29.1

Since the two masses are connected through the rope and pulley system, their motions will be related. The relationships between the motions of the bodies can be established by evaluating the geometry of the system. In doing so, position coordinates x and y, measured from a fixed reference point (the upper pulley in this case) can be used. As shown in Figure 29.1 above, x defines the horizontal distance from the upper pulley to block A and y defines the vertical position from the upper pulley to block B. Considering the radius of each pulley to be r, an expression for the total length of the cable in the system can be written using the x and y coordinates, such as

$$L = x + \pi r / 2 + y + \pi r + y + b$$

In this expression the length b, the lengths of the cable around the pulleys, the radius of the pulleys, and the total length of the rope, will be constants. Differentiating this equation gives the time rate-of-change of the cable's length L as

$$dL / dt = dx / dt + 2dy / dt = 0$$

Since dx / dt represents the velocity of block A and dy / dt represents the velocity of block B, this equation can be written as

$$v_A + 2v_B = 0$$

which provides a relationship between the velocities of the blocks. Differentiating again gives the relationship between the accelerations of the blocks

$$a_A + 2a_B = 0$$

These constraints indicate that, for the coordinate system chosen, the sense of the velocities and accelerations of the two blocks will be opposite. Note that these results do not depend on the radius of either pulley or on the distance b that the upper pulley is located beneath the attachment of the cable since these values are constants. Since specification of either x or y will determine the position of both particles, this system is called a 'one degree of freedom' system.

An example of a 'two degree of freedom' system is shown in Figure 29.2.

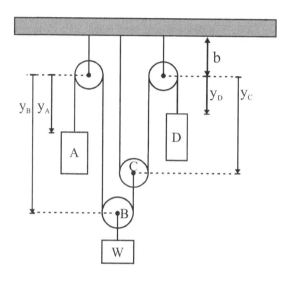

Figure 29.2

In this example the positions of pulley B and block W depend on the specification of two coordinates, either y_A or y_B and either y_C or y_D. Writing equations for the lengths of the cables attached to block A (length L_1) and block D (length L_2), where the portions of the cable around the pulleys and the distance b are considered to be constants, shows

$$L_1 = y_A + y_B + (y_B - y_C) + \text{constant} \quad , \quad L_2 = 2y_C + y_D + \text{constant}$$

The derivatives of these equations gives

$$v_A + 2v_B - v_C = 0 \quad , \quad 2v_C + v_D = 0$$

and

$$a_A + 2a_B - a_C = 0 \quad , \quad 2a_C + a_D = 0$$

Eliminating v_C and a_C from these equations gives

$$v_D + 2v_A + 4v_B = 0 \quad , \quad a_D + 2a_A + 4a_B = 0$$

These results provide the relationships between the velocities and accelerations of the blocks and pulleys of the system. Specification of any two velocities and any two accelerations are required to determine the motion of the complete system.

Example 29.1

In the mass and pulley system below, the end of the cable at D is being pulled downward at the rate of 0.5 m/s. Calculate the rise h of the weight W after 3 seconds.

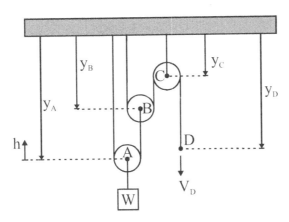

Solution: Writing expressions for the lengths of both cables using the defined displacements gives

$$L_1 = y_A + (y_A - y_B) + \text{constant} \quad , \quad L_2 = (y_D - y_C) + (y_B - y_C) + y_B + \text{constant}$$

Differentiating both equations gives the relationships

$$2v_A - v_B = 0$$
$$v_D + 2v_B = 0$$
$$v_A = -v_D / 4$$
$$= -0.5 / 4$$
$$\Rightarrow v_A = -0.13 \text{ m/s} = 0.13 \text{ m upward}$$

This indicates the sense of the motion of W will be opposite to the direction of y_A, or upward, and

$$h = v_A t$$
$$= -0.13(3)$$
$$\Rightarrow h = 0.39 \text{ m upward}$$

Example 29.2

In the figure below, the collars A and B slide along the rods and are connected by a solid bar AB having length L. In the position shown, collar B has a constant velocity of 0.5 m/s to the right. Determine the velocity and acceleration of block A.

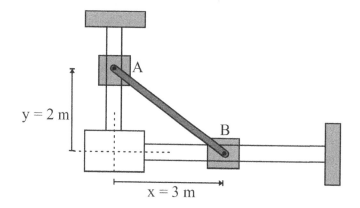

Solution: The length L of bar AB can be written as

$$L = [x^2 + y^2]^{1/2}$$

Differentiating gives

$$x(dx/dt) + y(dy/dt) = 0$$
$$xv_B + yv_A = 0$$
$$v_A = -xv_B/y$$
$$= -3(0.5)/2$$
$$\Rightarrow v_A = -0.75 \text{ m/s} = 0.75 \text{ m/s downward}$$

Differentiating the velocity equation above yields

$$(dx/dt)v_B + x(dv_B/dt) + (dy/dt)v_A + y(dv_A/dt) = 0$$
$$v_B^2 + xa_B + v_A^2 + ya_A = 0$$
$$a_A = [-v_B^2 - xa_B - v_A^2]/y$$
$$= [-(0.5)^2 - 3(0) - (-0.75)^2]/2.0$$
$$\Rightarrow a_A = -0.41 \text{ m/s}^2 = 0.41 \text{ m/s}^2 \text{ downward}$$

Problems

29.1 Block A has a velocity of 4 m/s and an acceleration of 7 m/s², both to the right. Determine the velocity and acceleration of block B.
(Ans. $v_B = 1.33$ m/s downward, $a_B = 2.33$ m/s² downward)

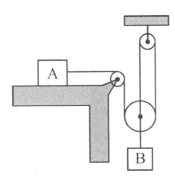

29.2 Calculate the velocity of block A if block B has a velocity of 0.4 ft/sec upward.
(Ans. $v_A = 0.4$ ft/sec downward)

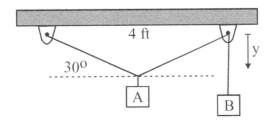

29.3 In the system shown below, block B has a upward velocity of 7.5 in/sec. Determine the velocity of block A.
(Ans. $v_A = 0.94$ in/sec downward)

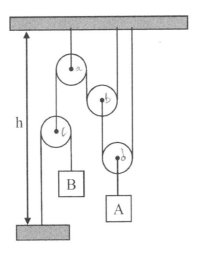

29.4 For the system shown in Problem 29.3, the upward displacement of block A is given by $y = 3.5t^2 - 4t + 5$ in. Calculate the velocity and acceleration of block B.
(Ans. $v_B = -56t + 32$ in/sec, $a_B = -56.0$ in/sec² downward)

29.5 For the system shown in Example 29.2, block A has a velocity of 2.5 m/s downward and is speeding up at the rate of 0.5 m/s^2. Determine the velocity and acceleration of block B.
(Ans. v_B = 1.67 m/s to the right, a_B = 2.68 m/s^2 to the left)

29.6 In Problem 29.2, calculate the acceleration of block B if block A has a velocity of 3 ft/sec upward, which is increasing at the rate of 0.75 ft/sec^2 at the instant shown.
(Ans. a_B = 6.59 ft/sec^2 downward)

29.7 Consider Example 29.2 for the case of y = 2.5 m, v_A = 0.3 m/s upward, and a_A = 0.1 m/s^2 downward. Compute the velocity and acceleration of block B.
(Ans. v_B = 0.29 m/s to the left, a_B = 0.76 m/s^2 to the right)

29.8 In Problem 29.4, the upward displacement of block A is given by $y = t^3 + t^2 + t + 1$ in. Calculate the velocity and acceleration of block B after 1.5 sec.
(Ans. v_B = 110.0 in/sec upward, a_B = 65.0 in/sec^2 upward)

MODULE 30: Kinetics of Particles

Kinetics is the study of the relationships between unbalanced forces and the motions they produce. In kinetics, the sum of the forces and/or moments acting on a body are not zero, therefore equilibrium does not exist. The motion resulting from the unbalanced forces or moments can be determined by three different solution techniques: the use of Newton's Laws of Motion (Modules 30-32, and 38-40), the use of work and energy methods (Module 33), and the use of methods of impulse and momentum (Module 34).

Newton's Laws of Motion state the following:

1. A body in equilibrium (at rest or moving in a straight line with constant speed) remains in equilibrium unless an external force acts on the body to change its state.

2. The sum of the external forces acting on a body is equal to the time rate-of-change of the linear momentum of the body.

3. For every action there is an equal and opposite reaction.

While all three of Newton's Laws play an important role, Newton's Second Law provides the basis for the study of kinetics. This law can be expressed mathematically as

$$\Sigma \mathbf{F} = d(m\mathbf{v})/dt = (dm/dt)\mathbf{v} + m(d\mathbf{v}/dt)$$

The first term on the right is a function of the time rate-of-change of mass. Variable mass problems are those in which mass is expended, as in the case of a thrusting rocket. For most problems, including those addressed in this text, the mass will be considered to remain constant. Under the assumption of constant mass, Newton's Second Law can be simplified to give

$$\Sigma \mathbf{F} = m(d\mathbf{v}/dt)$$

Since the time rate-of-change of velocity is equal to the acceleration, the equations of motion of a particle with constant mass can then be written as

$$\Sigma \mathbf{F} = m\mathbf{a}$$

Rectilinear Motion

Newton's Second Law can be applied to problems involving particles or bodies having rectilinear motion. In solving problems that involve bodies rather than particles, Newton's Second Law will describe the motion of the center-of-mass of the body. For two-dimensional problems in Cartesian coordinates, Newton's Second Law can be written in component form as

$$\Sigma F_x \mathbf{i} + \Sigma F_y \mathbf{j} = m(a_x \mathbf{i} + a_y \mathbf{j})$$

where

$$\Sigma F = [F_x^2 + F_y^2]^{1/2} \quad , \quad a = [a_x^2 + a_y^2]^{1/2}$$

In solving kinetics problems, the drawing of free-body-diagrams will once again play a crucial role in obtaining the correct solution.

Example 30.1

A 100 kg block is sliding along the floor with an initial velocity of 10 m/s at $x = 0$. If the coefficient of kinetic friction between the block and the surface is 0.3, how far will the block slide before it stops and how long will it take to stop.

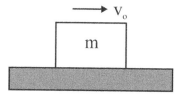

Solution: Drawing the free-body diagram (FBD) shows

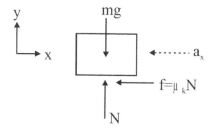

Writing Newton's Second Law in both the x and y directions shows

$\Sigma F_y = 0$ (since there is no motion in the y direction)
$N - mg = 0$
$N = mg$
$\quad = 100(9.81)$
$\Rightarrow N = 981.00 \text{ N}$

$\Sigma F_x = ma_x$
$-\mu_k N = ma_x$
$a_x = -\mu_k N / m = -0.3(981.00) / 100$
$\Rightarrow a_x = -2.94 \text{ m/s}^2$

Using kinematic relationships for the x direction motion shows

$v^2 = v_0^2 + 2a_x(x - x_0)$
$x = x_0 + (v^2 - v_0^2) / 2a_x$
$\quad = 0 + [0 - (10)^2] / [(2)(-2.94)]$
$\Rightarrow x = 17.00 \text{ m}$

$$v = v_0 + a_x t$$
$$t = (v - v_0) / a_x$$
$$= (0 - 10) / (-2.94)$$
$$\Rightarrow t = 3.40 \text{ s}$$

Example 30.2

The 50 lb block shown below is being pushed up the plane by force **P**. If the block starts from rest and moves a distance of 2 ft up the plane in 3 s, find the magnitude of **P**. The coefficient of kinetic friction is 0.4.

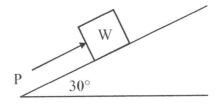

Solution: FBD:

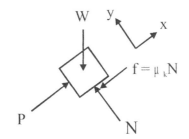

$$x = x_0 + v_0 t + a_x t^2 / 2$$
$$a_x = 2(x - x_0 - v_0 t) / t^2$$
$$= 2(2 - 0 - 0) / (3)^2$$
$$\Rightarrow a_x = 0.44 \text{ ft/sec}^2$$

$$\Sigma F_y = 0$$
$$N - mg \cos 30° = 0$$
$$N = mg \cos 30°$$
$$= 50(0.866)$$
$$\Rightarrow N = 43.30 \text{ lb}$$

$$\Sigma F_x = ma_x$$
$$P - \mu_k N - mg \sin 30° = ma_x$$
$$P = \mu_k N + mg \sin 30° + ma_x$$
$$= 0.4(43.30) + 50(0.500) + (50 / 32.2)(0.44)$$
$$\Rightarrow P = 43.00 \text{ lb}$$

Example 30.3

For the mass and pulley system shown below, block A has a mass of 40 kg and block B has a mass of 30 kg. If the masses are released from rest, calculate the tension in the cable. Neglect the mass and friction of the pulley.

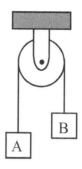

Solution: Free-body diagrams must be drawn for each body.

Block A:

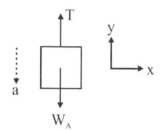

Block B:

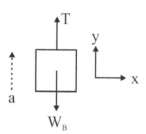

Since a cable connects the masses, they will both accelerate at the same rate, the larger mass accelerating downward and the smaller mass accelerating upward. Summing the forces in the y direction for each mass gives

A:

$\Sigma F_y = m_A a$
$-m_A g + T = -m_A a$
$a = g - T / m_A$
$\Rightarrow a = 9.81 - T / 40$

B:

$\Sigma F_y = m_B a$
$T - m_B g = m_B a$
$T = m_B g + m_B a$
$\Rightarrow T = 294.3 + 30a$

$T = 294.3 + 30(9.81 - T / 40)$
$\Rightarrow T = 336.3 \text{ N}$

Problems

30.1 Blocks A and B shown have masses of 12 kg and 5 kg, respectively. Consider μ_k between block A and the surface to be 0.35 and between block B and the surface to be 0.40. If the cord makes and angle of 8° with the horizontal, determine the tension in the cord if P = 150 N. (Ans. T = 43.92 N)

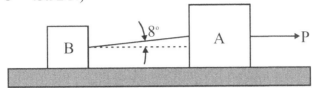

30.2 In the figure below, blocks A and B weigh 15 lb and 75 lb, respectively. If the coefficients of kinetic friction between block A and the plane is 0.4 and between block B and the plane is 0.2, determine the contact force between the blocks as they slide down the plane. (Ans. F = 1.96 lb)

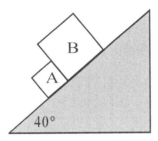

30.3 Solve Example 30.2 if force P is applied to the block in a horizontal direction. (Ans. P = 64.56 lb)

30.4 For the two cases shown below, calculate the acceleration of the 150 N block. Neglect the mass and the friction of the pulley.
(Ans. Case 1: a = 1.40 m/s²; Case 2: a = 3.27 m/s²)

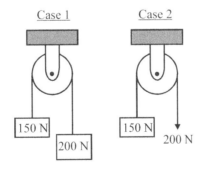

30.5 Blocks A and B and have masses of 10 kg and 35 kg, respectively. The coefficient of kinetic friction between A and the surface is 0.20 and the pulley is frictionless. Determine the acceleration of block B and the tension in the cord connecting the blocks.
(Ans. a = 7.19 m/s², T = 91.56 N)

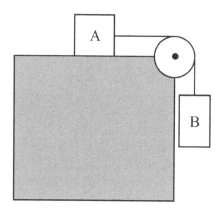

30.6 Determine the magnitude of the maximum force **P** that can be applied to m_2 (7 slugs) before m_1 (4 slugs) begins to slide off. The coefficient of static friction between the blocks is 0.35, while the friction between m_2 and the surface is negligible.
(Ans. P = 123.97 lb)

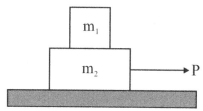

30.7 Solve Problem 30.5 for the case of m_B = 30 kg and μ_k = 0.15.
(Ans. a = 6.99 m/s², T = 84.6 N)

30.8 In Problem 30.6, calculate the acceleration of both blocks if P = 100 lb.
(Ans. a = 0.909 ft/sec²)

MODULE 31: Kinetics of Particles (cont.)

Plane Curvilinear Motion

As discussed in the study of kinematics in Module 27, plane curvilinear motion problems can be solved using either rectangular coordinates or normal and tangential coordinates. The equations of motion in rectangular coordinates were presented in the previous module.

Assuming that the mass is constant, Newton's Second Law can be written in component form in normal and tangential coordinates as

$$\Sigma F_n \, \mathbf{e}_n + \Sigma F_t \, \mathbf{e}_t = m(a_n \, \mathbf{e}_n + a_t \, \mathbf{e}_t)$$

where

$$\Sigma F = [F_n^2 + F_t^2]^{1/2} \quad , \quad a = [a_n^2 + a_t^2]^{1/2}$$

and $\mathbf{e}_n$ and $\mathbf{e}_t$ are the unit vectors in the normal and tangential directions respectively. The equations of motion of a particle can then be written in the normal and tangential directions for plane curvilinear motion problems as was done in the x and y directions for rectilinear motion problems.

Example 31.1

A car weighing 1,800 lb is traveling on a circular path having a radius of 2,000 ft. If the speed of the car is 60 ft/sec, calculate the friction force necessary to keep the car on the road. Also, if $\mu_k = 0.25$, calculate the maximum speed the car can travel before it slides off the road.

Solution: FBD: (looking down on the car)

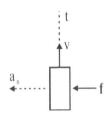

(a) Writing the equations of motion in the normal direction gives

$\Sigma F_n = ma_n$
$f = (W / g)(v^2 / r)$
$\quad = (1,800 / 32.2)[(60)^2 / 2,000]$
$\Rightarrow \ f = 100.60 \text{ lb}$

(b) For the maximum value of the friction force

$f_{max} = (W / g)(v_{max}^2 / r)$
$\mu_k W = (W / g)(v_{max}^2 / r)$

$$v_{max} = (r\mu_k g)^{1/2}$$
$$= [2,000(0.25)(32.2)]^{1/2}$$
$$\Rightarrow v_{max} = 126.90 \text{ ft/sec } (= 86.50 \text{ mph})$$

Example 31.2

A block with a mass of 3 kg slides down a curved track. At the bottom of the track the velocity of the block is 5 m/s. Determine the normal force that the track exerts on the block if the radius of curvature of the track is 2 m. Also calculate the number of g's, i.e., acceleration exerted by gravity, that the block would 'feel' at this point.

Solution: FBD: (bottom of track)

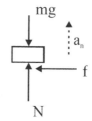

$\Sigma F_n = ma_n$
$N - mg = m(v^2 / \rho)$
$N = m(g + v^2 / \rho) = 3[9.81 + (5)^2 / 2]$
$\Rightarrow N = 66.93$ N

$a_n = N / m$
$= 66.93 / 3$
$= 22.31 \text{ m/s}^2$
$\Rightarrow a_n = 2.27$ g's (where 1 g = 9.81 m/s^2)

Example 31.3

A turn on a racetrack has a radius of curvature of 2,000 ft and a bank angle θ. If cars travel at 140 mph through the turn, find the minimum bank angle so the cars won't slip sideways during the turn. Neglect frictional forces.

Solution: FBD:

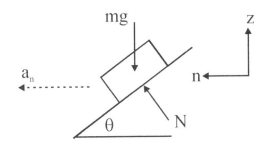

$\Sigma F_z = 0$
$N \cos \theta - mg = 0$
$\Rightarrow N = mg / \cos \theta$

$\Sigma F_n = ma_n$
$N \sin \theta = m(v^2 / \rho)$
$mg \sin \theta / \cos \theta = mv^2 / \rho$
$\tan \theta = v^2 / \rho g$
$\quad = [(140)(5,280) / 3,600]^2 / [(2,000)(32.2)]$
$\tan \theta = 0.654$
$\Rightarrow \theta = 33.2°$

Problems

31.1 A 3,200 lb car travels through a depression in the road at a speed of 60 mph. If the radius of curvature is 350 ft, find the force exerted on the springs of the car at the bottom of the depression.
(Ans. N = 5,398.83 lb)

31.2 The pendulum shown below consists of a 3 lb weight at the end of a cable. The mass is released from rest such that the velocity of the ball is 12 ft/sec when $\theta = 0°$. Determine the tension in the cable at that instant, if the length of the pendulum is 10 ft.
(Ans. T = 4.34 lb)

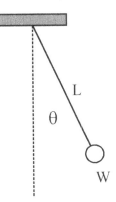

31.3 Arm OA rotates with an angular velocity of 0.8 rad/s in the clockwise direction (in the vertical plane) about point O as shown. When $\theta = 0°$, a small package is placed at a distance of 1 m from O. If the block slips off the arm when $\theta = 30°$, determine the coefficient of static friction between the block and the arm. Neglect the mass of arm OA.
(Ans. $\mu = 0.653$)

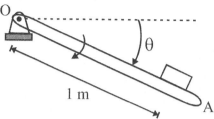

31.4 Using the results of Example 31.3, find the maximum speed (in mph) that the car can travel considering the coefficient of friction between the tires and pavement to be 0.35.
(Ans. v = 197.49 mph)

31.5 The block shown below has a mass of 0.75 kg. If the block has a speed of 7 m/s at point A and 5 m/s at point B, determine the normal force between the block and surface at both points.
(Ans. $N_A = 13.48$ N, $N_B = 9.79$ N)

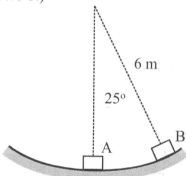

31.6 A pilot having mass M (kg) flies a plane in a vertical loop with a radius of 750 m at a constant speed of 520 km/h. Determine the force exerted on the pilot by the seat at both the top and bottom of the loop.
(Ans. top: F = 18.01M N; bottom: F = 37.63M N)

31.7 Consider the coefficient of static friction between the block and the arm in Problem 31.3 to be 0.55. Calculate the angular velocity of the arm if the block slips at an angle of 20°.
(Ans. $\omega = 1.31$ rad/s)

31.8 Solve Problem 31.5 for the case where the block has a mass of 0.65 kg and its speed is 8 m/s at point A and 3 m/s at point B.
(Ans. $N_A = 13.31$ N, $N_B = 6.75$ N)

MODULE 32: Kinetics of Particles (cont.)

This module presents additional material on particle kinetics in the form of more example problems.

Example 32.1

A plane flies on a high-arc trajectory in order to allow astronauts to experience weightlessness. (The 'feeling' of weightlessness will occur when the astronauts are being accelerated only by gravity as in the case of 'free-fall'.) If the radius of curvature of this arc is 24,000 ft, calculate the required speed of the plane in mph.

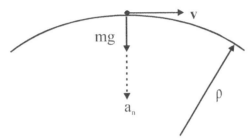

Solution: $\Sigma F_n = ma_n$
$mg = ma_n$
$mg = mv^2 / \rho$
$v = (\rho g)^{1/2}$
    $= [24,000(32.2)]^{1/2}$
$v = 879.10$ ft/sec (1mile / 5,280 ft) (3600 s/hr)
$\Rightarrow$ $v = 599.40$ mph

Example 32.2

Two cables support a ball of mass m until the horizontal cable is cut. Determine the ratio of the tension in the vertical cable before the cut is made to the tension in the vertical cable immediately after the cut is made.

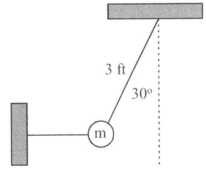

Solution: FBD before cut: FBD after cut:

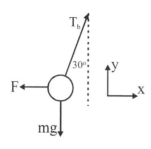 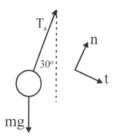

Before cut:

$\Sigma F_y = 0$
$T_b \cos 30° - mg = 0$
$\Rightarrow T_b = mg / \cos 30°$

After cut:

$\Sigma F_n = 0$
$T_a - mg \cos 30° = 0$
$\Rightarrow T_a = mg \cos 30°$

$T_a/T_b = mg \cos 30° / (mg / \cos 30°)$
$\qquad = (\cos 30°)^2$
$\Rightarrow T_a/T_b = 0.75$

Example 32.3

In the figure below, mass m is placed on the side of a disk that is rotating about the vertical z-axis. Calculate the maximum angular velocity of the disk for which the mass will not slip. The coefficient of static friction between the mass and the disk is 0.4. (Neglect the effects of the angular acceleration of the disk.)

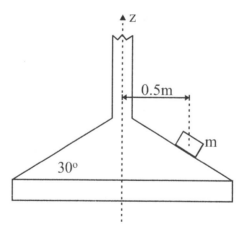

Solution: FBD:

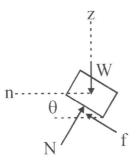

$\Sigma F_z = 0$
$N \cos \theta - mg + \mu_s N \sin \theta = 0$
$\Rightarrow N = mg / (\cos \theta + \mu_s \sin \theta)$

$\Sigma F_n = ma_n$
$N \sin \theta - \mu_s N \cos \theta = mr\omega^2$
$N(\sin \theta - \mu_s \cos \theta) = mr\omega^2$
$mg(\sin \theta - \mu_s \cos \theta) / (\cos \theta + \mu_s \sin \theta) = mr\omega^2$
$\omega = [g(-\mu_s \cos \theta + \sin \theta) / r(\cos \theta + \mu_s \sin \theta)]^{1/2}$
$= [(9.81)(-0.4 \cos 30° + \sin 30°) / (0.5)(\cos 30° + 0.4 \sin 30°)]^{1/2}$
$\Rightarrow \omega = 1.68$ rad/s

Problems

32.1 A ball weighing 8 lb is attached to a cord 10 ft in length and travels in a horizontal circle at constant speed as shown below. If the cord forms a constant angle of 32° with the vertical, determine the tension in the cord and the speed of the ball.
(Ans. T = 9.43 lb, v = 10.35 ft/sec)

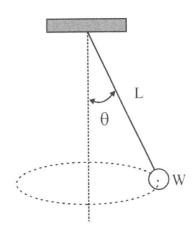

32.2 A ball of mass m is suspended by two cables as shown, each having a tension T to maintain equilibrium. If one of the cables is cut, determine the ratio k of the tension in the remaining cable immediately after the first cable is cut to the initial tension in the cable.
(Ans. k = 0.826)

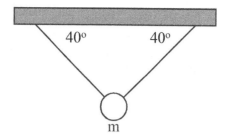

32.3 A pilot weighing 190 lb flies a plane through a vertical loop that has a radius of curvature of 450 ft. Calculate the speed of the plane at the top and bottom of the loop if the pilot experiences weightlessness at the top and feels a load of 3.5 g's at the bottom.
(Ans. top: v = 82.07 mph; bottom: v = 129.77 mph)

32.4 A plane flies an arc-shaped trajectory that will allow astronauts to experience 'weightlessness' for short periods of time. If the radius of curvature of this arc is 28,000 ft, determine the required speed of the plane at the highest point of the arc.
(Ans. v = 647.40 mph)

32.5 A coin is resting on a flat, circular table that rotates about its center. Determine the maximum constant angular velocity of the table before the coin begins to slide if the coin is located a distance of 0.75 m from the center of rotation. Consider the coefficient of static friction between the coin and the table to be 0.30.
(Ans. ω = 1.98 rad/s)

32.6 In Example 32.2, determine the angular acceleration of the remaining cable immediately after the first cable is cut. Assume the cable is 4.5 m in length.
(Ans. α = 1.09 rad/s²)

32.7 In Example 32.3, calculate the coefficient of static friction between the mass and the disk if the mass begins to slip when the angular velocity of the disk is 2.0 rad/s.
(Ans. μ = 0.425)

32.8 In Problem 32.1, calculate the angle θ and the tension in the cord if the speed of the ball is 10.0 ft/sec.
(Ans. T = 9.33 lb, θ = 30.97°)

MODULE 33: Work and Energy Methods

As mentioned in Module 30, the use of work and energy methods can also be used to solve problems in kinetics. This module describes those methods.

Work

For translational motion, work is done on a body when an externally applied force moves the body in the direction in which the force is applied. Therefore, the work done by the force will be a scalar quantity given by

$$U = Fs$$

where F is the magnitude of the applied force and s is the displacement of the body in the direction in which the force acts. The units of work will be kg-m^2/s^2 (or N-m) in the SI system and slug-ft^2/s^2 (or lb-ft) in the US system.

Kinetic Energy

The kinetic energy of a body in translation is a scalar quantity given by

$$T = mv^2 / 2$$

where v is the speed of the body. The units of kinetic energy are kg-m^2/s^2 (N-m) in SI units and slug-ft^2/s^2 (lb-ft) in the US system.

Potential Energy

The potential energy of a body can take two forms, gravitational and elastic. Gravitational potential energy is defined as the negative work done against gravity. In other words, the potential energy due to gravity can be calculated by

$$V_G = mgh$$

where h is a height defined above some reference or datum. Increasing h will increase the potential energy of a body and reducing h will decrease the potential energy of the body. The units of potential energy are the same as those for kinetic energy.

A mechanical element commonly used in many dynamics problems is a spring. The elastic potential energy of a spring is defined as

$$V_E = k(\Delta x)^2 / 2$$

where Δx is the amount of compression or elongation present in the spring and k is the spring constant in lb/ft (or lb/in) or N/m. The total potential energy of a body will be the sum of gravitational and elastic potential energies as

$$V = V_G + V_E$$

Relationship Between Work and Energy

The work done on a body between positions 1 and 2 is equal to the change in the total energy, which is the sum of the change in kinetic energy plus the change in potential energy. Therefore

$$U_{1 \to 2} = \Delta E = \Delta T + \Delta V$$
$$\Rightarrow U_{1 \to 2} = (T_2 - T_1) + (V_2 - V_1)$$

Conservation of Energy

If there are no external forces acting on the body and therefore no work being done, the change in the total energy of the body is zero. In this case, the total energy is said to be 'conserved,' and the Law of Conservation of Energy can be expressed as

$$\Delta E = 0$$
$$\Rightarrow T_1 + V_1 = T_2 + V_2$$

Example 33.1

A 20 lb block is released from rest at a height of 24 in above an uncompressed spring. If the spring constant is 75 lb/in, determine the amount the spring compresses when the block stops moving.

Solution: Since there are no external forces acting on the block, the total energy will be conserved. However, since both the initial and final velocities of the block will be zero, the change in kinetic energy will be zero and the initial gravitational energy of the block will be converted to elastic potential energy of the spring. If Δx is the compression of the spring, and considering the maximum spring compression to be the datum, then

$T_1 + V_1 = T_2 + V_2$
$V_1 = V_2$
$\Rightarrow V_{1G} = V_{2E}$
$mg(h+\Delta x) = k(\Delta x)^2 / 2$
$k(\Delta x)^2 / 2 - W\Delta x - Wh = 0$
$\Rightarrow 75(\Delta x)^2 / 2 - 20\Delta x - 480 = 0$

Using the quadratic formula to solve for Δx gives a compression of 3.85 in.

Example 33.2

A cart, traveling at a velocity of 2 m/s, is transporting a large mass hanging from a 10 m cable as shown below. If the cart stops suddenly, determine the maximum angle θ in the figure below.

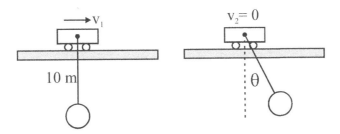

Solution: Consider the initial position of the hanging mass to define the datum so that the initial potential energy of the mass will be zero. Therefore, the initial kinetic energy of the moving mass will be converted to potential energy as a result of the mass swinging upward when the cart stops. Therefore, since there is no work being done on the mass, the total energy is conserved. Considering h to be the height that the mass rises above the datum, then

$T_1 = V_2$
$mv_1^2 / 2 = mgh$
$mv_1^2 / 2 = mg(L - L \cos \theta)$
$\theta = \cos^{-1}[1.0 - v_1^2 / 2gL] = \cos^{-1}[1.0 - (2.0)^2 / (2)(9.81)(10.0)]$
⇒ $\theta = 11.59°$

Example 33.3

A rocket-powered car with a mass of 500 kg has a velocity of 30 m/s at point A when the rockets are fired. The rockets provide a thrust F of 1,000 N between points A and C, where the rockets are turned off. Determine the distance d up the slope from point C to point D where the car stops.

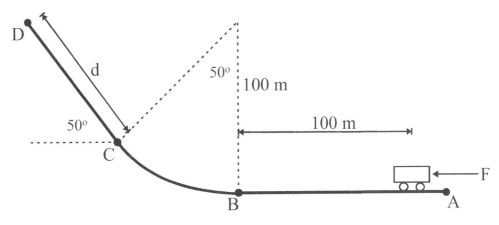

Solution: The car has an initial kinetic energy at point A, work is done on the car between points A and C, and the car only has a potential energy at point D. Therefore, the relationship between work and energy shows

$$U_{A \to D} = \Delta T + \Delta V$$
$$Fs = (T_D - T_A) + (V_D - V_A)$$
$$= (0 - mv_A^2/2) + (mgh_D - 0)$$
$$F(s_{A \to B} + s_{B \to C}) = -mv_A^2/2 + mg[r(1 - \cos\theta) + d\sin\theta]$$
$$F(s_{A \to B} + r\theta) = -mv_A^2/2 + mg[r(1 - \cos\theta) + d\sin\theta]$$
$$1{,}000[100 + 100\pi(50/180)] = -500(30)^2/2$$
$$+ 500(9.81)[100(1.0 - \cos 50°) + d\sin 50°]$$
$$187{,}266.46 = -225{,}000.00 + 175{,}212.68 + 3{,}757.45d$$
$$3{,}757.45d = 237{,}053.78$$
$$\Rightarrow d = 63.09 \text{ m}$$

Problems

33.1 A 12 lb block is attached to the end of a spring having a spring constant of k = 25 lb/in. In the position shown the spring is compressed 6 in. If the mass is released from rest, find the speed of the block as it passes through the location where the spring is unstretched.
(Ans. v_2 = 183.35 in/sec)

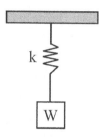

33.2 A force acts upon a block at rest having a mass of 15 kg as shown. If the coefficient of friction is 0.26, determine the speed of the block after it moves a distance of 30 m from its position of rest.
(Ans. v_2 = 21.14 m/sec)

33.3 At point A on the frictionless track, a 4 lb slider has a speed of 3.5 ft/sec to the right. At this point the spring is compressed a total of 1ft. If the spring constant is 3 lb/ft, determine the speed of the slider at point B.
(Ans. v_B = 10.53 ft/sec)

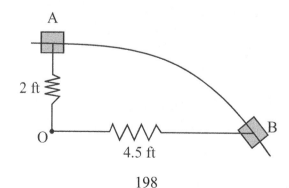

33.4 Assume the motion of the slider in Problem 33.3 occurs in the horizontal plane. If the slider weighs 9 lb and has a speed of 7 ft/sec to the right at point A, determine the spring constant if the speed of the slider at point B is zero.
(Ans. k = 10.96 lb/ft)

33.5 A block having a mass of 12 kg is released from rest at position A and slides down the ramp and impacts the spring. Neglecting friction, determine the maximum compression of the spring if k has a value of 450 N/m.
(Ans. Δx = 1.45 m)

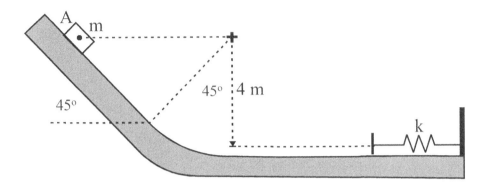

33.6 A pendulum 3 m in length is nudged from rest from the vertical position shown. If the ball at the end of the pendulum has a mass of 4 kg, determine the tension in the rod when $\theta = 180°$.
(Ans. T = 196.20 N)

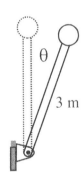

33.7 A 10 lb block initially at rest, is dropped from a height of 9 inches onto a spring having a spring constant of 45 lb/in. Determine the maximum speed the block achieves and the maximum compression of the spring.
(Ans. v = 6.95 ft/sec, Δx = 2.0 in)

33.8 Solve Problem 33.6 considering the mass at the end of the rod to have an initial tangential velocity of 3 m/s when $\theta = 0°$.
(Ans. F = 208.3 N)

MODULE 34: Impulse and Momentum Methods

The use of impulse and momentum methods is the third technique mentioned in Module 30 that is commonly used in the solution of problems in kinetics. Both linear impulse and linear momentum and angular impulse and angular momentum will be discussed in this Module.

Linear Impulse and Linear Momentum

Linear momentum is defined as the product of the mass of a body and its velocity as

$$\mathbf{G} = m\mathbf{v}$$

As previously discussed, Newton's Second Law states that the sum of the external forces acting on a body is equal to the time rate-of-change of linear momentum. If the forces are applied over a short period of time, the integral of these forces over that time period, called the linear impulse, is equal to the change in linear momentum. This can be shown mathematically as

$$\int (\Sigma \mathbf{F})\, dt = m\mathbf{v}_2 - m\mathbf{v}_1 = \mathbf{G}_2 - \mathbf{G}_1$$

If there are no external forces being applied to the body, the linear momentum of the body at position 1 is equal to the linear momentum of the body at position 2. In this case, it is said that the linear momentum is conserved. The Law of Conservation of Linear Momentum can then be stated as

$$m\mathbf{v}_2 = m\mathbf{v}_1$$

Angular Impulse and Angular Momentum

Angular momentum is defined as the moment of linear momentum about a point as

$$\mathbf{H} = \mathbf{r} \times m\mathbf{v}$$

where $\mathbf{r}$ is the moment arm from the point of interest to the mass. Newton's Second Law can also be used to show that the sum of the external moments (about the point) acting on a body is equal to the time rate-of-change of angular momentum. If the moments are applied over a short period of time, the integral of these moments over that time period, called the angular impulse, is equal to the change in angular momentum. This can be shown mathematically as

$$\int (\Sigma \mathbf{M}_o)\, dt = \mathbf{r}_2 \times m\mathbf{v}_2 - \mathbf{r}_1 \times m\mathbf{v}_1 = \mathbf{H}_2 - \mathbf{H}_1$$

If there are no external moments being applied to the body, the angular momentum of the body at position 1 is equal to the angular momentum of the body at position 2. In this case it is said that the angular momentum is conserved. The Law of Conservation of Angular Momentum can then be stated as

$$\mathbf{r}_2 \times m\mathbf{v}_2 = \mathbf{r}_1 \times m\mathbf{v}_1$$

Example 34.1

A 500 lb projectile is fired with an initial velocity of 1,800 ft/sec from a 175,000 lb canon. Determine the velocity of the recoil of the gun.

Solution: The explosion within the projectile's shell creates impulsive forces acting on both the projectile and the canon. These impulses will be equal in magnitude but opposite in direction. The relationship between the impulse and change in linear momentum can be written for both bodies as

projectile: $\int F_p \, dt = m_p(v_p)_2 - m_p(v_p)_1$

canon: $\int F_c \, dt = m_c(v_c)_2 - m_c(v_c)_1$

Since neither body will have an initial velocity the linear momentum at time 1 will be zero. Also, since the impulses will be equal but opposite, it can be written

$\int F_p \, dt = -\int F_c \, dt$
$m_p(v_p)_2 = -m_c(v_c)_2$
$(v_c)_2 = -m_p(v_p)_2 / m_c = -(500 / 32.2)(1,800) / (175,000 / 32.2)$
⇒ $(v_c)_2 = -5.14$ ft/sec (opposite to the direction of the projectile's velocity)

Example 34.2

A bullet with a mass of 200 g is fired with an initial velocity of 650 m/s and picks up four washers, each with a mass of 100 g. Find the velocity of the bullet and the washers and calculate the percentage of the total energy lost during this process.

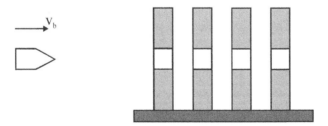

Solution: Since there are no external forces acting on the bullet or on the washers, the linear momentum will be conserved. Therefore,

$G_1 = G_2$
$m_1 v_1 = m_2 v_2$
$m_b v_b = (m_b + 4m_w) v_{b+w}$
$v_{b+w} = m_b v_b / (m_b + 4m_w)$
$= 0.2(650\, i) / [0.2 + 4(0.1)]$
⇒ $v_{b+w} = 216.67\, i$ m/s

During the process of the bullet picking up the washers, forces will occur due to the interaction of the bullet with the washers that will cause deformation and heat loss in both the bullet and the washers. Those forces are considered to be internal forces and the deformation will result in an energy loss during this process, therefore energy will not be conserved. The percentage of the total energy lost can be determined as the change in energy divided by the initial energy times 100% as

$$\% \Delta E = (E_2 - E_1) / E_1 \times 100\%$$
$$= (T_2 - T_1) / T_1 \times 100\%$$
$$= [(m_b + 4m_w)v_{b+w}^2 / 2 - m_b v_b^2 / 2] / (m_b v_b^2 / 2) \times 100\%$$
$$= \{[0.2 + 4(0.1)](216.67)^2 / 2 - 0.2(650)^2 / 2\} / [0.2(650)^2 / 2] \times 100\%$$
$$\Rightarrow \% \Delta E = -66.67 \%$$

Problems

34.1 The space transportation vehicle, with a mass of 98,000 kg, launches a 1,200 kg satellite upward from its bay with an ejection mechanism that applies an impulsive force. After ejection the velocity of the satellite relative to the vehicle is 0.24 m/s. Determine the velocity of the satellite and the velocity of the vehicle after ejection of the satellite.
(Ans. v_{sat} = 0.2371 **j** m/s, v_{veh} = -0.0029 **j** m/s)

34.2 A bullet with a mass of 85 g is fired horizontally and imbeds itself into a bag of sand having a mass of 30 kg as it hangs from a 2 m long cable. After impact the cable swings through an angle of $\theta = 18°$. Determine the initial velocity of the bullet and the percentage of the total energy lost during impact.
(Ans. v_1 = 490.56 m/s, %E lost = 99.72%)

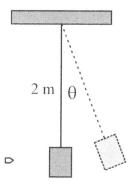

34.3 Three disconnected railroad cars move in the same direction with different speeds. Car A has a weight of 140,000 lb and a speed of 4 mph, car B has a weight of 100,000 lb and a speed of 2.5 mph, and car C has a weight of 110,000 lb and a speed of 2 mph. When the cars impact they become connected through the coupling mechanisms on each car. Neglecting friction, determine the final velocity of the three cars coupled together.
(Ans. **v** = 2.94 mph)

34.4 In Problem 34.2, consider a 65 g bullet imbedding into a 22 kg bag of sand. If the initial velocity of the bullet is 610 m/s, determine the maximum angle θ through which the cable swings.
(Ans. θ = 23.41°)

34.5 A 185 lb man runs horizontally and dives onto a 450 lb boat initially at rest. If the resulting velocity of the boat and the man is 4 ft/sec, find the initial speed of the man.
(Ans. v = 13.73 ft/sec)

34.6 A tennis ball with a mass of 0.05 kg approaches a tennis racket with a speed of 25 m/s and leaves at an angle of 12° from the approach direction with a speed of 40 m/s. Determine the magnitude of the impulse provided by the racket.
(Ans. $|\int \mathbf{F} dt| = 3.23$ kg-m/s)

34.7 Car A weighs 3,000 lb and is traveling from west to east at 40 mph. Car A collides with car B, which weighs 3,300 lb and is traveling from south to north at 30 mph. If the two cars become entangled and move together as a unit after the collision, calculate the magnitude of their velocity immediately after impact and the angle θ between the velocity vector and the north direction.
(Ans. v = 24.69 mph, θ = 50.49°)

34.8 Find the weight of railroad car B in Problem 34.3 if the final velocity of the three coupled cars is 1.65 mph.
(Ans. W_B = 88,554.2 lb)

MODULE 35: Kinematics of Rigid Body Plane Motion

General plane motion of rigid bodies, i.e., bodies that don't bend or deform, is described by the combination of translation and rotation. Translation considers a body moving in a particular direction with no angular motion, while rotation considers angular motion about a specified axis.

Consider the rigid body shown in Figure 35.1 which undergoes a combination of translation and rotation, where ω is the angular velocity of the body is α is the angular acceleration.

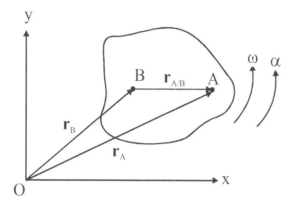

Figure 35.1

Relative Motion: Translating and Rotating Axes

The absolute position, velocity, and acceleration of point A is given by the relative motion equations

$$\mathbf{r}_A = \mathbf{r}_B + \mathbf{r}_{A/B} \quad , \quad \mathbf{v}_A = \mathbf{v}_B + \mathbf{v}_{A/B} \quad , \quad \mathbf{a}_A = \mathbf{a}_B + \mathbf{a}_{A/B}$$

Note that the position vector of point A relative to point B, $\mathbf{r}_{A/B}$, indicates the position vector from point B to point A. Since A and B are points on the rigid body, point A can neither get closer to nor farther from point B. Therefore, and motion of point A relative to point B can only be rotational. The relative velocity at point A relative to point B is then given by the vector equation

$$\mathbf{v}_{A/B} = \boldsymbol{\omega} \times \mathbf{r}_{A/B}$$

Since ω and $\mathbf{r}_{A/B}$ are perpendicular to each other, the magnitude of $\mathbf{v}_{A/B}$ is simply

$$v_{A/B} = \omega r_{A/B}$$

The relative velocity equation can then be written as

$$\mathbf{v}_A = \mathbf{v}_B + \boldsymbol{\omega} \times \mathbf{r}_{A/B}$$

In this equation, the velocity of point B can consist of translation and/or rotation about another point on the body. The relative acceleration, $\mathbf{a}_{A/B}$, is made up of two components, one in the normal direction and one in the tangential direction shown in vector form as

$$\mathbf{a}_{A/B} = (\mathbf{a}_{A/B})_n + (\mathbf{a}_{A/B})_t$$

where the vector forms of these components are given as

$$(\mathbf{a}_{A/B})_n = \boldsymbol{\omega} \times (\boldsymbol{\omega} \times \mathbf{r}_{A/B}) \quad , \quad (\mathbf{a}_{A/B})_t = \boldsymbol{\alpha} \times \mathbf{r}_{A/B}$$

Since these operations are performed using vectors that are mutually perpendicular, the magnitudes of these components can be written as

$$(a_{A/B})_n = r_{A/B}\omega^2 \quad , \quad (a_{A/B})_t = r_{A/B}\alpha$$

The normal component is also called the 'centripetal' acceleration of point A relative to point B. Using the relative acceleration equation, the absolute acceleration of point A can now be written as

$$\mathbf{a}_A = \mathbf{a}_B + \boldsymbol{\omega} \times (\boldsymbol{\omega} \times \mathbf{r}_{A/B}) + \boldsymbol{\alpha} \times \mathbf{r}_{A/B}$$

The normal acceleration results from point A having a circular velocity about point B and is in the direction from point A to point B. The tangential acceleration is equal to the time rate-of-change of velocity and is directed perpendicular to $\mathbf{r}_{A/B}$ and tangent to the circular path of point A at any instant. The directions of the relative acceleration components are shown in Figure 35.2.

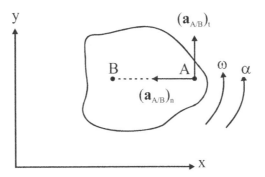

Figure 35.2

Example 35.1

Consider the wheel shown below to be rolling to the right with an angular velocity of 3 rad/s and an angular acceleration of 2 rad/s² in the clockwise direction. If the radius of the wheel is 1 m, determine the absolute velocity and absolute acceleration of point A.

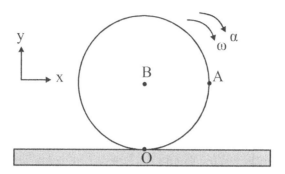

Solution: Since both the angular velocity and angular acceleration are clockwise, they can be written in vector form as

$$\boldsymbol{\omega} = -3\,\mathbf{k}\ \text{rad/s}\ ,\quad \boldsymbol{\alpha} = -2\,\mathbf{k}\ \text{rad/s}^2$$

The equation for the absolute velocity of point A is

$$\mathbf{v}_A = \mathbf{v}_B + \boldsymbol{\omega} \times \mathbf{r}_{A/B}$$

Since the absolute velocity of point B is to the right and parallel to the ground, it can be determined by considering it to be rotating about point O at this instant. Therefore, $\mathbf{v}_B$ can be expressed as $\boldsymbol{\omega} \times \mathbf{r}_B$, giving

$$\mathbf{v}_A = \boldsymbol{\omega} \times \mathbf{r}_B + \boldsymbol{\omega} \times \mathbf{r}_{A/B}$$
$$= (-3\,\mathbf{k}) \times (\mathbf{j}) + (-3\,\mathbf{k}) \times (\mathbf{i})$$
$$\Rightarrow\ \mathbf{v}_A = 3\,\mathbf{i} - 3\,\mathbf{j}\ \text{m/s}$$

Writing the equation for the absolute acceleration of point A shows

$$\mathbf{a}_A = \mathbf{a}_B + \boldsymbol{\omega} \times (\boldsymbol{\omega} \times \mathbf{r}_{A/B}) + \boldsymbol{\alpha} \times \mathbf{r}_{A/B}$$

However at this instant, $\mathbf{a}_B$ will have a tangential component but not a normal component because the center of the wheel is only moving in a straight line and not on a curved path. The acceleration equation can then be written as

$$\mathbf{a}_A = \boldsymbol{\alpha} \times \mathbf{r}_B + \boldsymbol{\omega} \times (\boldsymbol{\omega} \times \mathbf{r}_{A/B}) + \boldsymbol{\alpha} \times \mathbf{r}_{A/B}$$
$$= (-2\,\mathbf{k}) \times (\mathbf{j}) + (-3\,\mathbf{k}) \times [(-3\,\mathbf{k}) \times (\mathbf{i})] + (-2\,\mathbf{k}) \times (\mathbf{i})$$
$$= 2\,\mathbf{i} + (-3\,\mathbf{k}) \times (-3\,\mathbf{j}) - 2\,\mathbf{j}$$
$$\Rightarrow\ \mathbf{a}_A = -7\,\mathbf{i} - 2\,\mathbf{j}\ \text{m/s}^2$$

Example 35.2

For the slider-crank mechanism shown below, the angular velocity of link OB is 3 rad/s clockwise. Calculate the velocity of the slider A at this instant.

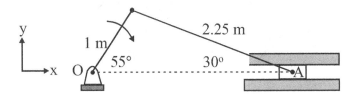

Solution: $\mathbf{v}_A = \mathbf{v}_B + \mathbf{v}_{A/B}$
$\mathbf{v}_A = \boldsymbol{\omega} \times \mathbf{r}_B + \mathbf{v}_{A/B}$

Since the direction of $\mathbf{v}_A$ must be in the x direction, and the direction of $\mathbf{v}_{A/B}$ must be in a direction perpendicular to link AB, this equation can be written as

$v_A \mathbf{i} = (-3 \mathbf{k}) \times (1.0 \cos 55° \mathbf{i} + 1.0 \sin 55° \mathbf{j}) + v_{A/B}(\cos 60° \mathbf{i} + \sin 60° \mathbf{j})$
$\Rightarrow v_A \mathbf{i} = (2.45 + 0.5 v_{A/B}) \mathbf{i} + (0.87 v_{A/B} - 1.72) \mathbf{j}$

Separating the vector components gives two equations as

i dir: $v_A = 2.45 + 0.5 v_{A/B}$, **j** dir: $0 = 0.87 v_{A/B} - 1.72$

Solving these two equations for v_A and $v_{A/B}$ gives the solutions

$v_{A/B} = 1.98$ m/s , $v_A = 3.44$ m/s

Therefore the absolute velocity of point A is $\mathbf{v}_A = 3.44\,\mathbf{i}$ m/s

Problems

35.1 Point P on the edge of the wheel has an acceleration of $\mathbf{a} = -6\,\mathbf{i} - 7\,\mathbf{j}$ m/s². Find the angular velocity ω and angular acceleration α of the wheel.
(Ans. $\boldsymbol{\alpha} = 8.00\,\mathbf{k}$ rad/s², $\boldsymbol{\omega} = 3.06\,\mathbf{k}$ rad/s)

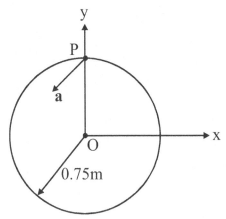

35.2 For the slider-crank mechanism shown in Example 35.2, determine the angular velocities of links OB and BA if the velocity of the slider at the instant shown is 7.5 m/s to the left.
(Ans. ω_{AB} = -1.92 **k** rad/s, ω_{OB} = 6.52 **k** rad/s)

35.3 In the piston mechanism below, the crank OB rotates counterclockwise at the constant rate of 75 rad/s. For the configuration shown, determine ω_{AB}, $\mathbf{a}_A$, and α_{AB}.
(Ans. ω_{AB} = 0, α_{AB} = -2,456.33 **k** rad/s^2, $\mathbf{a}_A$ = -245.63 m/s^2)

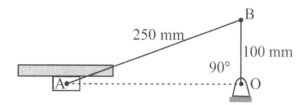

35.4 The wheel shown below rotates about point O. Point A has a velocity of -7 **j** in/sec and point B has a tangential acceleration of -4 **i** in/sec^2. Determine the absolute acceleration of point C.
(Ans. $\mathbf{a}_C$ = -0.62 **i** + 9.08 **j** in/sec^2)

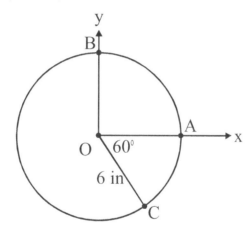

35.5 The wheel shown below has an angular velocity of 6 rad/s counterclockwise and an angular acceleration of 5 rad/s^2 clockwise. Determine the velocity and acceleration of point A relative to point C.
(Ans. $\mathbf{v}_{A/C}$ = 2.12 **i** + 5.12 **j** m/sec, $\mathbf{a}_{A/C}$ = -32.51 **i** + 8.47 **j** m/sec^2)

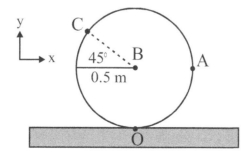

35.6 If the wheel shown in Problem 35.5 has an angular velocity of 4 rad/s and an angular acceleration of 7 rad/s², both in the clockwise direction, determine the absolute velocity and absolute acceleration of point C.
(Ans. $\mathbf{v}_C = 3.42\,\mathbf{i} + 1.41\,\mathbf{j}$ m/sec, $\mathbf{a}_C = 11.64\,\mathbf{i} + 11.19\,\mathbf{j}$ m/sec²)

35.7 Consider Example 35.1 where the angular velocity of the wheel is 2 rad/s and the absolute acceleration of point A is given as $\mathbf{a}_A = -3.50\,\mathbf{i} - 3.75\,\mathbf{j}$ m/s². Determine the radius and the angular acceleration of the wheel.
(Ans. r = 1.813m, $\boldsymbol{\alpha} = -2.07\,\mathbf{k}$ rad/s²)

35.8 If the absolute acceleration of point C in Problem 35.4 is given as $\mathbf{a}_C = 7.5\,\mathbf{i} + 14.0\,\mathbf{j}$ m/s², calculate the tangential acceleration of point A and the velocity of point B.
(Ans. $(\mathbf{a}_A)_t = 13.494\,\mathbf{j}$ in/sec², $\mathbf{v}_B = -7.086\,\mathbf{i}$ in/sec)

MODULE 36: Kinematics of Rigid Body Plane Motion (cont.)

This module presents additional material on the kinematics of rigid body plane motion in the form of more example problems.

Example 36.1

Slider B has a velocity of 6 in/sec downward. For the instant shown, determine ω_{OA} and ω_{AB}.

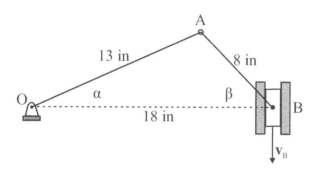

Solution: In order to solve this problem, the angles α and β must first be determined. The value of α can be found using the Law of Cosines, which states

$$c^2 = a^2 + b^2 - 2ab \cos \alpha.$$

For the case where c = 8 in, a = 13 in, and b = 18 in

$$(8)^2 = (13)^2 + (18)^2 - 2(13)(18) \cos \alpha$$
$\Rightarrow \alpha = 23.56°$

The value of β can then be found using the Law of Sines, which states

c / sin α = a / sin β
8 / sin 23.56° = 13 / sin β
$\Rightarrow \beta = 40.51°$

Using the relative velocity equation to calculate the absolute the velocity of B shows

$\mathbf{v}_B = \mathbf{v}_A + \mathbf{v}_{B/A}$
$-0.6 \, \mathbf{j} = \omega_{OA} \times \mathbf{r}_A + \omega_{AB} \times \mathbf{r}_{AB}$

Assuming that both OA and AB will rotate clockwise

$$-6.0 \mathbf{j} = -\omega_{OA} \mathbf{k} \times (13 \cos 23.56° \mathbf{i} + 13 \sin 23.56° \mathbf{j})$$
$$+ -\omega_{AB} \mathbf{k} \times (8 \cos 40.51° \mathbf{i} - 8 \sin 40.51° \mathbf{j})$$
$$= (-\omega_{OA})(11.92) \mathbf{j} + (-\omega_{OA})(5.20)(-\mathbf{i}) + (-\omega_{AB})(6.08) \mathbf{j} + (-\omega_{AB})(-5.20)(-\mathbf{i})$$

$\Rightarrow$ $-6.0 \mathbf{j} = (5.20\omega_{OA} - 5.20\omega_{AB}) \mathbf{i} + (-11.92\omega_{OA} - 6.08\omega_{AB}) \mathbf{j}$

Separating the vector components gives two equations as

i dir: $0.0 = 5.20\omega_{OA} - 5.20\omega_{AB}$, **j** dir: $-6.0 = -11.92\omega_{OA} - 6.08\omega_{AB}$

Solving these two equations for ω_{OA} and ω_{AB} gives

$\omega_{OA} = \omega_{AB} = 0.33$ rad/s
$\Rightarrow$ $\omega_{OA} = \omega_{AB} = -0.33$ **k** rad/s

Example 36.2

The linkage below has angular velocities of $\omega_{OA} = -10$ **k** rad/s, $\omega_{AB} = -2.5$ **k** rad/s, and $\omega_{BC} = -5.8$ **k** rad/s. If ω_{OA} is constant, determine the angular acceleration of links AB and BC.

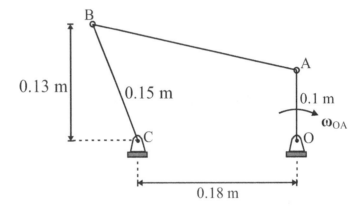

Solution: It will be assumed that both α_{AB} and α_{BC} act in the counterclockwise direction. The relative acceleration equation for point B is written below. Since the angular velocity of OA is constant, point A will not have a tangential acceleration component.

$\mathbf{a}_B = \mathbf{a}_A + \mathbf{a}_{B/A}$
$(\mathbf{a}_B)_n + (\mathbf{a}_B)_t = (\mathbf{a}_A)_n + (\mathbf{a}_{B/A})_n + (\mathbf{a}_{B/A})_t$
$\Rightarrow$ $\omega_{BC} \times (\omega_{BC} \times \mathbf{r}_{CB}) + \alpha_{BC} \times \mathbf{r}_{CB} = \omega_{OA} \times (\omega_{OA} \times \mathbf{r}_{OA}) + \omega_{AB} \times (\omega_{AB} \times \mathbf{r}_{AB}) + \alpha_{AB} \times \mathbf{r}_{AB}$

Substituting the known quantities gives

$$-5.8\,\mathbf{k} \times [-5.8\,\mathbf{k} \times (-0.075\,\mathbf{i} + 0.13\,\mathbf{j})] + \alpha_{BC}\,\mathbf{k} \times (-0.075\,\mathbf{i} + 0.13\,\mathbf{j}) =$$
$$-10\,\mathbf{k} \times (-10\,\mathbf{k} \times 0.1\,\mathbf{j}) + (-2.5\,\mathbf{k}) \times [-2.5\,\mathbf{k} \times (-0.255\,\mathbf{i} + 0.03\,\mathbf{j})]$$
$$+ \alpha_{AB}\,\mathbf{k} \times (-0.255\,\mathbf{i} + 0.03\,\mathbf{j})$$

$$\Rightarrow (2.523 - 0.13\alpha_{BC})\,\mathbf{i} + (-4.373 - 0.075\alpha_{BC})\,\mathbf{j} = (1.595 - 0.03\alpha_{AB})\,\mathbf{i}$$
$$+ (-10.188 - 0.255\alpha_{AB})\,\mathbf{j}$$

Separating the vector components gives two equations as

i dir: $0.928 = 0.13\alpha_{BC} - 0.03\alpha_{AB}$, **j** dir: $5.815 = 0.075\alpha_{BC} - 0.255\alpha_{AB}$

Solving for α_{BC} and α_{AB} gives $\boldsymbol{\alpha}_{BC} = 2.01\,\mathbf{k}$ rad/s² and $\boldsymbol{\alpha}_{AB} = -22.18\,\mathbf{k}$ rad/s².

Example 36.3

At the instant shown for the linkage below, $\omega_{OB} = -5\,\mathbf{k}$ rad/s and $\alpha_{OB} = 0$. Determine the absolute acceleration of slider A and the angular acceleration of link AB.

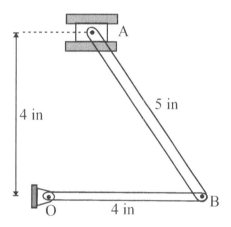

Solution:
$$\mathbf{v}_A = \mathbf{v}_B + \mathbf{v}_{A/B}$$
$$\mathbf{v}_A = \boldsymbol{\omega}_{OB} \times \mathbf{r}_{OB} + \boldsymbol{\omega}_{BA} \times \mathbf{r}_{BA}$$
$$v_A\,\mathbf{i} = -5\,\mathbf{k} \times 4\,\mathbf{i} + \omega_{BA}\,\mathbf{k} \times (-3\,\mathbf{i} + 4\,\mathbf{j})$$
$$\Rightarrow v_A\,\mathbf{i} = -4\omega_{BA}\,\mathbf{i} + (-20 - 3\omega_{BA})\,\mathbf{j}$$

Solving the component equations give $\omega_{BA} = -6.67\,\mathbf{k}$ rad/s and $\mathbf{v}_A = 26.67\,\mathbf{i}$ in/sec.

Writing the acceleration equation shows

$$\mathbf{a}_A = \mathbf{a}_B + \mathbf{a}_{A/B} = (\mathbf{a}_B)_n + (\mathbf{a}_{A/B})_n + (\mathbf{a}_{A/B})_t$$
$$a_A\,\mathbf{i} = \boldsymbol{\omega}_{OB} \times (\boldsymbol{\omega}_{OB} \times \mathbf{r}_{OB}) + \boldsymbol{\omega}_{BA} \times (\boldsymbol{\omega}_{BA} \times \mathbf{r}_{BA}) + \boldsymbol{\alpha}_{BA} \times \mathbf{r}_{BA}$$
$$= -5\,\mathbf{k} \times (-5\,\mathbf{k} \times 4\,\mathbf{i}) + (-6.67\,\mathbf{k}) \times [-6.67\,\mathbf{k} \times (-3\,\mathbf{i} + 4\,\mathbf{j})] + \alpha_{BA}\,\mathbf{k} \times (-3\,\mathbf{i} + 4\,\mathbf{j})$$
$$\Rightarrow a_A\,\mathbf{i} = (33.47 - 4\alpha_{BA})\,\mathbf{i} + (-177.96 - 3\alpha_{BA})\,\mathbf{j}$$

Separating the vector components gives two equations gives

i dir: $a_A = 33.47 - 4\alpha_{BA}$, **j** dir: $0 = -177.96 - 3\alpha_{BA}$

And solving for α_{BA} and a_A yields α_{BA} = -59.32 **k** rad/s² and $\mathbf{a}_A$ = 270.74 **i** in/sec².

Problems

36.1 In the mechanism below, link AB rotates with a constant angular velocity of 6 rad/s in the clockwise direction. Determine the angular velocities of links BC and CD.
(Ans. ω_{BC} = 1.50 **k** rad/s, ω_{CD} = 4.96 **k** rad/s)

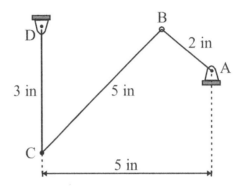

36.2 In Example 36.1, determine the acceleration of slider B if the angular velocity of link OA is constant.
(Ans. a_B = 2.32 in/s² upward)

36.3 Using the results of Problem 36.1, calculate the angular accelerations of links BC and CD.
(Ans. α_{BC} = -32.38 **k** rad/s², α_{CD} = -17.38 **k** rad/s²)

36.4 In the figure below, link AB rotates clockwise with a constant angular velocity of 5 rad/s. Determine the acceleration of point B and the angular acceleration of link BC.
(Ans. $\mathbf{a}_B$ = -2.50 **i** + 4.33 **j** m/s², α_{BC} = -10.15 **k** rad/s²)

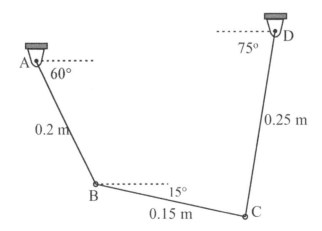

36.5 For the mechanism shown in Problem 36.1, determine the angular velocities and angular accelerations of links BC and CD if link AB has a clockwise angular velocity of 4 rad/sec and a counterclockwise angular acceleration of 2.5 rad/sec^2.
(Ans. ω_{BC} = 1.00 **k** rad/s, ω_{CD} = 3.31 **k** rad/s, α_{BC} = -15.02 **k** rad/s^2, α_{CD} = 20.24 **k** rad/s^2)

36.6 Consider the linkage shown in Example 36.3. If block A has an absolute velocity of 15 in/sec to the right and an absolute acceleration of 6 in/sec^2 to the left, determine the angular velocities and angular accelerations of links OB and BA.
(Ans. ω_{AB} = -3.75 **k** rad/s, ω_{OB} = -2.81 **k** rad/s, α_{AB} = 4.13 **k** rad/s^2, α_{OB} = 17.16 **k** rad/s^2)

36.7 In Problem 36.1, calculate the angular velocities of links AB and BC if link DC rotates with an angular velocity of 5 rad/s in the clockwise direction.
(Ans. ω_{AB} = 5.49 **k** rad/s, ω_{BC} = -1.37 **k** rad/s)

36.8 Calculate the angular acceleration of links AB and BC in Example 36.2 if α_{OA} = 1.0 rad/s^2 in the clockwise direction.
(Ans. α_{AB} = -22.5 **k** rad/s^2, α_{BC} = 0.94 **k** rad/s^2)

MODULE 37: Mass Moments of Inertia

Similar to the concept that mass is a measure of a body's resistance to acceleration, mass moment of inertia is a measure of a body's resistance to rotational acceleration. Generally the mass moments of inertia of a body are described in a coordinate system which is fixed to the body so that the values of these terms don't change with time. Consider the three-dimensional body shown in Figure 37.1, whose centroidal axes are designated as x^*, y^*, and z^*.

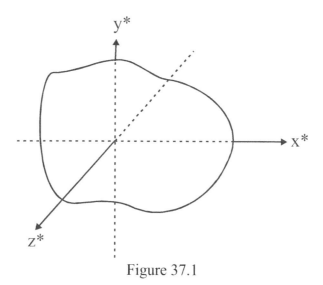

Figure 37.1

The mass moments of inertia of the body about each centroidal axis are determined by the expressions

$$I^*_{xx} = \int (y^2 + z^2)\, dm \quad , \quad I^*_{yy} = \int (x^2 + z^2)\, dm \quad , \quad I^*_{zz} = \int (x^2 + y^2)\, dm$$

which represent the second moments of the mass about each axis. Units for mass moments of inertia are kg-m^2 in SI units and slug-ft^2 in US Customary units.

The radius of gyration k^* of a body is a measure of the distribution of the body's mass from a particular axis, i.e., if all of the mass of the body was concentrated at a distance k^* from an axis. In the Cartesian coordinates shown above, these quantities are defined as

$$k^*_x = [I^*_{xx} / m]^{1/2} \quad , \quad k^*_y = [I^*_{yy} / m]^{1/2} \quad , \quad k^*_z = [I^*_{zz} / m]^{1/2}$$

For common shapes, simple formulas for I^* about each centroidal axis of a body can be used without the need for integration. Table 37.1 provides a summary of commonly shaped bodies and formulas for their respective mass moments of inertia about each of the coordinate axes.

Table 37.1 Mass Moments of Inertia of Commonly Shaped Bodies

Rectangular Solid:

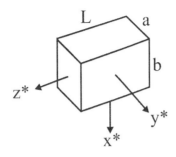

$I^*_{xx} = m(a^2 + L^2) / 12$
$I^*_{yy} = m(b^2 + L^2) / 12$
$I^*_{zz} = m(a^2 + b^2) / 12$

Circular Cylinder:

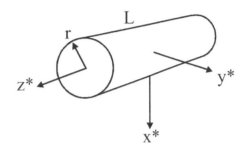

$I^*_{xx} = mr^2 / 4 + mL^2 / 12$
$I^*_{yy} = mr^2 / 4 + mL^2 / 12$
$I^*_{zz} = mr^2 / 2$

Circular Cylindrical Shell:

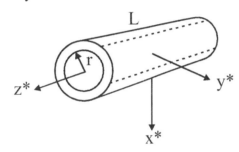

$I^*_{xx} = mr^2 / 2 + mL^2 / 12$
$I^*_{yy} = mr^2 / 2 + mL^2 / 12$
$I^*_{zz} = mr^2$

Sphere:

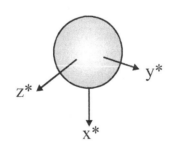

$I^*_{xx} = 2mr^2 / 5$
$I^*_{yy} = 2mr^2 / 5$
$I^*_{zz} = 2mr^2 / 5$

Uniform Slender Rod:

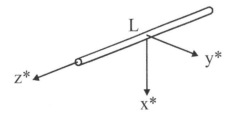

$I^*_{xx} = mL^2 / 12$
$I^*_{yy} = mL^2 / 12$
$I^*_{zz} = 0$

Parallel Axis Theorem

The mass moments of inertia about a body's centroidal axes are often the most important set of axes in the solution of rigid body kinetics problems. However, when the mass moments of inertia about non-centroidal axes are required, as may be the case of fixed-axis rotation, the parallel axis theorem is used for their computation. Consider an arbitrarily shaped body of mass m, whose centroidal axes and a set of arbitrary axes designated x, y, and z, are indicated in Figure 37.2.

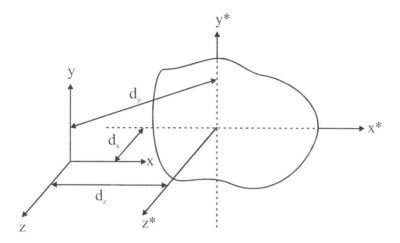

Figure 37.2

The quantities d_x, d_y, and d_z are defined as the distances between the x and x^* axes, the y and y^* axes, and the z and z^* axes, respectively. The parallel axis theorem provides formulas for the calculation of the moments of inertia about the x, y, and z-axes as

$$I_{xx} = I^*_{xx} + md_x^2 \quad , \quad I_{yy} = I^*_{yy} + md_y^2 \quad , \quad I_{zz} = I^*_{zz} + md_z^2$$

Here, the terms md_x^2, md_y^2, md_z^2 are known as the transfer terms. For the transfer of the radius of gyration of a body, the formulas are

$$k_x^2 = k^{*2}_x + d_x^2 \quad , \quad k_y^2 = k^{*2}_y + d_y^2 \quad , \quad k_z^2 = k^{*2}_z + d_z^2$$

Method of Composite Bodies

The Method of Composite Bodies can be used to determine the mass moments of inertia of a body that can be divided into two or more commonly shaped bodies. This is done using the following formulas, along with the formulas presented in Table 37.1, for the computation of mass moments of inertia about an arbitrary set of coordinates x, y, and z.

$$I_{xx} = \Sigma I^*_{xx} + \Sigma md_x^2 \quad , \quad I_{yy} = \Sigma I^*_{yy} + \Sigma md_y^2 \quad , \quad I_{zz} = \Sigma I^*_{zz} + \Sigma md_z^2$$

The terms I^*_{xx}, I^*_{yy}, I^*_{zz}, md_x^2, md_y^2, and md_z^2 represent the mass moments of inertia about the centroidal axes of each common shape and their associated transfer terms.

Products of Inertia

In addition to mass moments of inertia, products of inertia terms are defined by the expressions

$$I_{xy} = I_{yx} = \int xy \, dm$$
$$I_{xz} = I_{zx} = \int xz \, dm$$
$$I_{yz} = I_{zy} = \int yz \, dm$$

These quantities can also be expressed using the parallel axis theorem as

$$I_{xy} = I^*_{xy} + m d_x d_y$$
$$I_{xz} = I^*_{xz} + m d_x d_z$$
$$I_{yz} = I^*_{yz} + m d_y d_z$$

For a rigid body, an 'inertia matrix' can be defined in body-fixed coordinates as

$$I = \begin{bmatrix} I_{xx} & -I_{xy} & -I_{xz} \\ -I_{yx} & I_{yy} & -I_{yz} \\ -I_{zx} & -I_{zy} & I_{zz} \end{bmatrix}$$

If the coordinate system is selected so that the product of inertia terms will be zero, then

$$I = \begin{bmatrix} I_{xx} & 0 & 0 \\ 0 & I_{yy} & 0 \\ 0 & 0 & I_{zz} \end{bmatrix}$$

In this case, the chosen x, y, and z-axes are called 'principal axes of inertia,' and the quantities I_{xx}, I_{yy}, and I_{zz} are called 'principal moments of inertia'. For the bodies provided in Table 37.1, all axes shown are principal axes of inertia, therefore all products of inertia for these bodies are zero.

Example 37.1

The cylindrical body is made of a material with a density of 12 slugs/ft³ and contains a 4 in diameter cutout. Find the mass moment of inertia of this body about the z-z axis.

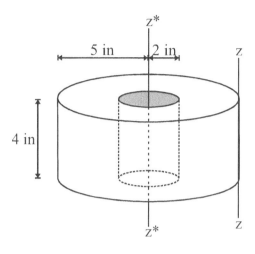

Solution: This body can be broken into two commonly shaped bodies, a solid cylinder and a cylindrical cutout that are designated as bodies 1 and 2, respectively. The masses and mass moments of inertia will be computed for each body. Those for body 2 will be computed as negative quantities since it represents the cutout portion of the body.

$m_1 = \rho \pi r_1^2 L_1$
$\quad = 12\pi(5/12)^2(4/12)$
$\Rightarrow m_1 = 2.182$ slugs

$m_2 = -\rho \pi r_2^2 L_2$
$\quad = -12\pi(2/12)^2(4/12)$
$\Rightarrow m_2 = -0.349$ slugs

The table below provides the quantities m, I^*_{zz}, d_z, and $I^*_{zz} + md_z^2$ for each body, where I^*_{zz} is calculated from the formulas provided in Table 37.1. The column for $I^*_{zz} + md_z^2$ is then added and the results is I_{zz} for the composite body.

Area	m (slugs)	I^*_{zz} (slug-ft²)	d_z (ft)	$I^*_{zz} + md_z^2$ (slug-ft²)
1	2.182	0.189	0.417	0.569
2	-0.349	-0.005	0.417	-0.066

Total: 0.503 slug-ft²

Therefore, for the composite body, $I_{zz} = 0.503$ slug-ft²

Example 37.2

The slender rod shown below has a mass of 100 kg. Determine the mass moments of inertia of this rod about the x, y, and z-axes.

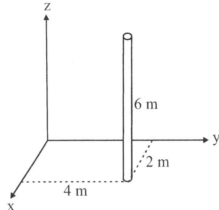

Solution: The values of the mass moments of inertia of the rod about its centroidal axes are calculated using the formulas presented in Table 37.1. From the figure above, the values of d_x, d_y, and d_z are determined as

$d_x = [(4)^2 + (3)^2]^{1/2}$
$\Rightarrow d_x = 5.00$ m

$d_y = [(2)^2 + (3)^2]^{1/2}$
$\Rightarrow d_y = 3.61$ m

$d_z = [(2)^2 + (4)^2]^{1/2}$
$\Rightarrow d_z = 4.47$ m

The values of I^*_{xx}, I^*_{yy}, and I^*_{zz} are then added to the transfer terms in order to obtain I_{xx}, I_{yy}, and I_{zz} as

$I_{xx} = mL^2 / 12 + md_x^2$
$\quad = 100(6)^2 / 12 + 100(5)^2$
$\Rightarrow I_{xx} = 2{,}800$ kg-m^2

$I_{yy} = mL^2 / 12 + md_y^2$
$\quad = 100(6)^2 / 12 + 100(3.61)^2$
$\Rightarrow I_{yy} = 1{,}603$ kg-m^2

$I_{zz} = 0 + md_z^2$
$\quad = 0 + 100(4.47)^2$
$\Rightarrow I_{zz} = 1{,}988$ kg-m^2

Problems

37.1 For the body in Example 37.1, determine the mass moments of inertia of about the centroidal x and y-axes.
(Ans. $I^*_{xx} = I^*_{yy} = 0.109$ slug-ft^2)

37.2 The aluminum ($\rho = 2,700$ kg/m^3) block shown below contains a cylindrical cutout through the center of the block having a diameter of D = 1.50 m. Determine the mass moments of inertia about the centroidal axes of the block.
(Ans. $I^*_{xx} = 1,375,869.2$ kg-m^2, $I^*_{yy} = 1,641,632.3$ kg-m^2, $I^*_{zz} = 1,078,089.2$ kg-m^2)

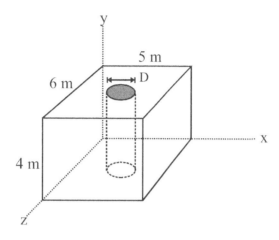

37.3 In the composite steel ($\rho = 7,850$ kg/m^3) body shown below, the large cylinder has a radius of $r_1 = 0.5$ m, while the small cylinder has a radius of $r_2 = 0.2$ m. Determine the mass moments of inertia about the x, y, and z-axes.
(Ans. $I_{xx} = I_{yy} = 499,683.1$ kg-m^2, $I_{zz} = 3,942.2$ kg-m^2)

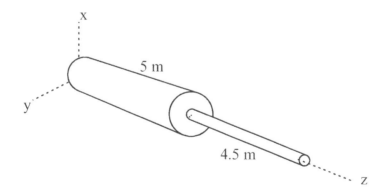

37.4 The wooden block shown has a density of 1,500 kg/m³. Determine the mass moments of inertia about the x, y, and z-axes provided.
(Ans. I_{xx} = 41.600 kg-m², I_{yy} = 51.200 kg-m², I_{zz} = 10.880 kg-m²)

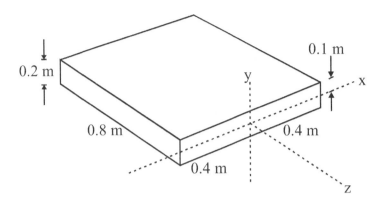

37.5 For the block in Problem 37.2, determine the mass moments of inertia about the x, y, and z-axes provided.
(Ans. I_{xx} = 5,339,761.6 kg-m², I_{yy} = 6,291,583.0 kg-m², I_{zz} = 4,204,185.9 kg-m²)

37.6 For the composite body in Problem 37.3, the large cylinder has a radius of r_1 = 0.65 m, while the small cylinder has a radius of r_2 = 0.10 m, determine the mass moments of inertia about the centroidal x and y-axes.
(Ans. I_{xx}^* = I_{yy}^* = 140,431.49 kg-m²)

37.7 Solve Example 37.2 for the case where the coordinate system is located at the bottom end of the slender rod and m = 125 kg.
(Ans. I_{xx} = 1,500 kg-m², I_{yy} = 875 kg-m², I_{zz} = 0)

37.8 Solve Example 37.1 for the case where the z-z axis is located on the inside edge of the solid cylindrical body.
(Ans. I_{zz} = 0.236 slug-ft³)

MODULE 38: Kinetics of Rigid Body Plane Motion

When unbalanced forces act on a rigid body they can create both translational and rotational motion. Translational motion is motion of the body's mass center in two or three-dimensional space, while rotational motion is a rotation about a particular axis. In this module, the combined translational and rotational motion that a body exhibits will be confined to a plane, i.e., the motion will be two-dimensional. That is, the body on which the forces are acting will be considered to be a thin slab and all of the motion of the body will occur in the plane of the slab. Since only two-dimensional motion will be considered here, the bodies will be said to have three degrees-of-freedom. This means that the body can move in both the x and y directions (translation) as well as rotate about an axis perpendicular to the plane of motion (rotation). The applied forces may create accelerations in the x and y directions as well as an angular acceleration about an axis of rotation. Therefore, it will be possible to write three equations of motion for the body: one force equation in the x direction, one force equation in the y direction, and one moment equation about the axis of rotation of the body. In this module, the axis of rotation will be considered to pass through the body's center-of-mass, G.

The translational equations of motion in the x and y directions are

$$\Sigma F_x = ma_x \quad , \quad \Sigma F_y = ma_y$$

and the rotational equation of motion about the body's mass center us

$$\Sigma M_G = I^* \alpha$$

where I^* is the mass moment of inertia about the centroidal z-axis, and α is the angular acceleration of the body. To better depict the concept of rigid body motion, consider the system of forces acting on the body as shown in Figure 38.1. The system of forces can be replaced by an equivalent system consisting of a resultant force **R** and resultant moment M_G both acting at the center of mass. This equivalent system creates both a translational acceleration **a** and a rotational, or angular acceleration α as indicated.

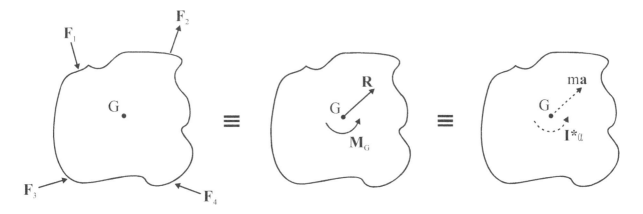

Figure 38.1

In the study of rigid body motion, problems consisting of pure translation with no rotation (Module 38), translation with rotation about the body's mass center (Module 39), and rotation about a fixed axis with no translation (Module 40) are considered. The more difficult problem of translation and rotation about a fixed axis not passing through the body's mass center isn't addressed in this text.

Pure Translation

In the case of pure translation the equations of motion can be expressed as

$$\Sigma F_x = ma_x \quad , \quad \Sigma F_y = ma_y \quad , \quad \Sigma M_G = 0$$

Example 38.1

Consider a rod 1 m in length having a mass of 5 kg and being pushed by the force **P** as shown. If the force has a magnitude of 100 N, determine the orientation angle θ of the rod and its acceleration if the rod does not rotate. Neglect the effects of friction.

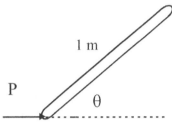

Solution: FBD:

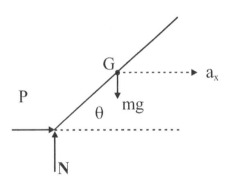

Since there's no rotation of the rod, three equations of motion can be written as

$\Sigma F_y = 0$
$N - mg = 0$
$N = mg$
$\quad = 5(9.81)$
$\Rightarrow N = 49.05 \text{ N}$

$\Sigma F_x = ma_x$
$P = ma_x$
$a_x = P / m$
$\quad = 100 / 5$
$\Rightarrow a_x = 20.0 \text{ m/s}^2$

$\Sigma \mathbf{M}_G = 0$
$\mathbf{r} \times \mathbf{P} + \mathbf{r} \times \mathbf{N} = 0$
$(-0.5 \cos\theta \, \mathbf{i} - 0.5 \sin\theta \, \mathbf{j}) \times (100 \, \mathbf{i} + 49.05 \, \mathbf{j}) = 0$
$-24.53 \cos\theta \, \mathbf{k} + 50.0 \sin\theta \, \mathbf{k} = 0$
$\theta = \tan^{-1}(24.53 / 50.0)$
$\Rightarrow \theta = 26.13°$

Example 38.2

In the figure below the rigid frame and rod are being accelerated at the rate of 10 m/s² by the force **P** as shown. If the mass of rod AB is 2 kg, determine the force on the spacer at point B.

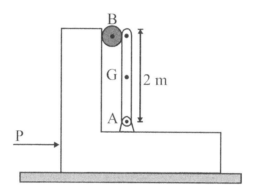

Solution: FBD:

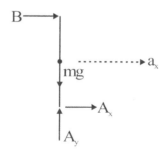

Writing the equations of motion of the rod shows

$\Sigma F_y = 0$
$A_y - mg = 0$
$A_y = mg$
       $= 2(9.81)$
$\Rightarrow A_y = 19.62$ N

$F_x = ma_x$
$B + A_x = ma_x$
$A_x = 2(10) - B$
$\Rightarrow A_x = 20 - B$

$$\Sigma M_G = 0$$
$$\mathbf{r}_1 \times \mathbf{B} + \mathbf{r}_2 \times \mathbf{A}_x = 0$$
$$\mathbf{j} \times B\mathbf{i} + (-\mathbf{j}) \times A_x \mathbf{i} = 0$$
$$-B\mathbf{k} + A_x \mathbf{k} = 0$$
$$B = A_x$$
$$= 20 - B$$
$$\Rightarrow B = 10 \text{ N}$$

Problems

38.1 A 2.0 m diameter sphere with a mass of 18 kg is pushed along the floor with no rotation by a force P as shown below. If the coefficient of kinetic friction is 0.20 and the sphere is being accelerated at the rate of 3.0 m/s^2, determine the magnitude of P and the distance above the floor d at which P acts.
(Ans. P = 89.32 N, d = 0.605 m)

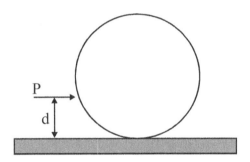

38.2 A 15 lb block resting on a cart is accelerated to the right by force **P**. The block is prevented from slipping by a small support between it and the cart. Neglecting friction, find the magnitude of the maximum acceleration the block can have without tipping.
(Ans. a_x = 8.05 ft/sec^2)

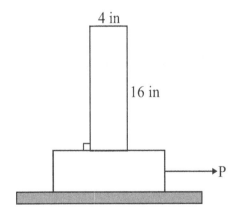

38.3 The block shown below is accelerating to the right at the rate of 7.0 m/s². A rod 3.0 m in length having a mass of 4 kg is hanging from a frictionless pin at point O. Determine the angle θ that the rod makes with the block.
(Ans. θ = 35.51°)

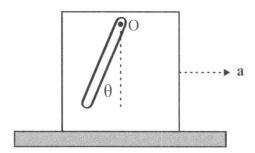

38.4 In the figure below, block A weighs 60 lb and block B weighs 120 lb. Neglecting friction, determine the range of values of the distance h for which block A will slide without tipping.
(Ans. 5.00 in ≤ h ≤ 23.00 in)

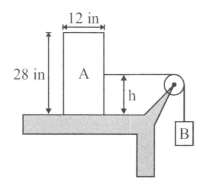

38.5 The log shown below has a mass of 75 kg and is suspended by three cables attached at points A, D, and E. For the case of θ = 30°, calculate the acceleration of the log and the tension in cables BD and CE immediately after cable AB is cut.
(Ans. a = 4.91 m/s², T_{BD} = T_{CE} = 318.6 N)

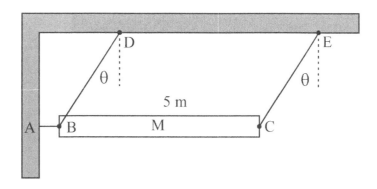

38.6 Solve Problem 38.4 considering that the coefficient of kinetic friction between block A and the surface is 0.20.
(Ans. $3.00 \text{ in} \leq h \leq 18.00 \text{ in}$)

38.7 For the block shown in Problem 38.3, determine its acceleration if the rod has a length of 2.5 m, a mass of 3 kg, and $\theta = 36°$.
(Ans. $a = 7.13 \text{ m/s}^2$)

38.8 Solve Problem 38.5 for the case of M = 75 kg, $\theta = 25.0°$, and L = 6 m.
(Ans. $a = 4.15 \text{ m/s}^2$, $T_{BD} = 333.4 \text{ N}$, $T_{CE} = 333.4 \text{ N}$)

MODULE 39: Kinetics of Rigid Body Plane Motion (cont.)

Fixed Axis Rotation About the Mass Center

For the case of rotation about the body's mass center, the rotational equation presented at the beginning of Module 38 will apply, which was provided as

$$\sum \mathbf{M}_G = I^* \boldsymbol{\alpha}$$

where I^* is the mass moment of inertia about the centroidal z axis in problems restricted to plane motion, and $\boldsymbol{\alpha}$ is the angular acceleration of the body.

Fixed Axis Rotation About an Arbitrary Point

For the case of rotation about a fixed axis which does not coincide with the body's mass center, the equations of motion presented in Module 39 must be modified. First, it's generally more practical to write the translational equations of motion in the normal and tangential directions, as

$$\sum F_n = ma_n = mr\omega^2 \quad , \quad \sum F_t = ma_t = mr\alpha$$

Second, the rotational equation of motion must be written about the fixed axis of rotation, point O, and not the mass center G. If the point of rotation is fixed and not accelerating, the moment equation about O can be written as

$$\sum \mathbf{M}_O = I^*\alpha + \sum mad = I_O \boldsymbol{\alpha}$$

where $\mathbf{a}$ is the acceleration of the mass center, d is the perpendicular distance from point O to the line-of-action of $\mathbf{a}$, and I_O is the mass moment of inertia about the axis of rotation passing through point O. The mass moment of inertia at point O is obtained by transferring the mass moment of inertia about the centroidal z axis (through the mass center) to the axis of rotation using the parallel axis theorem as discussed in Module 37.

Example 39.1

The pulley shown below has a mass of 10 kg and a radius of gyration of 0.25 m. Block A has a mass of 15 kg and block B has a mass of 9 kg. The system is released from rest and a frictional moment of 0.35 N-m is applied to the pulley as it rotates. If $r_1 = 0.5$ m and $r_2 = 1.0$ m, determine the angular acceleration of the pulley.

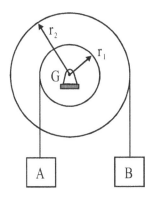

Solution: FBD:

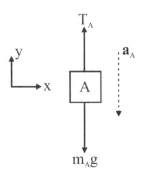 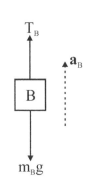 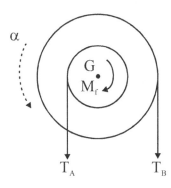

Block A:

$\sum F_y = m_A a_A$
$T_A - m_A g = -m_A a_A$
$T_A = m_A g - m_A a_A$
$\quad = 15(9.81 - a_A)$
$\Rightarrow T_A = 147.15 - 15 a_A$

Block B:

$\sum F_y = m_B a_B$
$T_B - m_B g = m_B a_B$
$T_B = m_B g + m_B a_B$
$\quad = 9(9.81 + a_B)$
$\Rightarrow T_B = 88.29 + 9 a_B$

Since the acceleration of each rope, and therefore each block, is equal to $r\alpha$, the equations above can be written in terms of α as

$T_A = 147.15 - 15 r_1 \alpha$
$\quad = 147.15 - 15(0.5)\alpha$
$\Rightarrow T_A = 147.15 - 7.5\alpha$

$T_B = 88.29 + 9 r_2 \alpha$
$\quad = 88.29 + 9(1.0)\alpha$
$\Rightarrow T_B = 88.29 + 9.0\alpha$

The rotational equation of motion written about the center-of-mass of the pulley is

$$\Sigma M_G = I^* \alpha$$
$$-r_1 \mathbf{i} \times (-T_A \mathbf{j}) + r_2 \mathbf{i} \times (-T_B \mathbf{j}) - M_f \mathbf{k} = I^* \alpha$$
$$0.5 T_A \mathbf{k} - T_B \mathbf{k} - M_f \mathbf{k} = mk^{*2} \alpha \mathbf{k}$$
$$\Rightarrow 0.5 T_A - T_B - 0.35 = 10(0.25)^2 \alpha$$

Substituting the results of the translational equations gives

$$0.5(147.15 - 7.5\alpha) - (88.29 + 9.0\alpha) - 0.35 = 0.63\alpha$$
$$\alpha = -1.13 \text{ rad/s}^2$$
$$\Rightarrow \boldsymbol{\alpha} = -1.13 \, \mathbf{k} \text{ rad/s}^2$$

Example 39.2

A 90 lb-ft moment is applied to disk A, which weighs 128.8 lb and has a radius of 1 ft. Disk B weighs 257.6 lb and has a radius of 2 ft. If there is no slipping between the disks, determine the angular acceleration of each disk.

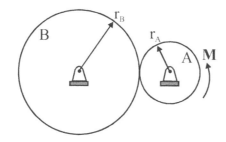

Solution: FBD:

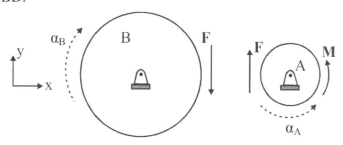

Since no slipping occurs, the accelerations of the disks are related by the expression

$$\mathbf{a}_A = \mathbf{a}_B$$
$$\boldsymbol{\alpha}_A \times \mathbf{r}_A = \boldsymbol{\alpha}_B \times \mathbf{r}_B$$
$$-\alpha_A \mathbf{k} \times (r_A \mathbf{i}) = \alpha_B \mathbf{k} \times (-r_B \mathbf{i})$$
$$\Rightarrow \alpha_A r_A = \alpha_B r_B$$

Writing the rotational equation of motion for both disks shows

Disk A:

$\Sigma (M_G)_A = I^*_A \alpha_A$
$M\mathbf{k} + (-r_A \mathbf{i} \times F \mathbf{j}) = 0.5 m_A r_A^2 \alpha_A \mathbf{k}$
$90.0 - (1.0)F = 0.5(128.8 / 32.2)(1.0)^2 \alpha_A$
$\Rightarrow F = 90.0 - 2.0\alpha_A$

Disk B:

$\Sigma (M_G)_B = I^*_B \alpha_B$
$(r_B \mathbf{i} \times -F \mathbf{j}) = -0.5 m_B r_B^2 (r_A / r_B)\alpha_A \mathbf{k}$
$-r_B F = -0.5 m_B r_B r_A \alpha_A$
$F = 0.5(257.6 / 32.2)(1.0)\alpha_A$
$\Rightarrow F = 4.0\alpha_A$

Substitution into the rotational equation for block A and solving for α_A and α_B gives

$\alpha_A = 15.0 \mathbf{k}$ rad/s²
$\alpha_B = -7.5 \mathbf{k}$ rad/s²

Example 39.3

The pendulum shown has a mass of 10 kg and has an angular velocity of 2.5 rad/s when $\theta = 30°$. Determine the magnitude of the reaction force at point O at this instant.

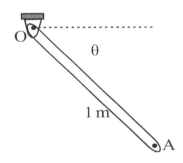

Solution: FBD:

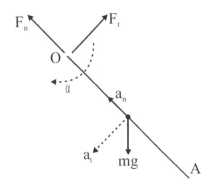

Writing the rotational equation about point O gives

$\Sigma \mathbf{M}_O = I_O \boldsymbol{\alpha}$
$(L/2) \cos\theta \, \mathbf{i} \times (-mg \, \mathbf{j}) = -[mL^2/12 + m(L/2)^2]\alpha \, \mathbf{k}$
$\alpha = 3g \cos\theta / 2L = 3(9.81)(0.866) / [2(1.0)]$
$\Rightarrow \boldsymbol{\alpha} = 12.74 \, \mathbf{k} \text{ rad/s}$

Writing the translational equations in the normal and tangential directions gives

$\Sigma F_n = ma_n$
$F_n - mg \sin\theta = mr\omega^2$
$F_n = m(L/2)\omega^2 + mg \sin\theta$
$\quad = 10(1.0/2)(2.5)^2 + 10(9.81)(0.5)$
$\Rightarrow F_n = 80.3 \text{ N}$

$\Sigma F_t = ma_t$
$mg \cos\theta - F_t = mr\alpha$
$F_t = mg \cos\theta - m(L/2)\alpha$
$\quad = 10(9.81)(0.866) - 10(1.0/2)(12.74)$
$\Rightarrow F_t = 21.2 \text{ N}$

$F = [F_n^2 + F_t^2]^{1/2}$
$\quad = [(21.2)^2 + (80.3)^2]^{1/2}$
$\Rightarrow F = 83.0 \text{ N}$

Problems

39.1 A weight of 75 lb is attached to a cable that is wrapped around a 325 lb drum as shown. The radius of gyration of the drum is 1.4 ft. If the system is released from rest, find the speed of the weight after it has moved a distance of 15 ft.
(Ans. v = 16.33 ft/sec)

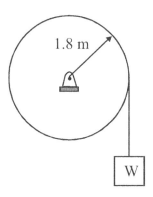

235

39.2 In the figure below, m_A is 20 kg, m_B is 12 kg, and the mass of the pulley is 4 kg. If the system is released from rest, determine the accelerations of the masses and the angular acceleration of the pulley. The pulley mount provides a resisting moment of 0.2 N-m.
(Ans. $a_y = 2.30$ m/s^2, $\alpha = 3.83$ rad/s^2)

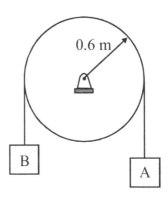

39.3 In Problem 39.2, consider m_A to be 18 kg and m_B to be 6 kg. Determine the mass of the pulley, having r = 0.5 m, if the angular acceleration is 5.0 rad/s^2.
(Ans. m = 45.86 kg)

39.4 The L-shaped bar has a mass of 12 kg and is released from rest from the position shown and rotates about point O. Calculate the acceleration of point A at the instant of release.
(Ans. $\mathbf{a}_A = -7.28\,\mathbf{i} + 10.19\,\mathbf{j}$ m/s^2)

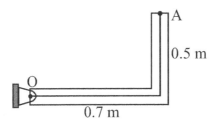

39.5 A thin disk is positioned in the horizontal plane and fastened atop a vertical shaft at point O. If the shaft provides a counterclockwise moment of 65 lb-ft to the disk and the disk starts from rest, how long will it take until the normal and tangential reaction forces at point O are equal. The mass of the disk is 25 slugs and the disk radius is 4.0 ft.
(Ans. t = 2.15 sec)

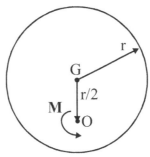

39.6 A bar having a mass of 6 kg is released from rest in the position shown. If the initial angular acceleration is 4 rad/s², determine the frictional moment provided by the pinned joint at O and determine the reaction force components at O at the instant of release.
(Ans. M_f = 26.86 N-m, O_y = 34.86 N, O_x = 0)

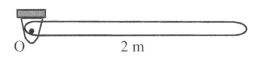

2 m

39.7 In Example 39.3, determine an expression for ω (in terms of α and θ) at the instant when the normal and tangential components of the reaction force at O are equal.
(Ans. $\omega = 2g(\cos\theta - \sin\theta) / L - \alpha$)

39.8 For Problem 39.6, calculate the length of the bar and the reaction force components at O if the frictional moment is 7.0 N-m and the angular acceleration is 6.5 rad/s².
(Ans. L = 1.99, 0.27 m, O_y = 20.0, 53.6 N, O_x = 0)

MODULE 40: Kinetics of Rigid Body Plane Motion (cont.)

General Plane Motion

The dynamics of a rigid body in general plane motion combines both translation of the mass center and rotation of the body about the mass center. The equations for general plane motion were presented in Module 38. The translational equations of motion of the mass center in the x and y directions are

$$\Sigma F_x = ma_x \quad , \quad \Sigma F_y = ma_y$$

and the rotational equation of motion about the body's mass center is

$$\Sigma M_G = I^* \alpha$$

where I^* is the mass moment of inertia about the centroidal z-axis, and α is the angular acceleration of the body. This module presents some additional applications of general plane motion.

Example 40.1

A solid sphere weighing 10 lb and having a radius of 10 in is released from rest and rolls down the incline without slipping. If $\theta = 30°$, determine the acceleration of the mass center of the cylinder and the friction force between the sphere and the plane.

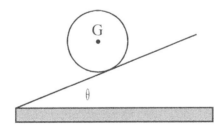

Solution: FBD:

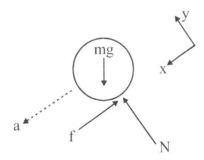

Writing the equations of motion in translation and rotation shows

$\Sigma F_x = ma$
$W \sin 30° - f = ma$
$f = W \sin 30° - (W/g)a$
$\quad = 10(0.5) - (10/32.2)a$
$\Rightarrow f = 5.0 - 0.31a$

$\Sigma \mathbf{M}_G = I^* \boldsymbol{\alpha}$
$-r\mathbf{j} \times (-f\mathbf{i}) = -0.4mr^2\alpha \mathbf{k}$
$\Rightarrow f = 0.4mr\alpha$

Since $a = r\alpha$ for the case of no slipping, then

$f = 0.4ma = 0.4(10/32.2)a$
$\Rightarrow f = 0.12a$

$0.12a = 5.0 - 0.31a$
$\Rightarrow \mathbf{a} = 11.49 \mathbf{i} \text{ ft/sec}^2$

The friction force can then be calculated as

$f = 0.12(11.49)$
$\Rightarrow \mathbf{f} = -1.38 \mathbf{i} \text{ lb}$

Example 40.2

A long bar having mass m is released from a ledge in the position shown below. Determine an expression for the angular acceleration of the bar.

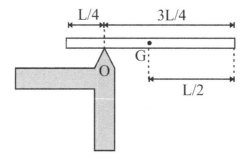

Solution: FBD:

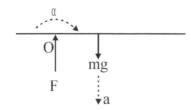

Since the bar will rotate about point O rather than about the mass center, the mass moment of inertia of the bar about point O must be calculated. The parallel axis theorem gives

$$I_O = I^* + md^2$$
$$= mL^2/12 + m(L/4)^2$$
$$\Rightarrow I_O = 0.15mL^2$$

Writing the rotational equation of motion about point O then gives

$$\Sigma \mathbf{M}_O = I_O \boldsymbol{\alpha}$$
$$(L/4)\,\mathbf{i} \times (-mg\,\mathbf{j}) = -0.15mL^2\alpha\,\mathbf{k}$$
$$-mgL/4\,\mathbf{k} = -0.15mL^2\alpha\,\mathbf{k}$$
$$\alpha = 1.71g/L$$
$$\Rightarrow \boldsymbol{\alpha} = -1.71g/L\,\mathbf{k}$$

Problems

40.1 A slender rod has a mass of 8 kg and hangs freely from a hinge at point O. If a horizontal force of P = 25 N is applied as shown, determine the angular acceleration of the rod and the reaction force components at O.
(Ans. $\alpha = 6.37$ rad/s^2, $O_x = 0.50$ N, $O_y = 78.48$ N)

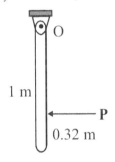

40.2 A large thin disk weighing 60 lb is released from rest as shown. Determine the acceleration of the mass center of the disk and the tension in the cable that is wrapped around the disk.
(Ans. a = 21.47 ft/sec^2, T = 20.01 lb)

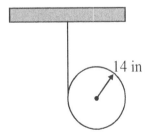

40.3 A cylinder of mass m and radius r rolls down an incline. If the coefficient of static friction is μ_s, determine an expression for the largest angle of inclination θ for which the cylinder doesn't slip.
(Ans. $\theta = \tan^{-1}[3\mu_s]$)

40.4 The sphere shown in Example 40.1 has a radius r and weight W, is released from rest and rolls down the incline. Determine the minimum value of the coefficient of static friction between the sphere and incline in order for rolling to occur without slipping.
(Ans. $\mu_s = 0.165$)

40.5 In the absence of friction, the ladder shown below, having a mass of 40 kg, is released from rest. Determine the angular acceleration of the ladder.
(Ans. $\boldsymbol{\alpha} = 1.42\ \mathbf{k}\ \text{rad/s}^2$)

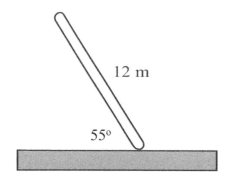

40.6 The wheel shown below has a mass of 30 kg, and a radius of gyration of 0.2 m. A force P of 25 N is applied to a cord wrapped around a groove cut into the wheel at a radius of 0.1 m. If μ_s between the wheel and the floor is 0.15, calculate the angular acceleration of the wheel if it starts from rest.
(Ans. $\alpha = 1.28\ \text{rad/s}^2$ CW)

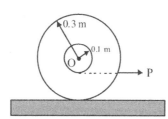

40.7 In Problem 40.5, determine the angular acceleration of the ladder considering that the coefficients of friction between the ladder and floor are $\mu_s = \mu_k = 0.10$.
(Ans. $\boldsymbol{\alpha} = 1.31\ \mathbf{k}\ \text{rad/s}^2$)

40.8 Solve Problem 40.6 for the case where the force P is applied on the top side of the inner cylinder instead of the bottom side.
(Ans. $\alpha = 2.56\ \text{rad/s}^2$ CW)

INDEX

Acceleration of gravity, 10-11

Area moments of inertia, 107
    common shapes, 109-110
    parallel axis theorem, 107
    radius of gyration, 108

Beams, 71, 77
    bending, 119, 131, 142
    deflections in bending, 135-137
    distributed loads, 71-72, 77
    normal stresses in bending, 131-132
    shear and moment diagram
        construction, 119-121, 127
    shear forces and bending moments, 119, 127
    shear stresses in bending, 131
        types of loading, 71
    types of supports, 119

Buckling, 157
    critical load, 157
    critical stress, 157
    effective column length, 157-158
    Euler formula, 157-158
    radius of gyration, 157
    slenderness ratio, 157

Centroids, 65, 77
    common shapes, 66

Conservation of energy, 196

Constrained motion, 175
    one degree of freedom, 176
    two degrees of freedom, 176

Coordinate systems, 4, 169
    Cartesian, 4
    normal and tangential, 169

Coplanar force systems, 27, 41
    conditions of equilibrium, 33
    equivalent systems, 28
    resultants, 26

Design stress, 95
    brittle material, 95
    ductile material, 95

Direct shear stress, 101
    double shear, 102
    fillet welds, 102
    single shear, 102

Failure modes, 152-153
    maximum normal stress theory, 153
    maximum shear stress theory, 153

Force-couple system, 21

Free-body diagrams, 33-34
    two-dimensional supports, 34
    two-force member, 41

Friction, 53, 59
    coefficient of kinetic friction, 53
    coefficient of static friction, 53
    maximum friction, 53

Impulse and momentum methods, 201
    angular impulse and angular
        momentum, 201
    linear impulse and linear momentum, 201

Kinematics of particles, 163-164, 169
    constant acceleration, 163
    curvilinear motion, 163-164, 169
    normal and tangential coordinates, 169
    rectangular coordinates, 164
    rectilinear motion, 163

Kinematics of rigid body plane motion, 205-206, 211

Kinetics of particles, 181, 187, 191
    plane curvilinear motion, 186
    rectilinear motion, 181

Kinetics of rigid body motion, 225, 231, 239
    fixed axis rotation about an arbitrary point, 231
    fixed axis rotation about mass center, 231
    general plane motion, 239
    pure translation, 226
    rotational equations, 225, 231, 239
    translational equations, 225, 231, 239

Mass moments of inertia, 217
    commonly shaped bodies, 218
    parallel axis theorem, 219
    principal axes of inertia, 220
    products of inertia, 220
    radius of gyration, 217

Material properties, 88
    SI, 88
    U.S. Customary, 88

Method of composite areas, 65, 110

Method of composite bodies, 219

Moment of a force, 15
    components, 15-16
    magnitude, 15, 21
    projection, 16

Newton's Laws of Motion, 181, 187, 191

Principle of superposition, 135, 140

Principal stresses, 147-149, 152
    Mohr's circle, 151-152
    stress element, 147-149

Relative motion, 170, 205-206
    translating and rotating axes, 205-206
    translating axes, 170

Statically indeterminate
    beams, 71
    structures, 35

Stress and strain, 85-87, 95
    axial loads, 85-87, 142
    compound bars, 96
    Hooke's law, 87
    Poisson's ratio, 87
    proportional limit, 86
    relationship between stress and strain, 86
    ultimate strength, 86
    yield strength, 86

Stresses under combined loadings, 141

Systems of units, 9-10, 88
    conversions, 10, 88
    SI, 10, 88
    U.S. Customary, 10, 88

Thermal expansion, 95
    coefficients, 95
    thermal stresses, 96

Torsion, 115, 142
    shear strain, 116
    shear stress, 115

Trusses, 47
    method of sections, 45-46

Vectors, 3-6
    addition/subtraction, 3-4
    magnitude 5, 182
    projection, 7
    resultant, 3-4, 7
    scalar product, 9
    unit vectors, 4-6
    vector product, 9

Weight, 10

Work and energy methods, 195
    kinetic energy, 195
    potential energy, 195
    relationship between work and energy, 196
    work, 195

Made in the USA
Columbia, SC
16 August 2021